D0208464

THE MYTH OF THE LAZY NATIVE

THE MYTH OF THE LAZY NATIVE

A study of the image of the
Malays, Filipinos and Javanese
from the 16th to the 20th century
and its function
in the ideology of colonial capitalism

SYED HUSSEIN ALATAS

Professor of Malay Studies,
University of Singapore

FRANK CASS : LONDON

First published 1977 in Great Britain by
FRANK CASS AND COMPANY LIMITED
Gainsborough House, Gainsborough Road,
London E11 1RS, England

and in the United States of America by
FRANK CASS AND COMPANY LIMITED
c/o International Scholarly Book Services Inc.
Box 555, Forest Grove, Oregon 97116

ISBN 0 7146 3050 0

Photoset, printed and bound in Great Britain by R. J. Acford Ltd., Industrial Estate, Chichester. Sussex.

To my parents
Syed Ali Alatas
and
Sharifah Raguan Alaydrus

Contents

Introduction

This book attempts to analyse the origins and functions of the "myth of the lazy native" from the 16th to the 20th century in Malaysia, the Philippines and Indonesia. The methodological approach is by way of the sociology of knowledge. The function of myth as a significant element in colonial ideology is illustrated by recourse to historical and sociological examples. Two concepts which have been consistently used here need clarification: they are ideology and colonial capitalism. A great deal of confusion has arisen over the definition of ideology particularly in the United States, a confusion generated partly by the phenomena to be contained in the definition and partly by the confused logic of some who attempted the definition. Without entering into the discussion we shall simply state how we define the term here. Our choice of meaning is neither haphazard nor born of mere convenience. Relying heavily on Mannheim's concept of ideology, it reflects that segment of the thought world which has characterized the political philosophy of colonialism in the Asian setting. It reflects an objective reality — the ideology of colonialism.

For present purposes, an ideology is a system of belief characterized by the following traits: (a) it seeks to justify a particular political, social and economic order, (b) in this attempt, it distorts that part of the social reality likely to contradict its main presuppositions, (c) it exists primarily in the form of a manifest thought content which is different from its latent content,[1] (d) it is authoritative in nature, (e) it expresses the interests of a distinctive group, (f) when it is dominant it creates a false consciousness among the group it represents as well as the group it dominates, (g) it can draw its ideas from any source, science, religion, culture, economics, history, etc., (h) it arises out of the conflicting interests of separate groups,[2] in a society with a pronounced division of labour and social classes, and (i) its major ideas are eventually to a large extent conditioned by the mode of production in a given time and place.

1

There are the ideologies of the ruling class and there are the ideologies of the subjugated classes; There are what Mannheim calls total ideologies and particular ideologies.[3] While the study of ideologies has affected numerous analyses and categories, here we may mention the classification into four major types—the conservative ideology, the reform ideology, the revolutionary ideology, and the counter ideology.[4] For our purpose it is sufficient to employ these classifications. In its historical empirical manifestation the colonial ideology utilized the idea of the lazy native to justify compulsion and unjust practices in the mobilization of labour in the colonies. It portrayed a negative image of the natives and their society to justify and rationalize European conquest and domination of the area. It distorted elements of social and human reality to ensure a comfortable construction of the ideology. The pieces of ideas patched together to construct the picture of native society will be displayed in the succeeding chapters.

As to colonial capitalism, it was characterized by the following traits: (a) predominant control of and access to capital by an alien economic power, (b) the control of the colony by a government run by members of the alien power, acting on its behalf, (c) the highest level of business, trade and industry, held by the alien dominating community, (d) direction of the country's export and import trade to suit the interest of the alien ruling power, (d) a bias towards the agrarian mode of production as opposed to that of industry, (e) the minimal expansion of technological and scientific skill, (f) the organization of production around semi-free labour, (g) the absence of guilds or trade unions as a counterweight to exploitation, (h) the non-involvement of large sections of the population in direct capitalist enterprise, and (i) the presence of a set of antitheses in the colonized society described by the term dualism.[5] The effective period of colonial capitalism, for our purpose, covered the 18th and 19th centuries and the first half of the 20th century. It is impossible to establish a rigidly demarcated onset of colonial capitalism, and it is sufficient for us to say that by the 18th century in Malaysia, the Philippines and Indonesia, the power of colonial capitalism was firmly entrenched. Within this time span a great many changes had taken place in the structure of indigenous society.

As to capitalism itself, the term is not easy to define. Quoting Weber, Sombart wrote that the modern capitalist organization was a huge cosmos into which the human unit was born. Like others before and after him, Sombart isolated the spirit of capitalism from its institutional trappings.[6] The use of capital alone does not constitute capitalism, for capitalism is an economic system associated with a certain outlook; it is characterized by the following features: (a) the purpose and ultimate aim of economic activity is the acquisition of greater and greater wealth; (b) the central measurement of wealth is money; (c) the source of increasing wealth, the capital, has to be constantly increased; (d) the boundary of this acquisition of profit has to be constantly expanded; (e) other non-economic values have to be subordinated to this urge for profit; (f) rational methods are used and devised in the effort to produce wealth and profit; (g) the organization involved in capitalist undertaking must be free of public control; (h) the capitalist owners and organizers are a minority; (i) the value of commodities is decided by the market; (j) capital is considered more important than labour in the distribution of profit; (k) there is a recognition of the right of different groups to compete in the production and sale of the commodities regarded as the sources of wealth and profit; (l) the vital roles of the financiers of capital are acknowledged; (m) free choice of activity on the part of the economic agent is present; and (n) there is private ownership of the means of production.[7]

When a system is governed by these features it is said to be capitalistic. Other factors which attended the development of capitalism in Western Europe such as the expansion of industry, the banking system, the growth of science and technology and its application to profit making, although parts of the historical phenomenon of capitalism do not strictly speaking belong to its essence. They are the means and results of capitalism. The distinction between the two has been maintained by many investigators. As the essence of capitalism Weber stressed the pursuit of profit, forever renewed by means of a continuous, rational capitalistic enterprise. "The impulse to acquisition," he wrote, "pursuit of gain, of money, of the greatest possible amount of money, has in itself nothing to do with capitalism. This impulse exists and has existed among waiters, physicians, coachmen, artists, prostitutes, dishonest officials, soldiers, nobles, crusaders, gamblers, and beggars. One may say that it has been common to all sorts and conditions of men at all times and in all countries of the earth, wherever the objective possibility of it is or has been given. It should be taught in the kindergarten of cultural history that this naive idea of capitalism must be given up once and for all. Unlimited greed for gain is not in the least identical with capitalism, and is still less its spirit. Capitalism *may* even be identical with the restraint, or at least a rational tempering, of this irrational impulse. But capitalism is identical with the pursuit of profit, and forever *renewed* profit, by means of continuous, rational, capitalistic enterprise. For it must be so; in a wholly capitalistic order of society, an individual capitalistic enterprise which did not take advantage of its opportunities for profit-making would be doomed to extinction". [8]

A fruitful attempt to isolate the essence of capitalism has also been made by Amintore Fanfani who compares it with the pre-capitalist spirit. The capitalist spirit, he holds, does not impose any limitation on the use of lawful and useful means of acquiring wealth and no non-economic restraint is allowed to inhibit the acquisition of profit. The pre-capitalist spirit assessed the price of an object according to the cost of its production while the capitalist spirit evaluates an object according to the general demand. The pre-capitalist adjusted wages according to the needs of the worker, the capitalist according to his output. The pre-capitalist recognized a socially imposed limitation on the enjoyment of his wealth while the capitalist does not. "It is in such differences of conception," observed Fanfani, "that we find the essential distinction between the capitalist and pre-capitalist spirit. And it is this differentiation that, above and beyond institutions, forms, economic means, allows us to declare whether a system is capitalistic or not. In making this our testing-rod in distinguishing between one economic age and another, we do not leave out of account the differences of institutions, forms, technical means. On the contrary, we shall see how these are more or less closely and directly bound up with the prevailing economic conception. Nor does our approach to the problem imply any denial that practical circumstances may determine a transition from one conception to another". [9]

Our reliance on such a concept of capitalism is directed not only by its legitimacy but also by historical necessity. Nowhere is the cultural and historical relativity of a concept more clearly revealed than in the Western-bound concept of historical capitalism. An explanation is necessary here. Fanfani's concept of the essential characteristics of capitalism was derived from European history; These characteristics emerged in the Italian cities of the 14th century, if not earlier, and also elsewhere in Europe. Discussing the more comprehensive definition of the sociologist and historian, he notes the various restricted definitions of capitalism: "At bottom, this is the opinion of many who speak of capitalism and mean now a system in which capital is predominant, now a system characterized by free labour, and now a system in which competition is unbridled, credit expands, banks prosper, big industry assumes gigantic dimensions, and the world market becomes one. For such authors the existence of capitalism depends on the scale of the means of production; on the range of the means for circulating wealth; on the elaboration of tools and plant. It may justly be objected that if such criteria are accepted as the hall-mark of capitalism, the capitalist system has no original features and no novelty. Indeed, well-meaning men have not failed to note that, at bottom, the capitalism that others believed to have made a first tentative appearance in the fifteenth century, flourished in Florence and in Italy generally in the fourteenth century. Yet others have added that it could be found in the Flemish and French cities about the same period, and as early as the eleventh century in Venice." [10]

Weber considered the rational organization of free labour as an essential characteristic of modern capitalism. [11] This he too derived from European history, but Fanfani's definition is more universal and less relative. The modern Dutch capitalism of the 19th century in Java was not based on free labour. In Fanfani's definition free labour is a historical trait peculiar to a certain period of European history; hence the capitalism of 19th century Java, though based on free labour in Holland, was not so in Java. Thus from the point of view of Javanese society it was dominated by a system of modern capitalism not based on free labour. This form of capitalism was the same as the one defined by Fanfani, but since the historical configuration of capitalism in Southeast Asia is not the same as in Europe, it is this different configuration that we have called colonial capitalism. It is a mixture of the essential elements of capitalism as suggested by Fanfani and the institutional and historical factors arising in the Southeast Asian colonies. Furthermore the effects of colonial capitalism on the societies under its domination, in our case Malaysia, Indonesia and the Philippines, were the reverse of those produced by capitalism in Europe on European societies.

To illustrate the above let us quote the following description offered by two historians of the stages of capitalism as seen from the European point of view and as derived from Europe's history: "The first stage—commercial capitalism—is associated with geographical discoveries, colonization, and the astounding increase in overseas trade. At this time, early capitalists protected by governmental controls, subsidies, and monopolies, made profits from the transportation of goods. Beginning about 1750, the second phase— industrial capitalism—was made possible by the adoption of new energy sources and machines to manufacturing, the development of the factory system, and the rapid growth of wealth. The essence of industrial capitalism was profit making from the manufacturing process itself. In the mid-nineteenth century, this phase reached its zenith with large factories, efficient machines, and the concentration of capital in the hands of the middle class. In the last decades of the nineteenth century, when the ultimate control and direction of industry came into the hands of financiers, industrial capitalism gave way to financial capitalism. The establishment of mammoth industrial concerns or empires and the ownership and management of their assets by men completely divorced from production were the dominant features of this third phase." [12]

The first stage was present in Southeast Asia; the second and third stages were not present in Southeast Asian societies, where the internal effects of finance and industrial capitalism generated in European societies were not similarly generated in Southeast Asian societies until the end of European colonialism there. The middle class was destroyed by the colonial powers much earlier in the 18th and 19th centuries. Furthermore, monopoly capitalism, which Lenin considered as the highest stage of capitalism leading to the scramble for empire, was operative in this region by the 17th century. The Dutch, the Spaniards and the Portuguese were responsible for this, but it was the Dutch who exerted the most influence there. Thus monopoly capitalism was introduced into the region, centuries earlier than Lenin had expected, [13] while finance capitalism was operative in Indonesia long before it dominated Western society. The historical configuration called capitalism in the West differed fundamentally from that of the colonial societies of Southeast Asia. We are therefore justified in using a different concept — colonial capitalism. We have listed some of the basic constituents of the concept, and others might be found in data available. This would, however, require the kind of economic historical study which has not hitherto been attempted. The mercantile capitalism of Southeast Asia before 1600, that is before the coming of the Europeans, should be compared with that of Western Europe. Some central questions can be raised around which the comparison can be made. What was the role of money and capital? What was the nature of the leading merchant, sedentary or mobile? [14] How did distance and climate influence trade and shipping? What was the mode of exchange? What was the relation between the commercial towns and the countryside? Was there an emergence of new classes? These are some of the questions which could be raised.

The effort to construct new concepts for the study of Southeast Asian societies is in keeping with a genuine application of the social sciences. The general universal and abstract concept of the modern social sciences which developed in the West should not automatically be applied to non-Western societies. The universal and the particular constituents of the concept have to be isolated; we have attempted to do this in the case of capitalism and in turn suggested the concept of colonial capitalism derived from the particular circumstances of the region. The same thing may be said of ideology, for colonial ideology in at least one respect is not representative of ideology in the West. Ideology in the West was born out of conflicts between groups, and so too were these ideologies in Asia. But the ideology of colonial capitalism, as an overall ideology of the ruling Western power in the colonies, was not born of conflict between groups, though some elements of that ideology, like the myth of the lazy native, were accentuated by the conflict between groups. Yet again this conflict was not between the dominating and the subjugated group but between the dominating groups themselves, as with the Dutch debate on the Javanese in the 19th century. Hence the notion of a conflict genesis of ideology does not belong to its universal essence: ideology can come into being with or without conflicts.

The ideology of colonial capitalism sought a justification of Western rule in its alleged aim of modernizing and civilizing the societies which had succumbed to Western powers. One of the most outspoken ideologists in this region was Thomas Stamford Raffles, the colonial founder of Singapore. [15] Whether it was in Malaysia, the Philippines or Indonesia, or whether it was the British, the Spaniards or the Dutch, the same type of arguments prevailed. The historical forms of the civilizing process differed; Catholicism in Malaysia and Indonesia, for example, was not considered as necessary to the civilizing process as it was in the Philippines. But all three powers were agreed that Western rule and Western culture were superior; that Western peoples should lead the world; that they were most suited to exploit the natural wealth of the East; and that they were the best administrators. Consequently, the ideology of colonial capitalism played down the capacities of Southeast Asian societies. Every conceivable item was invoked to denigrate the Southeast Asian, including his size and physiognomy. Thus Geoffrey Gorer, an anthropologist specializing in the study of national character, a discipline intended to correct prejudices and arrive at true understanding, early in his career observed of the Javanese: "I did not personally find the Javanese very sympathetic; despite their fertility they give somehow the impression of being a race of old and exhausted people, only half alive. This impression may I think be due partly to their religion, and to the abysmal poverty of the greater number. Poverty, especially uncomplaining and involuntary poverty, is numbing and repulsive anywhere; and Mohammedanism is the most deadening of all creeds. A purely personal point which prevented me enjoying their company was the question of size; I do not like being among people who appear smaller and weaker than I am, unless they have corresponding superiority elsewhere; I dislike the company of those I feel to be my inferiors." [16]

The ideological denigration of the native and of his history and society ranged from vulgar fantasy and untruth to refined scholarship. A vulgar fantasy was Jagor's suggestion that the Filipinos made oars from bamboo poles in order to rest more frequently. "If they happen to break, so much the better, for the fatiguing labor of rowing must necessarily be suspended till they are mended again." [17] Jagor was a German scientist who knew Rizal, and such opinions were held by other scholars and educated people. Their persistence and repetition over at least two centuries in thousands of books and reports written by administrators, scholars, travellers and journalists, revealed their ideological roots. Since the independence of Malaysia, Indonesia and the Philippines, the negative image of the native is no longer conspicuous in foreign writings. There are writings critical of the economic or political situations in the country but on the whole they do not contain direct denigration of the natives, their society and history. The political and economic relationship between Southeast Asia and the West has changed. Similarly the image of the native has changed. The ideological elements have been transformed, and have assumed a new garb. The image of the indolent, dull, backward and treacherous native has changed into that of a dependent native requiring assistance to climb the ladder of progress.

It is not our intention here to trace the ideological roots of the post-independence image; we are concerned rather with the colonial image. That there is a link between ideology and scholarship is a proposition whose truth is borne out by all ages. Marx and Engels, in their pioneering study of the modern capitalist ideology, suggested the instance of the doctrine of the separation of powers as an example of the role of ideology. In an age and in a country where royal power, the aristocracy and the bourgeoisie are contending for mastery, and where mastery is shared, the doctrine of the separation of powers becomes dominant and is conceived as an eternal law. [18] Ideology intrudes upon scholarship not only in the formation of concepts but also in the selection of problems. As Mannheim has pointed out, an observer could escape the distorting influence of ideology provided he became conscious of the social roots of his ideas and general attitudes. [19] Thus the statement that scholarship is conditioned by ideology should not be taken in the absolute sense that each and every scholar is necessarily and unconsciously influenced by his ideology. What we are saying is that during the colonial period and to a large extent thereafter, the study of the Malays, Javanese and Filipinos has been overwhelmingly dominated by ideological forces of the uncritical and superficial kind. A scholar who is mature and objective may allow ideological considerations in his choice of subject but his study on the subject itself will have to follow normal scientific procedures and seek objectivity.

My own ideological considerations in this book affect the choice of subject. It is an effort to correct a one-sided colonial view of the Asian native and his society. I believe in the primarily negative influence of colonialism. [20] I believe in the need to unmask the colonial ideology, for its influence is still very strong. Colonial scholars have on the whole avoided the study of the negative aspects of colonialism; an attempt to correct this should not be considered automatically as a reversal of the coin. It is the facts adduced, the evidence marshalled, the themes introduced, the analyses accomplished, and the attitudes of the scholar which should finally decide whether the attempt is merely a reversal of the coin or a real extension and supplementation of existing knowledge. That objectivity in scholarship is possible despite the influence of ideology on the choice of theme—but not on the reasoning and analysis—can be shown by the example of a Burmese scholar.

U Khin Maung Kyi, Professor of Research, Institute of Economics, Rangoon, had extended the scope and problems of Burmese economic history by raising the questions of whether Western colonial enterprise in Burma had promoted technical progress and generated an indigenous entrepreneurial class. Some aspects of the colonial capitalist economy had already been studied, but they were the structural sides of the colonial economy such as the dependence on export of raw materials, whether the colony's economy was able to grow into a self-generating one, the "free-trade" resulting in the elimination of the less competitive Burmese, the skimming tactics of foreign investors, the withdrawal of capital after the opportunity for quick returns was exhausted, and similar items of interest. U Khin Maung Kyi's problems were posed owing to his ideological background: he is a Burmese concerned with the national development of Burma; his criteria of significance when selecting his problems are Burmese national interests. He wrote: "Since the long term economic progress of a country could only be furthered by the development of native entrepreneurial activity and technical improvement, we would like to offer as an alternative criterion in evaluating the performance of Western enterprise the question of whether it had promoted technical progress and generated the emergence of a local entrepreneurial class. We would ask such questions as what diffusion of technology had occurred in Burmese society during the colonial period and what were the prospects of development of a native entrepreneurial class. Why did the Burmese entrepreneurial class fail to develop, as was the case, apart from the usual explanation of Burmese lack of business acumen or the lack of capital? These questions can be answered only when the growth of Western enterprise is considered in relation to its impact on the local conditions."[21]

The fact that his motivation and ideological perspective conditioned the direction of his research does not detract from its value. His able and original presentation further increased our understanding of colonial capitalism in Burma. The ideological perspective of the scholar or any other author is there, but the problem is to be conscious of it and prevent it from impairing the objectivity of the study. Otherwise the censure of Marx and Engels on 19th century European historians should apply. "Whilst in ordinary life every shopkeeper is very well able to distinguish between what somebody professes to be and what he really is, our historians have not yet won even this trivial insight. They take every epoch at its word and believe that everything it says and imagines about itself is true."[22] The uncritical scholar accepts the traditional concepts of the period, the problematics, and the modes of analysis, without any reflection and hesitation. More than the shopkeeper he is prepared to believe the propagandist of ideology. One clear instance is sufficient.

An American historian of the Dutch East Indies, Clive Day, in comparing the merits of Dutch rule with native rule inclined to the view that native governments were fit only for evil. The impression he derived from reading the annals of native states was that good rulers were few, they were ineffective, and there was no good native government.[23] He devoted about 20 pages to describing the negative traits of native government including the tyranny of their rulers. He noted how one ruler had a house at court in which he enjoyed the performance of naked women fighting with tigers.[24] He described the ill effects of native government on the population, despite the difficulties of such a study, as he himself acknowledged.[25] He expressed a naive conception of history in observing: "It seems no exaggeration to say that half or more of the serious wars in which the native states engaged rose out of the futile question as to which of the two men equally bad should govern a certain territory. I have seen no evidence that princes or dynasties won the affection or loyalty of their people in the period of native rule. The Dutch Governor General wrote in 1677, at the time of a revolt in Mataram by a pretender to the crown, that it was surprising that a people used for centuries to obey this ruler's ancestors should, as they did, give their allegiance to the rebel with entire indifference."[26]

Such a view of native society and of the personal and despotic character of native wars was strongly propagated by colonial capitalism. The words Day employed to described injustices arising from Dutch rule were different in tone from his description of injustices arising from native rulers or the Chinese community. The double dealing and opportunism of the Dutch, their divide and rule policy, "was the natural motto to follow when in contact with the native political organization, and was the principle which accounts for the greater part of Dutch success".[27] The errors and injustice of the Dutch were given respectability in the following description: "In attempting to pick their way in the tortuous paths of native politics the Dutch made mistakes which were sometimes followed by disastrous results, and the course that they pursued in some cases is decidedly questionable from the standpoint of modern ethical standards. There is much to criticize, but there is something of boldness and sagacity that commands admiration in this side of Dutch policy."[28] So too was the exploitation inherent in the capitalist system. Day defended the middleman and considered his function as essential. Of the Chinese in Java he wrote: "The Chinese are always represented as great sinners in their relations with the natives, overreaching them in every way; they cheat in trade, advance money at usurious interest, and exploit their victims sometimes mercilessly. These facts cannot be denied, and yet it is very easy to base a false inference on them. The natives and the native organization are to blame rather than the Chinaman.

The Chinese take much the same position in modern Java that the Jews took in mediaeval Europe; they are giving the natives some primary economic education, and they are hated for it just as the Jews were hated."[29]

The victims were blamed rather than the exploiters; exploitation was observed as a form of education. The greed and exploitation of the Dutch East India Company who used the Chinese middlemen was however at most described as "decidedly questionable from the standpoint of modern ethical standards". No mention was made of the Chinese massacre by the Dutch in Batavia in 1740, or of the despotic personal behaviour of some of the Dutch Governor-Generals. In his book the dice were loaded against the Orientals. Under cover of dispassionate objectivity, the injustices of the Dutch were expressed in sober terms but not so those of the native rulers. He claimed that he had not been able to discover a single document to show the affection of the natives for their rulers. Had he found any for the Dutch? Day was an apologist for Dutch colonialism though he was critical of some of its aspects. His ideological position clearly intruded upon the objectivity of his scholarship. Another point was his total silence on the views of the natives. Having examined practically all the basic source materials Day used, I have discovered that much can be glimpsed of the attitude of the natives. The wars were no mere clashes between individual despots; social injustice had a great deal to do with them. Day also omitted to study or evaluate the Dutch contribution to these wars and the instability of the area.

Another instance of the negative influence of ideology on scholarship is furnished by the works of J. S. Furnivall. One cannot accuse Furnivall of antipathy towards the natives: he was quite genuinely sympathetic to them and did not hide the exploitation committed by the ruling colonial powers and groups with vested interest. But the guiding ideological motive affecting his study was his hesitation to recognize the need for independence. On the eve of the Second World War he published *Netherlands India*; twelve pages were devoted to a historical account of native movements in Indonesia, but there was not a single mention of Sukarno, Hatta, Shahrir, Tan Malaka, Alimin, or Muso. He did mention and discuss the moderate leaders, and his omission of Sukarno was no careless slip. Sukarno's trial in Bandung in 1930 was a sensation, while there were sufficient Dutch records about him. The same is true of the activities of the Communists, Tan Malaka, Alimin and Muso. Furnivall was not keen on nationalism as a basis for statehood, believing that nationalism within what he called a plural society was a disruptive force which tended to shatter rather than consolidate the social order.[30]

In 1939 Furnivall's commitment was to an enlightened colonial rule. Hence he did not discuss the question of independence suggested by the nationalists as an alternative to the colonial system. He apparently avoided discussing Sukarno and Hatta because they were the foremost representatives of the nationalism which insisted on independence. This did not accord with Furnivall's ideology. His ideological disdain for nationalism became more revealing in his book *Colonial Policy and Practice.* The preface was dated October, 1947; two years had elapsed since Sukarno and Hatta proclaimed the Republic of Indonesia, August 17, 1945 and thus made world headlines. The Indonesian revolution against the Dutch was a major event after the War. It was impossible for Furnivall to have overlooked Sukarno and Hatta, yet no mention was made of their role in pre-war Indonesian politics. It was like writing the modern politics of India without reference to Gandhi and Nehru, or the Russian Revolution without Lenin and Trotsky.

In 1947 when independence had became a tidal wave washing across the colonial territories, when the colonial government was preparing to withdraw from Asia, Furnivall declared his support for independence. His earlier distrust for nationalism was modified. "Nothing less than independence could transform nationalism from a destructive fever into a creative force."[31] In other words he saw nationalism during the pre-independence period as a destructive force. It was because of this ideological bias that during the colonial days he paid scant attention to the independence movement. He regretted that in the past, more had not been done to equip the people and their leaders for the responsibility of independence.[32] That the colonized people were not loyal to the British Furnivall deplored. "It is lamentable that we failed to capture the imagination of the people so as to inspire an instinctive loyalty to the British connection, but we cannot escape the consequences of the past."[33] Only at the time when the colonies were already at the threshold of independence did Furnivall raise the question of the difficulties surrounding independence. He said: "The problem of endowing a tropical dependency with an instructed social will, so that it can find a place among the comity of nations, has much in common with the problem, simpler though not yet completely solved, of enabling the convict to live as a free citizen. Like the time-expired convict, a people that has known subjection is in need of after-care.

And a subject people resembles not only a convict but an invalid; it suffers from debility as a result of its confinement. Under foreign rule political and military traditions degenerate, cultural life decays and economic activities, losing their national significance, are distorted to meet the requirements of the colonial power."[34]

Thus the freedom of the colonies was compared to that of a convict; both needed after-care. The nurse was of course his former jailer! Yet he was explicit about the interest he was upholding — if the granting of independence was essential for the survival of Western civilization, then it should be assumed that it was possible.[35] Furnivall represented the ideology of late colonialism, an ideology that recognized the need to improve native welfare and for the eventual independence of the country but only after a certain amount of "training and preparation". This was a familiar chorus during the period before independence, and Furnivall had analysed it in a book. His ideology favoured the reform of colonial capitalism but not its abolition. This ideology dominated colonial scholarship but not in the sense of a procedural technique. For instance the method used for gathering and utilizing statistics was not motivated by ideology but the choice of subject and its interpretation were. Thus the growth of a colonial capitalist economy in a colonial territory was called "economic progress", while changes of administrative policy were called "reform" without any attempt to evaluate critically what "progress" and "reform" actually meant.

Furnivall was perhaps the most outspoken critic of the current colonial practices; yet his ultimate ideological orientation was colonial. An independent government, in his opinion, should lose its independence if it failed to conform to standards imposed by the world (in this instance, by implication, the Western world): "If a Government does not provide adequately for economic progress, it will be unable to maintain itself against external economic forces; it will not be permitted to survive. And if it does not attain a reasonable minimum in respect of human well-being, and especially in preventing epidemics of men, cattle and crops, then in the interest of world welfare it must be subjected to some measure of control. Tropical peoples forfeited their independence because, under the guidance of their native rulers, they were unable to qualify as citizens of the modern world by complying with its requirements. The usual type of colonial Government complies with them more adequately than the native tropical rulers whom it has superseded. Doubtless colonial powers, in the management of colonial affairs, look primarily to their own interest, and one source of weakness in colonial rule is the feeling in the outer world that they do not sufficiently regard the interests of non-colonial powers. Still, it is generally true, at least in British and Dutch dependencies, that the Government, though primarily responsible to the colonial power, does on the whole act as a trustee on behalf of the modern world."[36]

Here again the modern Western world was considered by Furnivall to be the sole arbiter of the destiny of men. He even justified Western colonialism by recourse to historical distortion. Was the motive of colonial expansion in fact the prevention of epidemics of men, cattle and crops; were the Dutch, the Portuguese and the Spaniards in Southeast Asia in the 16th, 17th and 18th century moved by such altruistic motive? According to this criterion Furnivall should have recommended the colonization of modern Spain and the Latin American republics. His criterion for independence was meant only for the non-Western world, and his thinking is an instance of the negative and unconscious influence of ideology on scholarship. It is that type of ideological influence that impairs objectivity in scholarship and a rational extension of the theme of enquiry. This orientation has focused attention on one field, namely the interests of the colonial power, and suppressed attention relating to the interests of the native population. Hence during the colonial period no colonial scholar ever examined the question of independence from the point of view of a desirable event to be realized in the near future. If some of them did, it was with a view to controlling the process or merely to account for it, and not in order to develop it as a legitimate historical force, in the way they studied Western education in the colonies.

We would consider it a legitimate and positive influence of ideology if Furnivall had exhaustively studied in an unbiased manner the role of nationalism and equally the role of colonialism. His conclusion might have affirmed the need for colonialism. His concepts should have been critically evaluated; his logic should have been consistent; his perspective on a problem should have been seen from various significant angles. For instance, when he made the prevention of epidemics a criterion of a legitimate government he should also have included the prevention of drug addiction. But this he could not do because he was certainly aware that a substantial part of the revenue of the British colonial government came from the official monopoly of opium. In British Malaya (including Brunei) and Singapore between 1918 and 1922 approximately 30 per cent on average of government revenue was derived from the opium sale. If Furnivall suggests health as a measure of legitimate and proper government he should impartially consider the promotion of drug addiction by the colonial government and compare it with the native government's ignorance of how to fight an epidemic, instead of suppressing this aspect of colonial rule and highlighting the inability of native rulers to fight epidemics.

In a total and fundamental sense, no scholarship is free from the influence of ideology. The influence of ideology can be vulgar, and it can be refined. A sociologist who studies dispassionately the problem of unemployment does not deliver any value judgement; he uses a technique of research free from ideological biases, but this does not mean that ideology has no influence on him. Already at the outset it conditions his study. Is the purpose of his study to understand unemployment with a view to increase it or to minimize it? Is he to study the effect of unemployment on the unemployed themselves, on society, or on the employers? Whatever decision he takes is based on a certain system of values which are in turn related to his ideology. The influence of ideology at this level is unavoidable but once the scholar is aware of it and if he is sincerely devoted to an ideal of objectivity he can proceed without allowing his initial ideological commitment to distort his analysis and conclusions. It should be possible for a native scholar committed to the ideal of independence to recognize the merits of colonialism without distorting them—similarly the converse should be true. What we are concerned with here is the negative influence of ideology, the distorting, uncritical, inconsistent streak in a scholar's reasoning which arises from an unconscious attachment to his ideology.

Judgements on the nature of Asian natives during the colonial period which are discussed in this book occurred under the negative influence of ideology, among both colonial scholars and laymen, i.e. those from Western countries who upheld the colonial system and who dominated the thought world of the colonies. Not every British or Dutch scholar interested in the colonies has been a colonial scholar in this sense; exceptions were J. A. Hobson and the Dutch scholar W. F. Wertheim. A colonial scholar, journalist, or author is one with a colonial mind whether refined or vulgar. The products of such a mind labouring under the negative influence of ideology can best be evaluated by the method of the sociology of knowledge. The roots of the distortion of native character can be traced and a comparison with reality made in this manner. An attempt is made here to correct the image of the native created in the colonial period by those in power. For Malaysia, this is not merely an exercise in historical scholarship: there is a pressing need to correct the colonial image of the Malays for this image still exerts a strong influence amongst an influential section of non-Malays, and it has also influenced a section of the Malay intelligentsia. The persistence of this image will impair the effort towards national integration. It has led to certain discriminatory practices in the employment of Malays—a number of employers have avoided Malays because they believe them to be lazy. Many people thought that by nature Malays are not endowed with the capacity to do business. All these ideas derive their origin from the colonial image of the Malays.

One need not be a Marxist to recognize that a dominant ruling elite upholding a definite social, economic and political order will utilize all channels of influencing thought and behaviour to impart its ideology to the minds of the people. The higher seats of learning, the press, the church, the party, the school, the books, all have been used for this purpose. The vigorous outburst of colonialism in the 19th century was accompanied by intellectual trends which sought to justify the phenomenon. Colonialism, or on a bigger scale, imperialism, was not only an extension of sovereignty and control by one nation and its government over another, but it was also a control of the mind of the conquered or subordinated.[37] It is not the intention here to enter into the controversy concerning the exact nature of the causes and forces responsible for the expansion of the West by 1900. The great bulk of Asia and Africa was colonized in the 19th century. In 1934, Great Britain, a country of 95,000 square miles and a population of 46,610,000, controlled a territory of approximately 5,217,000 square miles with a population of 415,595,000. Holland, a country of 13,000 square miles and a population of 8,290,000, controlled a territory of 792,000 square miles and a population of 60,971,000.[38] Malaysia came under British domination in the 19th century while the Philippines and Indonesia came under Spanish and Dutch rule respectively much earlier. British acquisition of territory in Malaysia started in Penang, in 1786. Malacca was taken from the Dutch in 1795, and Singapore acquired in 1819. The colonialism and its ideology which form the theme of the present work started long before the outburst of colonialism during 1870–1900 which attended the industrialization of Europe and the rise of industrial finance capital.

The second phase of colonial expansion, 1870–1900, does not affect our theme. Between 1819 and 1942 in Malaysia the ideology of colonial capitalism with its denigration of the native population, and its image of the native, remained basically the same. Though in terms of the economic and social history of the colonies the industrial and technological revolution of Europe in the 19th century had definite influences, this was not so in terms of its ideological history. The ruling ideology of colonial capitalism remained substantially the same because it was tied to a mode of production which did not experience drastic changes in vast areas of activity. Up to the outbreak of the Second World War, Malaysia, Indonesia, and the Philippines were basically plantation economies in a colonial capitalist setting. The economy was labour intensive and, as we shall see later, it was partly the question of labour which gave rise to the negative image of the native and to the ideology of colonial capitalism. The Industrial Revolution affected the colonies in the sense that they became markets for industrial goods in addition to being the producers of raw materials and cash crops. But that revolution did not scientifically and technologically transform the colonial societies in the institutional and structural sense as it did European societies. In Europe the Industrial Revolution converted existing classes, the essential professions and institutions into something different and this difference was the penetration of these classes, professions and institutions by the attributes of modern science and technology and the entire industrial life complex. In the colonies, the institutions, the profession, and the classes that were not functional to colonial capitalism were either eliminated or left to stagnate;[39] with the exception of a few like the administrative structure, they were not transformed.

This is not to say that colonialism did not effect major changes in the colonized societies; many such changes introduced by colonialism through its system of colonial capitalism, were different from those resulting from capitalism in Europe. In Europe capitalism corroded the forces of feudalism. In Southeast Asia, at least in the Philippines and Indonesia, colonial capitalism became a type of transformed feudal order with racial undertones. European domination over the Asian and African in the 19th century was everywhere accompanied by a rise in the social status of the white races and all their outward characteristics, such as their language, manners, dress and skin colour. A status system dominated by race was thus created. The Europeans formed the ruling class at the top of the hierarchy; next came those of mixed European blood and Christian in faith, then came the foreign Asian immigrant community, and finally the native population. In Indonesia only the native population were called upon for compulsory labour. "Discrimination was found everywhere in the fields of government and justice, eligibility for official positions and teaching. The native mother of a natural child of a European father had no rights of guardianship after the death of the latter. Her permission was not required before the child married. A person's position depended not on what he was himself but on the population group to which he belonged. Punitive measures were framed to ensure that the colour line should not be overstepped—it was forbidden to dress otherwise than in the manner customary in one's own population group. The colonial rulers even succeeded in large measure in forcing the Indonesians themselves to accept the system of values based on race. The members of the colonial ruling class were from their birth, or from the moment of their disembarkation on the shores of the Indies, conditioned to this pattern of behaviour and imbued with all the stereotypes connected with it."[40]

The colonial status system was a novel creation of colonial capitalism. The details differed in certain places and according to the dominating system, but in broad outline the status system was the same. In the economic system a similar situation prevailed with the European at the top, the foreign Asian in the middle, and the native at the bottom. Morally too the same hierarchy was upheld: Europeans were the most civilized, followed by the foreign Asian, and then the native. The social world of colonial capitalism was different from that of modern capitalism in the West. In the West there were extreme distances between rich and poor but the rich and the poor in England were both English. In the colonies there were no poor Europeans; there was also no very rich and economically powerful native capitalist class. In England the capitalists built industrial factories; in the colonies they did not. They planted cash crops and set up firms which received favoured treatment from the colonial government. The pattern of capitalism in the colonies was different from that in the colonizing countries. Mining and planting were the major capitalist investments in the colonies, not business and industry; industries started in the colonies were negligible in scope and level. Hence, as noted earlier, capitalism in the colonies did not promote the spread of modern science and technology because it was not attached to industry and because the system of mining and estate cultivation did not require much science and technology for the initial process of producing the raw materials which were then directly shipped to Europe. As the processing of the raw materials was done in Europe, the colonies did not benefit from the practice of modern science and technology associated with such processing.

The above factor led to the technological and scientific stagnation of native society during the colonial period. Colonial control of the economy, production, the school system, foreign relations, cultural contacts and the like, deprived the Malaysian, Indonesian and the Filipino societies of the freedom to select their own stimuli and react to them. This fact was very clearly attested by Rizal and other Filipino reformers during their sojourn in Spain in the latter part of the 19th century, when they complained about things Spain did not introduce into the Philippines. It was part of the colonial indoctrination that Western colonialism brought the benefits of Western civilization; the truth is that Western colonialism blocked the benefits of Western civilization. Developments after the independence of the Philippines, Indonesia and Malaysia attest to this. Schools multiplied by the hundreds, literacy spread very rapidly, newspapers sprang up like mushrooms, thousands of new buildings were constructed, tens of thousands of students went abroad to the West, numerous universities were set up. In all aspects of life there was a cultural explosion assimilating voluminous items from the Western civilization. The knowledge imparted, the method and the books were all from the West. It was the burst of a cultural dam once the wall of colonialism was broken; the former colonies derived far more from Western civilization after independence than before. A higher and more varied science and technology have now been assimilated from the West. This, despite the numerous problems Southeast Asian societies are facing, the problems of corruption, the distribution of income, and economic development, in short the general problem of backwardness. Despite all these, the countries have gained by comparison with colonial times. Contacts with the Western world have increased tremendously, and the inflow of science and technology have shot up significantly.

Hence the relatively static nature of Southeast Asian societies was due to colonial domination. Colonialism isolated these countries from each other and to a great extent from the Western world as a whole. Southeast Asian societies have been known for their assimilative nature long before the first Europeans arrived in the 16th century. Hinduism, Buddhism, and Islam together with their cultural traits had long been acquired by Southeast Asians. Numerous artifacts and processes of technology had been assimilated in the past, from India, China, and other regions.[41] Malays and Javanese had travelled to China, India, Persia and Arabia well before the coming of the Europeans. There was then already international cultural interaction, and contact with the Western world outside a colonial relationship would have speeded up the process. In fact it was colonialism which restricted and slowed down this process. Had there been no colonialism, by the end of the 19th century there would have been Malay and Javanese trading houses in the West. There would have been an independent, influential trading class in Indonesia and Malaysia, and possibly the Philippines, to spearhead the cultural contact. More elements of modern civilization would have been assimilated through this class. (Instead such a class was destroyed by colonialism, as we shall show in Chapter 12.)

What could have been emergence of commercial coastal towns, probably comparable to those of Italy in the 15th century and forging new forms of economic and social life, was hindered by the expansion of Dutch power in the 17th century. Thus what might have been the Renaissance of the Malay Archipelago was smothered before it was born.

The question whether the Philippines, Indonesia and Malaysia would have developed if Western imperialism had not intruded upon the scene is of cardinal importance. At this stage we can offer only the suggestion that the indigenous societies would have been more assimilative of the Western world, and hence the pace of economic and social change would now be further advanced. The mining class, instead of disappearing under British rule, in Malaysia, or of being dominated under Dutch rule in Malacca, would inevitably have acquired modern mining technology, just as they had other technologies in the past. An expanding European trade outside a colonial relationship would have provided the necessary incentive for growth within the context of non-colonial economic relations with the West. It was the growth of exports from the region that invited Western imperialism. The consciousness of cash crop exports had long existed. In Malaysia, the Philippines and Indonesia, as in the rest of Southeast Asia, there was a flourishing international trade and culture contact at least by the 15th century, if not earlier. The monopoly system was first effectively introduced by the Dutch, gradually and steadily, from the 17th century onwards.

This process is relevant to our theme. As a result of the effective Dutch monopoly affecting both Indonesia and parts of Malaysia, accompanied by a similar policy of the Spaniards in the Philippines, an independent, influential native trading class operating international business was eliminated. This was certainly obvious by the 18th century, when the vacuum was filled by a Chinese trading class. As colonial capitalism defined useful labour—the labour of traders, money making through commerce, selling goods to and from colonial European countries, or later in the 19th century managing cash crop plantations—the community which did not possess such a class was considered non-industrious. One of the reasons why 15th and early 16th century European visitors on the whole did not project an image of the lazy native was because there was a flourishing native trading class and the essential participation of the native population in commercial shipping. Politically relations were also different: Westerners did not rule the archipelago. The first major and effective Western rule there, apart from the Philippines, may be said to have started with the Dutch. The exact point in time is difficult to establish but it can safely be assumed that by the middle of the 18th century the Dutch was the major power in the archipelago; it was then that the theme of laziness began to develop. This theme was not intended for the native population, they were not asked for their opinion or told of opinions which others held about them. They were simply discussed. Until the present moment, with the exception of a few educated natives, the overwhelming majority of Southeast Asians are not aware that they have been the subject of discussion for centuries. The European colonial authors, administrators, priests and travellers wrote for a home audience. It was their own people they wish to convince of the laziness and backwardness of the natives.

Put into its historical and sociological context, the image of the lazy native will direct us to numerous historical and sociological phenomena. The rise and persistence of a governing idea are always linked to significant events and situations in the historical context. A governing idea is always part of a wider grouping of ideas; it forms a cluster, and its root has several ramifications. The image of the native is interwoven into the political and economic history of the region, the ethnocentricity of Western colonial civilization, the nature of colonial capitalism, the degree of enlightenment of the ruling power, the ideology of the ruling group, and certain events in history affecting colonial policy such as the rise of modern liberalism. It is these ramifications which the present work tries to understand and analyse. The first four chapters and the tenth chapter are primarily an exposition of various images of the native; the remainder discuss the problems arising from them. When presenting the view of an author, direct quotations as far as possible are given. This method is more reliable than paraphrase, for the full impact of what the author intended to say is diminished if it is not conveyed in his own words. An attempt is made to be as fair as possible to the author whose views are discussed; his whole work is carefully perused to avoid any misrepresentation out of context. Similarly in the use of historical documents, care is taken to place the issue within its proper context. Thus the citations selected to show how the Dutch crushed indigenous trade are not of isolated instances: they represented the general pattern. Hence the behaviour of the Portuguese captains of Malacca in extorting from traders is not considered as a determinant in the general strangulation of trade in the region, while the Dutch policy is.

The work of a scholar is sometimes similar to that of a judge and sometimes to that of a referee. Both require impartiality, but the referee applies the set of rules governing a game without any need to consider the question of truth based on circumstantial evidence; the judge, however, must evaluate the evidence. According to the nature of the facts the latter should pronounce judgement without being influenced by any party. Nevertheless it is the business of scholarship to face complication; for an avoidance of complication for the sake of simplicity can lead to a distortion of the truth. In historical and other scholarship, simplicity is sometimes advocated at the expense of truth. Events are assessed in terms of a clear-cut division. Simple and irrelevant motives are discussed which have no bearing on subsequent events; often this discussion is an attempt to minimize the guilt of a party in history. Colonial historical writing never fails to mention that the colonial powers were driven to acquire territories by sheer necessity. (They actually were interested in trade.) The advocate of simplicity takes this at its face value. The problem is, what is necessity? One set of necessities begets another. The image of the lazy and inferior native has also been conceived as a necessity.

As an illustration of the above consider the often-repeated statement that the Dutch established their rule in Indonesia under force of circumstances. When the Dutch State granted the United East India Company its charter in 1602, the charter envisaged territorial conquest as well, though diplomatic measures were preferred. Trade and war had been in the mind of the Company right from the very beginning, and the Dutch insistence on monopoly was a provocative factor. In Indonesia at the beginning of the 17th century, the native trading ports were open to several nationalities including Indians, Arabs, Persians, Turks, Abyssinians, the British, the French, the Portuguese and the Danes. For centuries the Archipelago had been practising free international trade. Suddenly a group emerged that assumed for itself the right of monopoly. This monopoly was directed not only against the English, the Portuguese and the Spaniards but also against native traders. It meant the strangulation of native trade, and national extermination was the price of resistance. Within the Company's circle there was disagreement regarding the use of violence. One of its dignitaries, Laurens Reael, was unable to associate himself with the policy of exterminating a whole population, the cutting off of food supplies and other essential commodities. This policy was to be applied against Banda, in East Indonesia.[42]

The above policy of force and violence was initiated barely a decade after the formation of the United East India Company. What historical necessity compelled them to territorial conquest except their intention to use force in order to trade? Other nations had profited from the Southeast Asian trade for centuries without feeling the need for territorial conquest. This does not imply that Dutch empire-builders like Jan Pieterszoon Coen at the beginning of the 17th century did not sincerely feel they should use force and acquire territories; he and the Directors of the Company did feel it was called for. But for historians to proclaim what the empire builders considered as necessary to be a historical necessity, is a suspension of the critical faculty. They deserve the censure of Marx and Engels, who declare such historians worse than the shopkeeper who knew the difference between what a man claimed to be and what he really was. The claims of the participants were uncritically accepted, and an air of inevitability was infused into the interpretation of events.

Similarly the degradation of the native population could be considered as a historical necessity. Once their country was taken they had to accept a subordinate place in the scheme of things. They had to be degraded and made to feel inferior and subservient for otherwise they would have cast off the foreign yoke. As Fanon put it: "Native society is not simply described as a society lacking in values. It is not enough for the colonist to affirm that those values have disappeared from, or still better never existed in, the colonial world. The native is declared insensible to ethics; he represents not only the absence of values, but also the negation of values. He is, let us dare to admit, the enemy of values, and in this sense he is the absolute evil. He is the corrosive element, destroying all that comes near him; he is the deforming element, disfiguring all that has to do with beauty or morality; he is the depository of maleficient powers, the unconscious and irretrievable instrument of blind forces."[43] But the colonial writers who degraded the natives implicitly or explicitly did not pose the question of its necessity. In their lack of awareness they did not even attempt to pause and think of the image they had created. Had they done so they would have discovered that the image each helped to create was born out of what was felt to be a colonial necessity. A most appropriate instance is furnished in the person of Sinibaldo de Mas, an emissary of the Spanish Crown sent to the Philippines to report on conditions there in 1842. His report is a unique and total presentation of the colonial philosophy of domination in its entire nakedness. It was a clear, frank, dispassionate and unambiguous discourse on how to impose one's rule.

Sinibaldo de Mas wrote in his official capacity on the assumption that Spain would retain the Philippines. Personally he was inclined to give the Philippines its independence, but his official views interest us here. He observed that the laws best for the Philippines depended on the purpose the government had in mind. This purpose could have been one of the following: to keep the islands as a colony forever; to consider the fate of the Spanish nationals living therein as of no importance whether or not the islands were lost by the Spaniards; or to "determine their emancipation and prepare the islands for independence".[44] If the second was preferred then the islands should have been left as they were. Mas was inclined to recommend the first although he agreed to the idea of an independence forced by historical circumstances as he saw them. To keep the islands as a colony de Mas suggested three basic policies: the Spaniards born in the Philippines should be reduced in number; the administration should undergo a thorough reform; and the most relevant to us, "the coloured population must *voluntarily* respect and obey the whites".[45] The reduction of the Spanish population was suggested because they became a burden creating discontent and subsequently generating the desire for independence arising from the prevalence of local interests. The Filipino Spaniard was a mislocated breed. "A Filipino Spaniard, for example, is in truth called a Spaniard and enjoys the rights of such, but he has never been to Spain and neither has he there friends nor personal relations. He has spent his infancy in the Philippines, there he has enjoyed the games of childhood and known his first loves, there he has all his companions, there he, has domiciled his soul. If sometime he should go to the Peninsula, soon he sighs for the skies of Asia. The Philippines is his native land. When he hears of Manila, of tobacco or money being sent to the government of Madrid, he experiences the same disgust that a Spaniard would feel if Spanish liquor or moneys were sent to Russia or England as tribute. Besides, the Philippine born Spaniards are for the most part the sons and grandsons of employees who dying in the colony left them nothing but a scanty education, the custom of acting as master and riding in carriages and the taste for dissolute living which laziness and vanity inspire. Hardly or not at all inclined to the religious life, discouraged by their lack of capital and their circumstances from engaging in mercantile, agricultural and industrial speculative enterprises and being too many for the scanty opportunities available in the legal or maritime careers, they seek solely to secure government positions."[46]

On extracting respect for the European from Filipinos, de Mas recommended the following: "To achieve this it is necessary to keep the former in such an intellectual and moral state that despite their numerical superiority they may weigh less politically than the latter, just as in a balance a pile of hay weighs less than a bar of gold. The work-hand, the goatherd do not read social contracts and neither do they know what occurs beyond their own town. It is not this kind of people who have destroyed absolutism in Spain, but those who have been educated in the colleges who know the value of constitutional liberties and accordingly fight for them. We must always keep this in mind if we are to think sincerely. It is indispensable that we avoid the formation of liberals, because in a colony, *liberal* and *rebellious* are synonymous terms."[47] In the military service the Filipino's rank should not be higher than that of a corporal. "It is better to let a Spanish rancher even if he can neither read nor write be an officer or sergeant rather than the most capable native. On the contrary, the more worthy and intelligent the latter may be the bigger the mistakes to be committed. Here one plays at a game of the loser winning. To bestow the rank of officer to the most vicious, cowardly and degraded is less dangerous and more permissible."[48] Religion was looked upon by de Mas as an instrument for power and a means to awaken respect for the Spaniards. "Taking religion as the foundation on which we base our rule it is clear that everything that will contribute to destroying the religious spirit will destroy and undermine this foundation. This being so nothing can be more directly injurious than the degradation and corruption of the ministers of worship and experience has demonstrated the truth that just as the first followers of Christ rapidly spread their beliefs due to their enthusiasm and their willingness to suffer martyrdom, so also in all parts where priesthood has given itself to gossip, pleasure, ambition and vice, the beliefs of the people immediately diminished and were converted into religious indifference. The government, hence, must consider the clergy as a power; and just as much care is taken not to allow in an army indiscipline and demoralization, so also must there be vigilance in the conduct of the priests. Let them have all the influence possible upon the towns, but let them always be European Spaniards and not feel any interest other than Spain's."[49] The laws also were to be used for the purpose of awakening respect and breaking pride. "It is also necessary to completely break the pride of the natives so that in all places and at all times they should consider the Spaniards as their masters and not their equal. Our laws of the Indies, dictated in the most beneficient spirit, but not always prudently, do not only concede them the same rights as a Spaniard but they seem to prefer them to the latter, particularly in the possession of lands."[50] He objected to Filipino members of the leading classes being given the title "don".[51] The Filipinos were not to be taught Spanish. "It is impossible to avoid circulating in the provinces papers and books which are inconvenient for them to read and experience has taught us that those who know our language are almost always the most headstrong of the towns and the ones who murmur, censure and go against the curate and the governors."[52] They should also not be taught to manage artillery and to manufacture firearms.[53]

If independence of the Philippines was the object of Spain then de Mas suggested measures opposed to those he proposed for retaining the colony. Personally he favoured preparing for independence not for idealistic reasons but because the Philippines were useless to Spain. It did not swell the Spanish coffers, it did not become a dumping ground of industrial goods from Spain as Spain lacked manufactured goods, and it was of no use as a cure for over-population as Spain did not have this problem.[54] He concluded his report with these prophetic words: "In conclusion if we keep the islands for love towards the natives, we are wasting our time and merit; because gratitude is found at times in persons but it is never to be expected of peoples; and if for our own sake, we fall into an anomaly because how can we combine the pretensions of liberty for our own selves and desire at the same time to impose our law on distant peoples? Why deny to others the benefits that we desire for our own native land? From these principles of morals and universal justice and because I am persuaded that in the midst of the political circumstances, in which Spain is in now, the state of that colony will be neglected; none of the measures (this is

my conviction) that I have proposed for keeping it will be adopted;
and the Philippines will become emancipated violently with great
loss to properties and lives of Europeans and Filipino Spaniards.
I think it would be infinitely much easier, more useful and more
glorious for us to achieve the merit of the work, by forestalling
it with generosity."[55]

His view of the Philippine problem was that of a realist. But
de Mas was a colonial writer despite his inclination to prepare the
Philippines for independence. It was the state of neglect of the
Philippines that compelled him to give up this wish. He recommended
a policy of divide and rule,[56] and subscribed to the view that might
was right, using it to justify Spanish rule in the Philippines. "I
love liberty but I am not one of those dreamers who desire the
end without the means. The Spaniards have a superb colony in
the Philippines and they want to keep it; they must, therefore,
use all the means within their reach to attain that goal. As for
the inhabitants of these islands will they be happier when left free
to themselves to wage war, one province against another, one village
against the other? No, certainly not. Thus for the good of the
motherland, in the very interest of the inhabitants of these islands,
the Spaniards must practice all wise and prudent measures necessary
to maintain the status and to keep their rights. But if someone
should inquire by what right do the Spaniards lay claim to remain
masters of the Philippines, this I must answer that without discours-
ing on rights, it is necessary to accept the fact. This exists everywhere. This is the law of might being right."[57] De Mas was enthusiastic about the achievements of the Catholic clergy in the
Philippines for they harmonized with his sense of Spanish patriotism.
"The Philippines is a conquest of religion. The first care of the
friars who arrived there was to proselytize the Indios and their
conversion was effected even before the islands had been admini-
stratively organized. The monks' influence grew more and more
and was strengthened by the very nature of this administration
whose governor-general only had a passing residence there and
whose various civil officials stayed only temporarily while the clergy
remained in the country maintaining their authority and exercising
it, in such a way as to make it cherished and respected. The
influence that the clergy exercises upon the Indios is all-powerful;
they do not abuse their authority unless it be to conserve it, but
they have known at least how to use it in the interests of the
Mother Country as well as their own; this has been noted in the
great crises which from time to time have menaced the colony;

they marched against the enemy at the head of their flock giving them an example of self-sacrifice and devotion to keep them in submission, a friar is worth more than a squadron of cavalry to duty. The only progress made in the Philippines, the roads and waterways, the public works, the social, political and charitable institutions are due to their efforts; and they have changed a race Malayan in origin into a population Spanish in customs and in beliefs. The conquests of the Catholic religion in America and in the Philippines are marked with a grandeur which impresses and sways all unprejudiced persons."[58] He was not oblivious to the faults of the friars: they hindered the industrialization of the Philippines.[59]

Sinibaldo de Mas' report on the Philippines submitted to the Spanish government in Spain is a most revealing document. It is a frank discourse on colonial policy. To a greater or lesser degree the British, the Dutch and the Portuguese had been practising his principles of domination. The destruction of the pride of the native was considered as a necessity; hence the denigration of native character. His attitude towards independence resembled that of the post-Second World War colonial who eventually came round to accept the desirability of independence, not because colonialism was morally wrong, but because it had become impractical for various reasons for the colonial power to retain the colonies. In this respect de Mas was well ahead of his times. His is clear proof that the question of independence could be raised during colonial times if one only has the interest to do so. Owing to the overwhelming influence of colonial ideology the topic was not even raised by almost all colonial writers and civil servants. Even de Mas discussed the topic within the context of the colonial ideology. Independence of the Philippines would be to him the result of a breakdown in Spanish rule, not an end in itself, namely, the freedom of a people. This was the ideology of late colonialism which de Mas anticipated a century before Furnivall and other colonial writers gave expression to it.

The sociology of knowledge has established that different people develop different perspectives depending on their location in the class structure, the intellectual stratum, the cultural milieu, the power hierarchy and the cultural group. These factors operated within the context of time, place and situation. Stereotypes of and prejudices against other groups have been a common occurrence in the history of man. The universal and particulars in the forms of these stereotypes and prejudices have to be isolated to arrive at a deeper understanding of the phenomenon. Let us examine the stereotype developed for the purpose of domination. The capitalist class in 19th century England had portrayed a degraded image of the working class. Many of the features of this image are also present in the image of the Southeast Asians. The British working class was thought to be morally inferior, disinclined to work, low in intelligence, and so forth. These traits were also suggested of the natives in colonized territory. But there was a vast difference between the two phenomena. When the British capitalist denigrated the British working class he was not denigrating the entire British nation. In the case of the colonial ideology, whole communities and ethnic groups were affected. Such prejudice tends to prevail for a very long time.[60]

The other difference is that colonial ethnic prejudice as represented by its image of the native was inflicted by a minority upon the majority. In non-colonial areas it is the majority which inflicts the prejudice upon the minority, for example with the Negro in the United States or the prejudice against gypsies and Jews in Europe. Yet another point of difference is that in non-colonial areas of the West the ethnic or racial stereotype functions in an interactional framework. The Negroes have been conscious of the stereotypes applied to them and they are reacting to them. The white image of the Negro becomes part of the interaction pattern of which both sides are conscious. In the case of the colonial image it was not part of the conscious interaction pattern of the natives but only of the European rulers. The lack of inhibition in the expression of the dominant minority is also a conspicuous factor. Imagination ran wild in forming the image of the native. Detailed accounts are given in the relevant chapters. This lack of inhibition, such as calling the natives animals who could be made to work only by force, characterized the colonial image-builders. Some openly preached in favour of the poverty of the natives on the grounds that poor people were easier to govern. This outlook had dominated colonial administration for centuries; it was only during the early decades of the 20th century that in Indonesia and Malaysia an honest attempt was made to look into the problem of native welfare.[61]

The British capitalist who entertained a distorted image of the working class did not insult the worker's religion, culture, race, language and customs—he shared these with him. The typology of prejudice within a tropical colonial setting is thus different from that which exists in the West. This is only one of the dimensions of research which bears on our theme, but we shall not follow this up as we are not primarily interested in the general typology of prejudice. Similarly we have excluded numerous subjects of enquiry into the nature and development of colonialism, selecting only those strictly relevant, the origin and function of the colonial image of the native. Subjects such as why the Dutch became the most formidable colonial power in Southeast Asia, the weaknesses of native states which caused them to succumb to colonial rule, the nature of each colonial rule and of the impact on native society, how colonial history was related to Western history, what would have happened if Western colonialism had not entered the scene, how colonialism contributed to the advancement or retardation of native society, all these and many others have been omitted, although reference is made to some of them. The drugging of the whole population by the colonial government might have had an effect on the kind of image of the native and other Asiatics in the colonial dependencies; it also reveals the ethical outlook of the colonial government. In this also we shall let the colonial ideologue speak his mind and then assess his defence of the opium policy.[62] The Asians were told they had no business mind after the native business class was eliminated by colonialism. This aspect of colonialism will be treated in the last part of the book.

NOTES

1. On this issue see Robert K. Merton, *Social Theory and Social Structure,* ch. 1, "Manifest and Latent Functions". Free Press, New York, 1969. Manifest thought is, for instance, the British discouraging the Malays from planting rubber on the grounds that they were better off cultivating rice. The latent thought, or motivation, could be to control the volume of rubber within profitable limits, or to avoid importing rice should more Malays leave the rice-fields to cultivate rubber.

2. Harry M. Johnson has conveniently listed five general sources of ideology. These are social strain, vested interests, bitterness about social change, limited perspective about social position, and persistence of outmoded traditions of thought. See his article "Ideology", II, in David L. Sills (ed.), *International Encyclopaedia of the Social Sciences,* vol. VII. Macmillan/Free Press, U.S.A. 1968.

3. Karl Mannheim, *Ideology and Utopia.* Routledge-Kegan Paul, London, 1948.

4. Harry M. Johnson, "Ideology", *op cit.*, p. 81.

5. The term dualism had been hotly debated ever since Boeke introduced it in 1930 to characterize Indonesian society. His fellow Western critics have not fully understood the implication of Boeke's typology of dualistic economic system in the colonies. Capitalism in the colonies did not have the same effect as in the West. Here is one instance: "The mass product of the new Western industries was thrown upon the Eastern market, sweeping away Native handicrafts, Native trade, and the Native system of distribution. There capitalism only offered new products, and did not provide any new sources of labour.

From a social point of view its effect was destructive rather than constructive. Instead of enriching the pattern of Oriental society, it made forms of social activity superfluous. As a result it broke off any number of local social props, but it did not open up the possibility for new ones to develop in their place. It forced a population with a rapid natural increase to revert to small-scale farming, and by bringing law and order stimulated the population's growth but at the same time stunted its differentiation." J. H. Boeke, "Dualistic Economics", p. 172, in *Indonesian Economics, W. Van Hoeve, the Hague, 1961. (Ed. chairman W. F. Wertheim.)

6. Werner Sombart, *The Quintessence of Capitalism.* Tr. M. Epstein. Howard Fertig, New York, 1967. "To understand the spirit that pervades all capitalist economies, we must strip them of their mechanical devices, their outer trappings, as it were. And these devices have always been the same, from the earliest dawn of capitalism down to this very day. A large sum of money is necessary for the production of marketable commodities; we call it capital. Someone has to provide this money; has to advance it, as it used to be called; perchance to enable a weaver to buy his raw material, perchance to provide the wherewithal to install a new pump in a mine; or, indeed for any and every industrial or commercial purpose. The money with which banks worked was from a very early period provided by deposits; the capital for commercial and shipping companies was forthcoming either by the underwriting of stock or through partnership contributions. Or, it might have been, that an individual had sufficient spare cash of his own with which to start a capitalist concern. But the different ways of collecting the capital had no influence on the spirit of the enterprise itself. The men who financed the scheme did not determine its spirit: that was done by the man who utilized the capital." Pp. 63–64.

7. See Zakir Husain, *Capitalism.* Asia Publishing House, London, 1967.

8. Max Weber, *The Protestant Ethic and the Spirit of Capitalism,* p. 17. Tr. Talcott Parsons. Charles Scribner, New York, 1958.

9. Amintore Fanfani, *Catholicism, Protestantism and Capitalism,* pp. 30–31. Sheed & Ward, London, 1938.

10. *Ibid.,* pp. 7–8.

11. Max Weber, *op. cit.,* p. 21.

12. T. Walter Wallbank, Alastair M. Taylor, *Civilization,* vol. 2, p. 87. Scott, Foresman, U.S.A., 1961. (Fourth edition.)

13. See V. I. Lenin, *Imperialism, the Highest Stage of Capitalism.* Foreign Languages Publishing House, Moscow. (Undated.) Eleventh Impression.

14. On the role of sedentary merchants, see N. S. B. Gras, "Capitalism-Concepts and History," in F. C. Lane, J. C. Riemersma, (eds.), *Enterprise and Secular Change.* Richard D. Irwin, Illinois, 1953.

15. On this see Syed Hussein Alatas, *Thomas Stamford Raffles (1781–1826): Schemer or Reformer?* Angus and Robertson, Singapore/Sydney, 1971.

16. Geoffrey Gorer, *Bali and Angkor,* p. 40. Michael Joseph, London, 1936.

17. Feodor Jagor in his "Travels in the Philippines", p. 36, in Austin Craig (ed.), *The Former Philippines thru Foreign Eyes.* Philippine Education, Manila, 1916.

18. Karl Marx, Frederick Engels, *The German Ideology,* p. 65. Part One, selected and edited by C. J. Arthur, Lawrence and Wisehart, London, 1970. Based on the complete Moscow edition of 1965.

19. Karl Mannheim, *Ideology and Utopia,* pp. 150, 266. Routledge and Kegan Paul, London, 1948.

20. This is merely a statement of belief. It requires substantiation but this will not be attempted here as it is not relevant and necessary.

21. U Khin Maung Kyi, "Western Enterprise and Economic Development in Burma", p. 26. *Journal of the Burma Research Society*, LIII, no. 1, June, 1970.
22. Karl Marx and Frederick Engels, *op. cit.*, p. 67.
23. Clive Day, *The Policy and Administration of the Dutch in Java*, p. 17. Macmillan, New York, 1904. Reproduced by Oxford University Press, Kuala Lumpur, 1966, under the title *The Dutch in Java*.
24. *Ibid.*, p. 17.
25. *Ibid.*, pp. 27–28.
26. *Ibid.*, p. 19.
27. *Ibid.*, p. 49.
28. *Ibid.*, p. 49.
29. *Ibid.*, p. 364.
30. J. S. Furnivall, *Netherlands India*, p. 468. Cambridge University Press, London, 1939.
31. J. S. Furnivall, *Colonial Policy and Practice*, p. XII. Cambridge University Press, London, 1948.
32. *Ibid.*, p. XI.
33. *Ibid.*, p. XII.
34. *Ibid.*, p. 468.
35. *Ibid.*, p. 469. His reasoning here, as in many other places, was not clear.
36. *Ibid.*, p. 489.
37. In this book colonialism and imperialism are considered basically the same with the only difference that imperialism is the control of vast foreign areas by one nation.
38. The figures are rounded off to the nearest thousand. The source is J. A. Hobson, *Imperialism*, p. 369, appendices, I, II. Allen and Unwin, London, 1938.
39. As an instance, see the development of horse-racing in Europe. It was there long before the Industrial Revolution. By the 20th century horse-racing had been transformed into a sport involving the application of modern science and technology to its development. Not so with cock-fighting in Southeast Asia. It remained traditional. Large areas of colonial society were not affected by the scientific and technological revolution.
40. W. F. Wertheim, *Indonesian Society in Transition*, pp. 137–138. W. van Hoeve, the Hague, 1969.
41. M. A. P. Meilink-Roelofsz, *Asian Trade and European Influence in the Indonesian Archipelago between 1500 and about 1630*. Martinus Nijhoff, the Hague, 1962. "In the 16th and early 17th centuries the Asians underwent considerable European influence in the technical field. By the second half of the 16th century these factors must already have increased Asia's powers of resistance and enabled the Asians to defeat the Portuguese efforts to secure a monopoly," p. 124.
42. M. A. P. Meilink-Roelofsz, *op. cit.*, p. 211. "In their letters the Directors had put forward plans to exterminate the Bandanese and repopulate the country with other peoples, and Reael begged them to consider whether a country could, in fact, be worth anything without its inhabitants, since it would then be left without a labour force for cultivating and harvesting the nutmegs. Elsewhere, after all, there had been plenty of bad experience gained through populating a country with other than its original inhabitants."
43. Frantz Fanon, *The Wretched of the Earth*, pp. 33–34. Tr. C. Farrington. MacGibbon and Kee, London, 1965.

44. Sinibaldo de Mas, *Report on the Condition of the Philippines in 1842*, III, *Interior Politics*, p. 121. Tr. C. Botor, revised A. Felix Jr., ed. J. Palazon. Historical Conservation Society, Manila, 1963. Sinibaldo de Mas was ahead of Dutch and British colonial writers by a hundred years in raising the question of independence.

45. *Ibid.*, p. 121.

46. *Ibid.*, p. 122.

47. *Ibid.*, p. 133.

48. *Ibid.*, pp. 133–134.

49. *Ibid.*, p. 147.

50. *Ibid.*, p. 156.

51. *Ibid.*, p. 161.

52. *Ibid.*, pp. 166–167.

53. *Ibid.*, p. 167.

54. *Ibid.*, p. 192.

55. *Ibid.*, p. 194.

56. *Ibid.*, p. 163.

57. *Ibid.*, p. 204, note 6.

58. *Ibid.*, pp. 202–203.

59. *Ibid.*, p. 203.

60. Colonial ethnic prejudice against the natives prevailed for more than three centuries in the Philippines and Indonesia. In Malaysia it lasted for more than one and a half centuries.

61. The indifference of the Dutch colonial government in Indonesia during the 19th century was attributed to this outlook. Highly educated Dutch civil servants, governor-generals and ministers were known to have shared this indifference. On this issue see F. de Haan, *Priangan*, vol. 1, pp. 430–431. Bataviasch Genootschap van Kunsten en Wetenschappen, Batavia, 1910.

62. On this matter see *Proceedings of the Committee appointed by His Excellency the Governor and High Commissioner to inquire into Matters relating to the Use of Opium in British Malaya*. Government Printing Office, Singapore, 1924. The revenue from opium between 1918 and 1922 was 30 per cent of the total revenue. (Appendix XVII, B19). 703 tons of prepared opium were sold to an adult Chinese population of 663,030, one ton to 9,043 during 1918–1922. The number of smokers must have been quite high.

CHAPTER 1

The Image of the Malays until the Time of Raffles

During the last four to five centuries, foreign observers have held definite opinions about the Malays. This opinion was directly formulated, without ambiguity. The Malays themselves had also an opinion on what they were, but this was not directly expressed. The Malay historical sources do not concern themselves with the problem. Nevertheless from them we can infer how the Malays think of themselves, their duties, their values, and their culture as a whole. But the foreign sources are full of accounts of the Malays. We may start with one of the earliest available of these, compiled by Tom Pires in 1512–1515 A.D. His description of the customs, laws and commerce of Malacca under the Malay Sultans (and written there), is perhaps the richest single source of information, unsurpassed until today. The tone of his writing is sober compared to many who wrote after him. As to the character of the Malays, Tom Pires mentions in passing that they were a jealous nation because the wives of the important people were never to be seen in public. When the wives did go out, they moved around in covered sedan chairs, with many of them together.[1]

The Portuguese Tom Pires was soon followed by another country-man, Duarte Barbossa. Barbossa's accounts, completed about 1518 A.D., is interesting in that his view of the Malays differs radically from that of the Javanese in Malacca and Java. He arrived in Malacca shortly after it was conquered by the Portuguese. He noted that the distinguished Malays of Malacca were serious Muslims, leading a pleasant life, in large houses outside the city with many orchards, gardens and water-tanks. They had separate trading houses in the city, and possessed many slaves with wives and children. Of their character Barbossa observed: "They are polished and wellbred, fond of music, and given to love".[2] Of the Javanese in Malacca, who were also Muslims, Barbossa had the following opinion: "They are very cunning in every kind of work, skilled in every depth of malice, with very little truth but very stout hearts (and are ready for every kind of wickedness). They have good weapons and fight without fear." [3]

His description of the Javanese in Java abounds in detail. We shall quote it in full since the material will be useful to a subsequent discussion. He writes, "The inhabitants are stout broad-chested men with wide faces, the most part of them go bare from the waist up, whereas others wear silk coats which come halfway down their thighs. Their beards are plucked out as a sign of gentility, their hair is shaven in the middle over the top of the head, they wear nothing on their heads, saying that nothing ought to be over the head; the greatest insult among them is to put the hand on any man's head. Nor do they build houses of more than one storey, so that none may walk over the heads of others. They are extremely proud, passionate and treacherous, and above all very cunning. They are very clever at cabinet-making. Other trades which they follow are the making of firelocks and arquebusses, and all other kinds of firearms; they are everywhere much sought after as gunners. Besides the *junks* which I have already mentioned they have well-built light vessels propelled by oars, and in these some of them go out to plunder, and there are great pirates among them. They are also very cunning locksmiths, and they make weapons of every kind very firm and strong and of good cutting steel. They are also great wizards and necromancers, and make weapons at certain hours and moments saying that he who carries them cannot die at the edge of the sword, and that they kill whensoever they draw blood, and of others they say that their owners cannot be vanquished when carrying them. Sometimes they will spend twelve years in making certain of these weapons, awaiting a favourable day and conjunction for the purpose. These the Kings value greatly and keep in their possession."

"Among them also there are many skilful riders and hunters; they have plenty of good riding-horses and nags and very many and excellent birds of prey; when they go a-hunting they take their wives with them in horse-waggons which are excellent and fair to see with coaches finely wrought in wood. Their women are exceedingly fair with very graceful bodies; their countenances are broad and ill-featured. They are great musicians and sempstresses who are very cunning in work of every kind, and are given to love-enchantments." [4]

In 1613, a century after Tom Pires and Duarte Barbossa, a distinguished Portuguese official, Emanuel Godhino de Eredia, submitted three treatises to the King of Spain. His description of the

Malays was written after a century of Portuguese domination in Malacca, while Tom Pires and Barbossa saw the Malays just after they lost their sultanate to the Portuguese. Eredia's observation on the Malays in Malacca thus refers to the period when they found themselves a subject community which had undergone a century of domination affecting various aspects of their life. After describing the appearance and dress of the Malays, Eredia claimed that the majority of them were cheerful, roguish, and very wanton. They were also ingenious and intelligent but negligent and careless about studies and arts. They spent their time amusing themselves. Hence few literati, mathematicians, or astrologers were to be found amongst them.[5]

He noted that the nobles occupied themselves with cock-fighting and music. Eredia thought better of the common people. "The common people have better characters, for they usually occupy themselves with mechanical arts to earn their livelihood; many of them are very accomplished craftsmen at carving and also at alchemy, imparting a fine temper to iron and steel for making arms."[6] About 35 years after the Dutch occupation of Malacca, an Italian traveller, and doctor of law, John Francis Gemelli Careri, arrived at Malacca in June 27, 1695. He complained that Malacca was an expensive city, and wrote that the Malays (*menangkabaus*) who were Muslim were very great thieves. They were such mortal enemies of the Dutch that they refused to have any commerce with them, and were, according to Careri, wild people living like beasts who could not easily submit to the Dutch. Hence the Dutch dominion reached not more than 3 miles around the city.[7]

Our next observer of Malay character is a Dutchman, Francois Valentyn, who completed his history of Malacca in 1726 A.D. We may perhaps consider Valentyn as one of the earliest Europeans who cultivated a scholarly interest in the Malays, their culture and language. He knew Malay and took great trouble to collect Malay literary and historical works. As to Malay character, he noted that the Malays were of a very lively nature, witty, with a great self-conceit. They were the most cunning, the most ingenious, and the politest people of the whole East, not much to be relied upon.[8] A contemporary of Valentyn, a certain Portuguese Captain de Vellez Guirreiro, in his account of Johore during the visit of a Portuguese governor designate of Macao to Johore from Goa, expressed the general Portuguese view that the Malays were barbarians.[9] He described the Malays in Johore who had retained their independence from Western colonial rule in Malacca. In his account there was no reference to the wildness, unreliability, or cunningness of the Malays as a nation. He was full of appreciation for the ruler of Johore but he condemned the coastal Malays as belonging to "the accursed Mohammedan sect, treacherous by nature and of little loyalty."[10] He was rather harsh on the Bugis Malays with whom the Portuguese Governor was involved in an incident.[11] On the other hand, Raffles, whom we shall now discuss, was well disposed towards the Bugis.

Sir Thomas Stamford Raffles, the founder of Singapore and British Lieutenant Governor of Java and Bengkulen, had his first contact with the Malays in Malacca when he became Agent for the Governor-General in 1810 A.D. Apart from his public life Raffles was deeply interested in the study of the Malays. It can be suggested that the study of the national character of the Malays had in Raffles a significant pioneer, despite the shortcomings of his method and conclusions judged by modern scientific standard. The development of his views on the subject is interesting, as is his bias and partiality. An assessment of Raffles's view and those of the others mentioned will be made later; for the moment we shall just present his views on the Malays as a whole. Raffles considered the Malays as a nation within the greater context of the racial and ethnic configuration embracing Indonesia and the Philippines. "I cannot," he writes, "but consider the Malayan nation as one people, speaking one language, though spread over so wide a space, and preserving their character and customs, in all the maritime states lying between the Sula Seas and the Southern Ocean, and bounded longitudinally by Sumatra and the western side of Papua or New Guinea."[12]

According to Raffles the Malays did not achieve a high intellectual stage of development. "From the comparative rude and uncivilized character of the Malay nation, learned disquisition is not to be looked for but simple ideas, simply expressed, may illustrate character better than scientific or refined composition."[13] He was particularly interested in the maritime codes of the Malays and their legal institutions. It was the absence of a well-defined and generally accepted system of law which, according to Raffles, was the greatest influence in the deterioration of the Malay character. The absence of this general system of law was attributed to the conversion of the Malays to Islam, but it was also due to the previous Hindu influence, which had led to diversification in the realm of law. The absence of a synthesis between customary law, generally derived from Indian sources, and Islamic law, contributed to the diversification and degradation deplored by him. Anomalous institutions had sprung up in different states. Such a situation opened the door to the caprice and tyranny of Malay rulers and a general insecurity both of person and property. [14]

Historically and sociologically Raffles's view on the causes of diversification is unsound. The diversification was there long before the coming of Islam. Logically it does not necessarily follow that diversification created insecurity of person and property. However, we mention this fact because of its relation to Raffles's conception of the Malays. It is his opinion that the Malays were degraded when the British found them. Before the coming of Islam, according to Raffles, the Malays had in general made considerable progress in civilization. The combined influence of Islam and the Arabs, the Dutch, and the Chinese led to their decline. [15] The causes leading to the decline of the Malays are summarized as follows: "The causes which have tended most to the depression of the Malays, and the deterioration of their character, are the following: the civil commotions to which every state is liable from the radical want of strength in the sovereign, and the constant wars between petty chieftains, and heads of villages or districts: the ill-defined succession to the throne, from the doctrine of primogeniture being imperfectly recognized in the Malay states: the prevalence of piracy in all the eastern seas: the system of domestic slavery, with all its concomitant evils, as wars for the purpose of procuring slaves, and the want of general confidence between family and family, man and man: the want of a generally established and recognized system of laws regarding all questions, civil and criminal, in the Malay states: the want of a similar system of commercial regulations respecting port duties, anchorage, and other charges, to prevent arbitrary exactions in the various Malay ports: the discouragement given to regular trade by the monopolies of the Malay Rajahs: the redress of these evils is, in a great measure in the power of the English nation; it is worthy of their general character, and there is no other nation that possesses the means in an equal degree, even if it possessed the inclination." [16]

In Raffles's opinion the historical and sociological circumstances affecting the Malays contributed to the emergence of certain generally perceived peculiarities such as the Malay inclinations to act on individual will and to express ferocious passion. [17] Raffles also noted other traits of Malay character as he conceived them. He thought it tolerably correct to see the Malay as being so indolent that when he has rice nothing will induce him to work. Accustomed to bear arms from infancy and to rely on his own powers for safety, and to fear those of his associate, he becomes the most polite of all savages. Yet he is very sensitive to insult and is resentful of conformity imposed by others. Long nurtured grievances sometimes express themselves in retaliation against the innocent. [18] The many negative traits of Malay character noted by Raffles were explained by him in a historical and sociological manner. It is this side of his works, his approach, rather than his diverse conclusions, which interests us at this juncture. Though Raffles saw certain elements in Malay culture and society constituting the psychological make-up of the Malays as a nation, he considered these as effects of situational factors. The Malay's readiness to draw his *kris* in self-defence, his sensitivity to insult, his recourse to piracy in some instances,[19] were all explained by Raffles in the light of situational exigencies. In his letter to the Earl of Buckinghamshire, he complained that the character of the peoples inhabiting Malaysia and Indonesia was then not known to Europe.[20]

Raffles suggested the following explanation for the prevalence of certain traits in Malay society. "The creeses is to the Malay what the practice of duelling is to European nations. There are certain points in the composition of every man's notions which cannot be regulated by courts of law; the property, the life, the character of the European is protected by law; but yet there are some points, and these are the very points on which all society hinges, which are not protected. In support of these he condemns the law which stigmatizes him as a murderer, and the very men who made the laws still say he is right. Neither the property, the life, nor the character of the Malay is secured by law — he proudly defends them with his own hand whenever they are endangered. The readiness with which an injury is thus redressed has a wonderful effect in the prevention of injuries; and except in warlike enterprise the Malay is seldom known to draw his criss, unless perhaps in defence of what he considers his honour. The certainty of resentment has produced that urbanity and consideration for the feelings of each other, that they are habitually wellbred, and if they are to be termed savages, certainly they are the most polite of all savages; but in truth they are very far from being savages."[21] The effect of exploitation on character was also noted by him. Exploitation through forced labour and oppressive taxation, characteristics of Dutch rule in Java, was strongly condemned by Raffles. Of this he noted the following: "The baneful influence of this system was but too clearly developed in the debasement of the popular mind and in that listless and apathetic feeling which appeared to characterize the Javanese nation. Whilst the rich and powerful were living in pampered luxury, the poor provincials laboured under all the horrors of penury and want; but blessed with a fruitful soil and an humble submissive mind, they were enabled to bear up under all these accumulated deprivations and misfortunes."[22]

Before we leave Raffles and hear our next observer, it is worthwhile to mention one more observation of Raffles which is, I believe, rather significant. He believed that the present Malay nation was more or less the creation of Islam. "The most obvious and natural theory on the origin of the Malays is, that they did not exist as a separate and distinct nation until the arrival of the Arabians in the Eastern Seas. At the present day they seem to differ from the more original nations, from which they sprung in about the same degree, as the Chuliahs of Kiling differ from the Tamul and Telinga nations on the Coromandel coast, or the Mapillas of Malabar differ from the Nairs, both which people appear, in like manner with the Malays, to have been gradually formed as nations, and separated from their original stock by the admixture of Arabian blood, and the introduction of the Arabic language and Moslem religion."[23] Raffles's conception of the Malay nation is the same as the one upheld in the present Constitution of Malaysia. Our appraisal of Raffles's study of the Malays will be included in a general discussion later.

The next person of interest is John Crawfurd, a British Resident at the court of the Sultan of Java. He wrote on the manners, arts, languages, religions, institutions, and commerce of the Indian Archipelago. He suggested that the region lacked geniuses and great events. The geographical situation of the country inhibited the exercise of great military talents. There were a few exceptions to this like Sultan Agung of Mataram and the Laksamana of Malacca during the Portuguese attack on the Sultanate. Like Raffles he endorsed the sociological explanation of what he considered as the intellectual backwardness of the Malay and Indonesian peoples. He said: "Such a feebleness of intellect is the result of such a state of society, and such a climate, that we may usually reckon that the greatest powers of the native mind will hardly bear a comparison, in point of strength and resources, to the ordinary standard of the human understanding in the highest stages of civilization, though they may necessarily be better suited for distinction in the peculiar circumstances in which they are called into action."[24]

NOTES

1. Tom Pires, *The Suma Oriental of Tom Pires,* p. 268. Tr. and ed. Armando Cortesao. Hakluyt Society. vol. 2, 2nd Series, no. 90, London, 1944.
2. Duarte Barbossa, *The Book of Duarte Barbossa,* p. 176, Tr. and ed. M. L. Dames. Hakluyt Society, vol. 2, 2nd Series, no. 49, London, 1921.
3. Duarte Barbossa, *ibid.,* p. 177. I guess Barbossa referred to the Javanese as people from Java, not necessarily as an ethno-linguistic group inhabiting the central and eastern part of the island.
4. Duarte Barbossa, *ibid.,* pp. 191–194.
5. E. G. de Eredia, "Description of Malacca and Meridonial India and Cathay", p. 31. Tr. from the Portuguese by J. V. Mills. *JMBRAS,* vol. VIII, pt. 1, April. 1930.
6. E. G. de Eredia, *ibid.,* p. 39.
7. J. F. G. Careri, *A Voyage Round the World,* p. 272. (Translator and publisher unknown.)
8. F. Valentyn, "Description of Malacca", pp. 52–53, Tr. D. F. A. Hervey. *JSBRAS,* no. 18, June, 1884.
9. J. T. de Vellez Guerreiro, "A Portuguese account of Johore". Tr. T. D. Hughes. *JMBRAS,* vol. XIII, pt. 2, October, 1935.
10. J. T. de Vellez Guerreiro, *ibid.,* p. 119.
11. J. T. de Vellez Guerreiro, *ibid.,* p. 127.
12. T. S. Raffles, *Memoir,* p. 29, vol. 1 (ed.), Sophia Raffles. James Duncan, London, 1835.
13. T. S. Raffles. *ibid.,* p. 30.
14. T. S. Raffles. *ibid.,* pp.98–99.
15. The Dutch and the Chinese were characterized as venal and crafty. The Arabs fared much worse. See Raffles, *ibid.,* pp. 80–83.
16. T. S. Raffles, *ibid.,* pp. 91–92.
17. T. S. Raffles. *ibid.,* p. 41.
18. T. S. Raffles. *ibid.,* pp. 258–259.
19. T. S. Raffles, *ibid.,* pp. 91–93.
20. T. S. Raffles. *ibid.,* p. 287.
21. T. S. Raffles. *ibid.,* pp. 288–289.
22. T. S. Raffles. *ibid.,* p. 244.
23. T. S. Raffles. *ibid.,* p. 40.
24. J. Crawfurd. *History of the Indian Archipelago,* vol. II, p. 287. Archibald Constable, Edinburgh. 1820.

CHAPTER 2

The British Image of the Malays in the Late 19th Century and 20th Century

During the 19th century, interest in the Malays took definite shape and direction. The number of publications and journals had strikingly increased. Two writers of this period, Hugh Clifford and Frank Swettenham, are of particular interest to us. Both were contemporaries and both were British Residents when their publications appeared. They were conscious of the major changes affecting Malay society. The Malays changed considerably after the introduction of British rule in Malaya. Both Swettenham and Clifford welcomed the change and considered it to be necessary progress, at least in so far as the government system and certain practices were concerned. Swettenham had, more than any single writer, written the most on Malay character. His earlier books on the Malays were completed in 1885 and 1899.[1] A later book first published in 1906 contains a chapter on the Malays.

The following is his picture of the Malays: "The Malay is a brown man, rather short of stature, thickset and strong, capable of great endurance. His features, as a rule, are open and pleasant: he smiles on the man who greets him as an equal. His hair is black, abundant and straight. His nose is inclined to be rather flat and wide at the nostrils, his mouth to be large; the pupils of his eyes are dark and brilliant, while the whites have a bluish tinge; his cheek bones are usually rather marked, his chin square, and his teeth, in youth, exceedingly white. He is well and cleanly made, stands firmly on his feet, and is deft in the use of weapons, in the casting of a net, the handling of a paddle, and the management of a boat; as a rule, he is an expert swimmer and diver. His courage is as good as most men's, and there is about him an absence of servility, which is unusual in the East. On the other hand, he is inclined to swagger, especially with strangers."[2] A Malay belonging to a poor family after receiving the traditional education, had to work, to help his father plant rice, fish in the river, tend goats, or collect jungle produce. "The young Rajas and other gilded youths took to top-spinning, cock-fighting, gambling, opium-smoking, love-making, and some of them to robbery, quarrelling, and murder." Swettenham's description refers to the Malays of 1874 in Malaya. He suggested another trait. "The leading characteristic of the Malay of every class is a disinclination to work."[3]

Swettenham also suggested that the Malay is a Muslim, fatalist, and very superstitious. Concerning his ruler and tradition, the Malay, according to Swettenham, has the following view: "Above all things, he is conservative to a degree, is proud and fond of his country and his people, venerates his ancient customs and traditions, fears his Rajas, and has a proper respect for constituted authority — while he looks askance on all innovations, and will resist their sudden introduction. But if he has time to examine them carefully, and they are not thrust upon him, he is willing to be convinced of their advantage. At the same time he is a good imitative learner, and, when he has energy and ambition enough for the task, makes a good mechanic."[4] Swettenham's conception of Malay character was considerably modified compared to some earlier writers. He did not agree in characterizing the Malays as treacherous. "The Malay has often been called treacherous. I question whether he deserves the reproach more than other men."[5] He further noted the traits of loyalty, hospitality, generosity, and extravagance which constituted the Malay character. In addition, he mentioned the tendency of the Malay to borrow money if he knows a person well, though he would seldom find it possible to repay the debt. But he would undertake any service on the lender's behalf until he had discharged himself of his obligation.[6]

As Raffles and a few others, Swettenham attempted by means of a sociological and historical approach to explain certain negative traits he believed to be in the Malay character. The traits in question are the alleged dislike of the Malay for hard and continuous work, either of the brains or the hands, and his lack of initiative. Regarding the first mentioned it was explained by Swettenham as due to the fact that interest in manual and intellectual labour was not situationally cultivated. "Whatever the cause," he explained, "the Malay of the Peninsula was, and is unquestionably opposed to steady continuous work. And yet, if you can only give him an interest in the job, he will perform prodigies; he will strive, and endure, and be cheerful and courageous with the best. Take him on the war-path or any kind of chase, or even on some prosaic expedition which involves travel by river, or sea, or jungle, something therefore which has a risk: then the Malay is thoroughly awake, and you wish for no better servant, no more pleasant or cheery companion. Perhaps it is these qualities which, a hundred years ago, made him such a dreaded pirate, a life to which he was driven by the unpardonable proceedings of early European navigators and adventurers, especially the Portuguese and the Dutch."[7]

As to the lack of initiative, or incentive for acquiring wealth, he offered the following explanation: "There was, in 1874, a very broad line indeed between the ruling classes in Malaya and the raiats, the people. The people had no initiative whatever; they were there to do what their chiefs told them—no more, no less. They never thought whether anything was right or wrong, advantageous to them personally or otherwise; it was simply, 'What is the Raja's order?' Wherever the Raja was recognized his order ran; the only exception would be where some local chief defied or disputed the authority of the Raja and told the people that they were only to take orders from him. Such a case would happen but seldom."[8] Apart from the preceding factor, geographical factors were noted by Swettenham. "Less than one month's fitful exertion in twelve, a fish basket in the river or in a swamp, an hour with a casting net in the evening, would supply a man with food. A little more than this and he would have something to sell. Probably that accounts for the Malay's inherent laziness; that and a climate which inclines the body to ease and rest, the mind to dreamy contemplation rather than to strenuous and persistent toil. It is, however, extremely probable that the Malay's disinclination to exert himself is also due to the fact that, in the course of many generations, many hundreds of years, he has learned that when he did set his mind and his body moving, and so acquired money or valuables, these possessions immediately attracted the attention of those who felt that they could make a better use of them than the owner."[9]

The preceding views and explanations of Malay character dating from the 16th century onward, are sufficiently variegated and provocative to merit further enquiry. With Hugh Clifford, however, a further dimension to the problem was introduced. Like Swettenham, Clifford was also concerned with the impact on traditional Malay society and character of the introduction of British rule in Malaya. Until the British Government interfered in the administration of the Malay States in 1874, the Malays of the Peninsula were, to all intents and purposes, living in the Middle Ages. The introduction of British rule released a set of reactions transforming Malayan society. Clifford himself was conscious of being an instrument of this rapid transformation when he expressed his task in 1896 as "to bring about some of those revolutions in facts and in ideas which we hold to be for the ultimate good of the race."[10]

Unlike any previous writer, he made the distinction between the Malays on the East Coast and those in the West Coast. Those on the West Coast, had, he claimed, "become sadly dull, limp, and civilized".[11] The East Coast Malays, who were more or less uncivilized, and whose customs were unsullied by European vulgarity, to use his own words, appeared to him to be more attractive as a type.[12] Both Clifford and Swettenham deplored the ignorance of the Europeans on matters relating to the Malays. In 1874, Malaya was conceived as an unknown, mysterious, and barbarous country. An impression prevailed that some kind of internal struggle for power was going on for the sheer pleasure of fighting.[13] The nature of Malayan society and the change it experienced under the impact of British influence were not properly understood. It was Clifford more than anyone else who touched at the very core of the problem when he emphasized the significance of British rule as an agent of change.

Writing in 1896, he suggested the following: "What we are really attempting, however, is nothing less than to crush into twenty years the revolutions in facts and in ideas which, even in energetic Europe, six long centuries have been needed to accomplish. No one will, of course, be found to dispute that the strides made in our knowledge of the art of government, since the thirteenth century, are prodigious and vast, nor that the general condition of the people of Europe has been immensely improved since that day; but, nevertheless, one cannot but sympathize with the Malays, who are suddenly and violently translated from the point to which they had attained in the natural development of their race, and are required to live up to the standards of a people who are six centuries in advance of them in national progress. If a plant is made to blossom or bear fruit three months before its time, it is regarded as a triumph of the gardeners's art; but what, then, are we to say of this huge moral-forcing system which we call 'Protection'? Forced plants, we know, suffer in the process; and the Malay, whose proper place is amidst the conditions of the thirteenth century, is apt to become morally weak and seedy, and to lose something of his robust self-respect, when he is forced to bear nineteenth-century fruit."[14]

The impact of British rule on traditional Malay society, with its negative as well as positive traits, as an explanation of the change in Malay character, is one which derives much support from sociological and anthropological analysis. In addition to citing the phenomenon, Clifford stressed the need to understand the Malays by viewing matters from their standpoint, an attitude which he considered as "the common European inability". [15] Both Swettenham and Clifford emphasized the methodological principle of understanding events from within as perceived by the participants. They stressed the necessity of knowing the Malay language, living intimately with the Malays, and studying them with a sympathetic attitude. This sound methodological principle had not always been applied by subsequent writers as a result of which they obtained a distorted picture of the object under examination.

Clifford, as we noted earlier, differentiated between the East and West coast of Malays. Apparently he had in mind two categories of differentiation. One, between Malays before British rule in 1874, the other after 1874. The other category of differentiation refers to the Malays before the coming of the British, and I assume the other Europeans. Clifford saw a difference in character between the Trengganu and Pahang Malays as such. According to Clifford, the Pahang Malays think chiefly of deeds of arms, illicit love intrigues, and sports forbidden by his religion. They are ignorant, irreligious, unintellectual and arrogant. Their good qualities are their manliness and recklessness. They are capable of extraordinary loyalty to their chiefs. [16]

Of their attitude towards labour, Clifford said the following: "He never works if he can help it, and often will not suffer himself to be induced or tempted into doing so by offers of the most extravagant wages. If, when promises and persuasion have failed, however, the magic word krah is whispered in his ears, he will come without a murmur, and work really hard for no pay, bringing with him his own supply of food. Krah, as everybody knows, is the system of forced labour which is a State perquisite in unprotected Malay countries, and an ancestral instinct, inherited from his fathers, seems to prompt him to comply cheerfully with this custom, when on no other terms whatsoever would he permit himself to do a stroke of work. When so engaged, he will labour as no other man will do. I have had Pahang Malays working continuously for sixty hours at a stretch, and all on a handful of boiled rice; but they will only do this for one they know, whom they regard as their Chief, and in whose sight they would be ashamed to murmur as to the severity of the work, or to give in when all are sharing the strain in equal measure." [17]

As to the Malays of Trengganu, Clifford regarded them as a very different type. First and foremost they are men of peace. Their sole interest is their trade and occupation. They have none of the pride of race and country alleged to be so marked among the Pahang Malays. They have none of the "loyal passion" for their intemperate rulers.[18] As artisans they excelled above other Malays. Of the Kelantan Malays, Clifford had much less pleasant things to say. They have less self-respect, touchy, sensitive, and when brave it is with the courage of the ignorant. They excelled in their proclivity to steal, enjoying the reputation of thieves among thieves.[19]

Before we pass on to the next observer, there is one more noteworthy observation made by Clifford on the psychology of the Malays. He claimed that the Malays were, as a whole, capable of developing a psycho-pathological disorder called *latah*. In the state of *latah*, which can be elicited by any sudden noise, shock, or a surprising command, the subject appears unable to realize his own identity, or to do anything but imitate, often accompanied by the use of vulgar language. Anyone who attracts his attention can make him do any action by simply feigning it. The condition can last for hours until the subject drops down in exhaustion, after which recovery to normal consciousness takes place. Only adults are known to have such a disorder.

According to Clifford any Malay is capable of developing into a typical case of *latah* if he is sufficiently persecuted, teased, and harassed. The difference between him and an advanced case is only a matter of degree.[20] Added to the theory that the Malays were decadent and degenerate when the British found them, is the theory that they were as a nation, potential victims to a pathological disorder of the mind, the seed of which already existed in their mental make-up. This aspect of Clifford's characterization of the Malays can be brushed aside without further ado. It has no empirical basis whatsoever. Should the theory be accepted, there would be no reason for us not to regard any other nation as potentially pathological. We may, for instance, suggest that the American people are potentially pathological exhibitionist because there are exhibitionists found in American society.

Approximately four decades after the introduction of British rule in Malaya, judgements on the Malays assumed a more sober tone. Thus Wright and Reid brushed aside some earlier references to Malay laziness and treachery. They said, "How unjust this assumption was has been proved strikingly by the later history of Malaya, which, with one or two exceptions, has shown that under proper treatment the Malay is as loyal and trustworthy as any of the subject races of the Crown."[21] According to them, those who are intimate with the Malays would subscribe to the following judgement on Malay character: "They recognize in him one of Nature's gentlemen, and are often enthusiastic in their testimony to the possession of instincts and habits of thought which mark him out from other Oriental races with whom they may have been brought in contact. Nevertheless, even the Malay's best friends are compelled to admit that he does not take kindly to manual labour. His tastes incline in the direction of sport—cock-fighting by preference—and these are incompatible with the strenuous life. He goes through existence with an easy grace born of long centuries of experience in the art of getting the best of things with the smallest exertion. Not so very many years ago he was accustomed to vary his daily exercises in killing time with a little indiscriminate piracy."[22]

Twenty-six years following the above observation, Wheeler, in a much more ambitious undertaking as far as national character goes, formed yet another opinion of the Malays. The traits which particularly impressed him were others, docility and friendliness. When discussing the problem of achieving harmony between the stability of the traditional order and the change introduced by the new one, he delivered the following judgement concerning the Malays: "Few races offer a better opportunity for the study of this problem than the Malays. Their old traditions and beliefs have suffered no violent break; their docility and friendliness create a favourable atmosphere for that progress which is certainly necessary and which has already made great strides. But on the other hand a certain lassitude and passivity, partly climatic, partly born of Islam, are favourable to a state of stagnation which, if not vitalized by new currents, can only end in decay."[23]

To conclude our presentation of foreign views on the Malays, we may note the one suggested by one of the most industrious British scholars of Malay subjects, Sir Richard Windstedt. References are made here to some of his most recent works. Among some of the traits mentioned by Windstedt were the lack of originality amongst the Malays, their racial pride, their adaptability, and their undeserved reputation for idleness. Here are some of his observations: "The Malay has great pride of race—due, perhaps, as much to his Muhammedan religion as to a past he has forgotten. He has, as Sir Frank Swettenham once wrote, 'as good a courage as most men', and a better sense of the values of what life offers than is generally gained from book philosophies. Even the aborigines of Malaya have attractive manners, and the Malay has not only undergone the discipline of Hindu etiquette but has been affected by his Muslim teaching much as an English boy has been affected by the public school, acquiring poise and confidence. Because he is an independent farmer with no need to work for hire, the Malay has got an undeserved reputation for idleness, which his Asiatic competitors take care to foster. In affairs he is not only diplomatic but intelligent and statesman-like, with a natural ability to weigh both sides of a question."[24]

On Malay literature he wrote the following: "As for Malay literature, hitherto it has been a literature of translation. The Malay is still a child of nature in a sophisticated world that awaits his exploration. If any Malay should develop an original literary bent, it is more likely that the impulse will come from densely populated Java or even from Sumatra rather than from the two and a half million Malays of the peninsula, though it is not always the probable that happens."[25] A similar opinion was expressed in another work. "Anyone who surveys the field of Malay literature will be struck by the amazing abundance of its foreign flora and the rarity of indigenous growth."[26]

NOTES

1. F. A. Swettenham, *The Real Malay*. John Lane, London and New York, 1907: and *Malay Sketches*, John Lane, London and New York, 1913.
2. F. A. Swettenham, *British Malaya*, p. 134. Allen and Unwin, London, 1955.
3. F. A. Swettenham, *ibid.*, p. 136.
4. F. A. Swettenham, *Malay sketches, ibid.*, p. 3.
5. F. A. Swettenham, *ibid.*, p. 4.
6. F. A. Swettenham, *British Malaya*, p. 140.
7. F. A. Swettenham, *ibid.*, pp. 139–140.
8. F. A. Swettenham, *ibid.*, p. 141.
9. F. A. Swettenham, *ibid.*, p. 137.
10. Hugh Clifford, *In Court and Kampong*, p. 53. The Richards Press, London, 1927.
11. Hugh Clifford, *ibid.*, p. 6.
12. Hugh Clifford, *ibid.*, p. 7. See also p. 20.
13. F. A. Swettenham, *The Real Malay*, pp. 7–8.
14. Hugh Clifford, *ibid.*, p. 3.
15. H. Clifford, *ibid.*, p. 2.
16. H. Clifford, *ibid.*, pp. 17–18.
17. H. Clifford, *ibid.*, p. 19.
18. H. Clifford, *ibid.*, p. 20.
19. H. Clifford, *ibid.*, p. 25.
20. H. Clifford, *Studies in Brown Humanity*, pp. 195–196. Grant Richards, London, 1898.

21. A. Wright, T. H. Reid, *The Malay Peninsula,* p. 314. Fisher Unwin, London, 1912.
22. *Ibid.,* p. 315.
23. L. R. Wheeler, *The Modern Malay,* p. 23. Allen and Unwin, London, 1928.
24. Sir Richard Windstedt, *Malaya and Its History,* p. 17. Hutchinson University Library, London, 1956.
25. Sir Richard Windstedt, *The Malays: A Cultural History,* p. 181. Routledge and Kegan Paul, London, 1956.
26. Sir Richard Windstedt, "A History of Classical Malay Literature", p. 5. Monograph on Malay subjects no. 5, *JMBRAS,* XXXI, pt. 3, 1958.

CHAPTER 3

The Image of the Filipinos during the 17th to the 19th Centuries

The Filipinos too had been negatively described by the Spaniards, and other European visitors. Careri, writing on the Filipinos after his visit to the Philippines in 1696, suggested that they resembled the Malays in their shallowness of judgement. Of the Bisayans he said that they had grown lazy since the Spaniards ruled over them. To quote him, "It is their laziness, that makes them appear less ingenious; and they are so entirely addicted to it, that if in walking they find a thorn run into their foot, they will not stoop to put it out of the way, that another may not tread on it."[1] The friar, Sabastian Manrique, visiting Manila during his travel to this part of the world (1629–1634) wrote of the Chinese in Manila as a group whose life's blood is the Spanish dollar. The scent of the Spanish dollar would attract the Chinese "with such vehemence that if it were possible they would descend into hell in order to produce new articles for sale, so as to get possession of the coveted silver and longed-for reales-of-eight".[2]

The French scholar, Le Gentil, in his rich and interesting record of his visit to the Philippines in the second half of the 18th century, suggested that the Filipinos were idle, easy-going and unambitious. He was also one of the early observers who blamed inhabitants of the Tropics for the vices of their colonial masters of which he gave many instances. He mentioned the ups and down of private fortunes leading to the impoverishment of many Spanish families. He also noted that the Spanish ladies in Manila were in the habit of receiving calls even when their husbands were absent, so much so that while in Manila he felt as much at ease as in France.[3] He found it difficult to show a city where morals were more corrupt than they were in Manila. The Filipinos were to blame for creating the climate of loose morals. Their men and women went bathing together, they flirted on the street. No wonder it was not rare for celibate priests to have children.[4]

A rather energetic portrayal of the Filipino character was

presented by the friar, Gaspar de San Agustin in his letter to a friend in Spain (1720) especially written for this purpose. His letter is the most far reaching pronouncement ever made on national character. More than 30 negative traits were listed. He started by defending his generalization. If one was known all would be known. The Filipinos were almost the same as other peoples of the East Indies. They were fickle, false, mendacious. Their physiognomy was cold and humid, because of the great influence of the moon.

They were untrustworthy, dull, and lazy, fond of travelling by river, sea, and lake. They were remarkable for their ingratitude, never repaying borrowed money to the friar, not attending mass, to avoid him. A borrowed object was never returned unless it was asked for on the ground that there was no previous request to the effect. "Their laziness is such that if they open a door they never close it; and if they take any implement for any use, such as a knife, pair of scissors, hammer, etc. they never return it whence they took it, but drop it there at the foot of the work."[5] If they received advance payment they would leave the job and keep the pay. They were also meddlesome and inquisitive to the extent that whenever one wanted to attend to bodily necessities, there came a Filipino before or behind him. They were rude by nature. When talking to a friar or Spaniard, they would first scratch themselves on the temples, women on the thighs, "but the more polished scratched themselves on the head".[6] They made a mess in folding a cloak. They walked in front of their wives. They always want to know every movement of the priest. They were always curious to see the content of letters and listened to private conversation which did not concern them.

They entered into the house and convents of Spaniards without being asked, searching for cracks to peep into if the doors were locked. Yet propriety was observed in their own houses. In their own homes they rose early but with their masters they followed him in rising late. When in the convent, their happiness was based on being in the kitchen. The seats were broken because of their manner of sitting and leaning with outstretched legs, that they could see the women. At night they threw their blazing torch wherever they liked. In houses or convents where there was no scent of women, they lived unwillingly.

San Agustin had much more to say on the Filipinos. We may perhaps note the following: "It is laughable to see them waken another who is sleeping like a stone, when they come up without making any noise and touching him very lightly with the point of the finger, will call him for two hours, until the sleeper finishes his sleep and awakens. The same thing is done when they call anyone downstairs, or when the door is shut; for they remain calling him in a very low tone for two hours, until he casually answers and opens to them."[7] The remarks so far have been all on the negative side but in the concluding part of his letter, he quoted a mystical writer, "we must not possess the nature of the dung beetle, which goes always to the dungheap, but that of the bee, which always seeks out the sweet and pleasant".

San Agustin then enumerated the positive side of the Filipinos. They were good at handicraft, they built the galleys and acted as sailors, artillerymen, and divers. They manufactured the powder, swivel-guns, cannons, and bells. They furnished the Spaniards with food and services. Their agricultural products furnished the Spaniards in Manila with great profit. San Agustin did not wish to exaggerate, magnify and heighten their laziness. It would have been sheer ingratitude to do so. Having been conquered in their own lands, they had served the Spaniards almost as slaves. They defended the Spaniards from their enemies. The many insurrections which took place were, in his opinion, due to "the authority and arrogance that every Spaniard assumes upon his arrival" in the Philippines. Some alcaldemayors and other Spaniards, "having been elevated from low beginnings, try to become gods and kings in the provinces, tyranizing over the Indians and their possessions". This was often the cause of the insurrections.[8]

One interesting fact to be noted in connection with the Philippines is that the subject of national character was a subject of debate and serious consideration between the Spanish observers themselves. Neither the British nor the Dutch had discussed the subject in the manner of the Spanish authors. Thus Juan Jose Delgado, who visited the Philippines in 1771, in his *Historia*, written during 1751–54, and Sinibaldo de Mas in his *Informe de las Islas Filipinos* (1842), commented and argued on some of the characteristics suggested by San Agustin. Delgado objected to San Agustin's tendency to generalize on the borrowing attitude of the Filipinos. Regarding the behaviour of the boys who served in the convent, he said the Spaniards themselves did so in their own country when they were boys like the Filipinos employed in the convent. The same thing applied to not shutting the doors.

On the manner of waking up a sleeping person, Delgado denied its universality. He had seen them awakened in another manner.

He had also been impressed by the honesty and sense of sin about stealing as expressed by the Filipinos. Their deceptiveness to the Spaniards was partly because the Spaniards often deceived them and taught them things which were not very good.[9] Mas objected to the general characterization of the Filipinos as a community prone to stealing, although theft was the greatest crime of the islands. The system of Spanish administration could be one of the causes.[10] Instances of authors as Delgado and Mas showed that the subject was much more seriously considered in Spanish circle than in Dutch or British circles.

The German scholar Feodor Jagor, writing in the second half of the 19th century echoed very much the earlier views on the Filipinos. He found them addicted to idleness and dissipation. In Manila he noted their passion for cock-fighting.[11] The native Filipinos were thought of by Jagor as imitative to a wearisome degree. "They imitate everything that passes before their eyes without using their intelligence to appreciate it."[12] Incentive was lacking in their labour. The oars used in the Philippines are usually made of bamboo poles, with a board tied to their extremities with strips of rattan. If they happen to break, so much the better; for the fatiguing labor of rowing must necessarily be suspended till they are mended again."[13] Along the river Pasig somebody might be seen asleep on a heap of coconuts. "If the nuts run ashore, the sleeper rouses himself, pushes off with a long bamboo, and contentedly relapses into slumber, as his eccentric raft regains the current of the river."[14]

The Spanish priest Zuniga whose work was first published in 1803, attributed the Filipinos liking for fish to his indolent ways. Food that easily grew in the country were better suited to his relaxed habit. Of the Filipino's fondness of fishing Zuniga said the following:

"In this occupation the inhabitants of these islands take more delight than in anything else, as it is a pursuit which at once indulges their indolent habits and gratifies their partiality to fish in preference to animal food. Throughout the country are found many other productions contributing to the support of life and which, though not so relishing as those enumerated above, are probably better suited to their relaxed habits; and the pith of the palm, shoots of the sugar-cane, green withes, and other succulent productions, serve for food to those who have no desire to labour for their subsistence."[15]

An unusually interesting writer on the Filipinos was Sinibaldo de Mas, mentioned earlier. In 1843 his report on the Philippine

Islands was published in Madrid. He was sent to the Orient as a diplomatic attaché to gather information on scientific, political and commercial subjects. His views on the Philippines were most consistently ideological in character. He saw the stirring for independence in the Philippines. In his report, de Mas recommended certain drastic measures with the object of keeping the Philippines as a Spanish colony. The natives should be taught to respect and obey the Spaniards. "To achieve this it is necessary to keep the former in such an intellectual and moral state that despite their numerical superiority they may weigh less politically than a bar of gold. The work-hand, the goatherd do not read special contracts and neither do they know what occurs beyond their own town. It is not this kind of people who have destroyed absolutism in Spain, but those who have been educated in the colleges who know the value of constitutional liberties and accordingly fight for them. We must always keep this in mind if we are to think sincerely. It is indispensable that we avoid the formation of liberals, because in a colony, *liberal* and *rebellious* are synonymous terms." [16]

To break the pride of the Filipinos was a necessity according to de Mas. The Spaniards ought to be distinguished by special clothes forbidden to the natives. [17] The natives should be treated differently. "When a Filipino or mestizo meets a Spaniard, he should be obliged to stop (except in Manila) and greet him. If seated, he should stand when the Spaniard talks to him or passes in front. Whosoever should raise his hand against a Spaniard, even in defense of his life, should be sentenced to hard labor for life; if the offense had been by word, the penalty should be lowered proportionately. A Spaniard should not seat a Filipino or mestizo in his house, much less eat with him and whosoever incurs in this breach of decorum shall be punished for the first and second time by a fine and for the third offense, with banishment from the colony. Under no pretext will a Spaniard be permitted to contract marriage with any Filipina or mestiza. Filipinos or mestizoes desiring the use of a carriage or to mount a saddled horse must procure a license which will be taxed annually so that there be only a few who can avail themselves of this luxury." [18] The Filipinos were not to be taught Spanish. In the army they should be no more than corporal. [19] He considered them rude, lazy, and defiant. "Many times in a road full of mud where there was only one clean track have Filipinos of the lowest class stopped, waiting for me to step into the mud to let them pass and if I touched the heads of their horses with my whip to open way for me, they murmured.

Some have laughed, as we say, right in front of my nose, seeing me, I believe, with eyeglasses. Once in the vicinity of a town, I wanted to buy some mangoes and ears of roasted corn from some who were selling these and other edibles and they did not want to sell for any apparent motive at all and upon asking my servant what this meant, he answered me: 'Sir, that man must be crazy'. Finally, in the few times I have been to the justices in the towns to ask for a guide or something similar (of course by paying for their service), despite my passport as captain, they have dealt with me with very little deference and respect and two or three times have I had to smell the noisy emanations of an outpouring which decency does not permit me to name, done in my presence, to the great enjoyment of those around. I, in all these things do not see any proof of security and preservation of our rule; it seems to me that we were more secure in those days when the natives knelt down when a Spaniard passed by."[20]

The report of de Mas is the manifestation of the ideology of imperialism in all nakedness. He saw the Catholic religion as the foundation of Spanish rule. Hence the priesthood should remain Spanish.[21] The divide and rule policy was to be applied to the Chinese and the Filipinos. "The skill of the government," de Mas said, "will lie in keeping them separate and at odds, so they can never form one mass nor have a common public spirit, but on the contrary, one should serve as the instruments to keep the other a subject."[22] The report expressed his official views. As a Spaniard, de Mas was in favour of preparing the Philippines for independence, since in his opinion the Philippines were in no way useful to Spain[23].

Another observer of the Filipinos of interest to us was the British merchant, Robert MacMicking. His book on the Philippines was published, in London in 1851. He was critical of Spanish rule in the Philippines. He was also critical of Spanish writings on the Filipinos. He said, "In the character of the native Indians there are very many good points, although they have long had a bad name, from their characters and descriptions coming from the Spanish mouths, who are too indolent to investigate it beyond their households, or at the most beyond their city walls; as very few, indeed, of all the Spaniards I met with have ever been in the country any distance from Manila, except those whose duty it has been to proceed to a distance, as an alcalde of the province or as an officer of the troops scattered through the islands—very many of whom remain at home in the residency or in their quarters, smoking, or drinking chocolate and bewailing their hard fate which has condemned them to live so far away from Manila, from the theatre, and from society. They come and go without knowing, or caring to know, anything about the people around them, except when a feast-day comes, when they are always ready enough to visit their houses, dance with the beauties, and consume their suppers."[24]

In judging the Filipinos to be indolent, MacMicking deserves the censure which he delivered against the Spaniards. He graded the personal strength and mental activity of the Filipinos higher than any of the Malays he had seen in Java or Singapore.[25] However he explained the Filipino's indolence by the hot climate. "In a tropical climate the elements of society are varied, and quite different from those of a country with a climate like that of Great Britain. A native Indian, under a tropical sun, could scarcely support a system of really *hard* labour for six days of the week for any length of time; and their indolent habits are in some degree necessary to their existence, perhaps as much as his night's rest is to the British labourer; for without days of relaxation to supply the stamina which they have lost during exposure to the sun and hard labour under it, it is my decided opinion that the men so exposed, and exhausted, would, after a very few years, knock themselves up and become unfit to work, thereby rendering themselves an unproductive class and burdens on their friends and on society."[26]

Sir John Bowring, a former governor of Hong Kong, visited the Philippines and wrote a book on the country. He disagreed with a European author who considered the Filipinos industrious. He blamed the Filipinos for the backwardness of the country owing to their indolence.[27] In addition to their indolence, Bowring noted the indifference and pliability of the Filipinos: He quoted a priest as saying, "Did all mankind hang on a single peg, and that peg were wanted by an Indian for his hat, he would sacrifice all mankind. They have no fear of death, but this is an infinite mercy of the Divine Being, who knows how fragile they are; they talk about death, even in the presence of the dying, without any concern. If condemned to the scaffold, they exhibit equal indifference, and smoke their cigar with wonted tranquillity. Their answer to the attendant priest is invariably, 'I know I am going to die. I cannot help it. I have been wicked—it was the will of God,—it was my fate.' But the approach of death neither interferes with their sleep nor their meals."[28]

Bowring himself had the following to say on the Filipinos: "It has been said of the Indian that he is more of a quadruped than a biped. His hands are large, and the toes of his feet pliant, being exercised in climbing trees, and divers other active functions. He is almost amphibious, passing much of his time in the water. He is insensible alike to the burning sun and the drenching rain. The impressions made upon him are transitory, and he retains a feeble memory of passing or past events. Ask him his age, he will not be able to answer: who were his ancestors? he neither knows nor cares. He receives no favours and cannot, therefore, be ungrateful; has little ambition, and therefore little disquiet; few wants, and hence is neither jealous nor envious; does not concern himself with the affairs of his neighbour, nor indeed does he pay much regard to his own. His master vice is idleness, which is his felicity. The labour that necessity demands he gives grudgingly. His health is generally good, and when deranged he satisfies himself with the use of herbs, of whose astringent or laxative powers he has had experience. He uses no soap to wash, no razor to shave; the river is his bathing-place, and he pulls out the hairs in his face with the assistance of a sharp shell; he wants no clock to tell him of the flight of time—no table, nor chairs, nor plates, nor cutlery, to assist him at his meals; a *hacha*, or large knife, and bag are generally hung at his waist; he thinks no music equal to the crowing of his cock, and holds a shoe to be as superfluous as a glove or a neck-collar."[29]

Such are the views on the Filipinos held by various authors from the 17th century onwards. On the whole they resemble the views on the Javanese and the Malays, held by the Dutch, the British, and other European observers. One striking work on the Philippines and the Filipinos has been omitted here, the book of Antonio de Morga, lieutenant-governor of the Philippines, first published in Mexico in 1609. Morga's account of the Filipinos was very different from other Spanish works. Morga's views will be discussed together with those of Rizal in another chapter. Our task here is to show the prevalence of the image of the indolent native and an evaluation of this image will be undertaken later.

NOTES

1. G. F. G. Careri, *A Voyage to the Philippines*, pp. 65, 71. Filipiniana Book Guild, Manila, 1963.
2. *The Travels of Fray Sebastian Manrique*, in Careri, *ibid.*, p. 202 (appendix).
3. G. J. H. J. B. Le Gentil de la Galaisiere, *A Voyage to the Indian Seas*, pp. 19, 79. Filipiniana Book Guild, Manila, 1963. Of the Tagalogs he thought that they were not inventive, very indolent, not ambitious, the great mediocrity, who would not stop dancing and fiddling until they spent their last centavo.

Only thereafter they would work again. The above has also been said by Dutch observers of the Javanese, except the dancing and fiddling.

4. Le Gentil, *ibid.*, pp. 87–88. Insanity appeared to attack many Spaniards in Manila, notably priests and women, according to Le Gentil. The Spaniards introduced the siesta, the afternoon nap between 12 and 3.00p.m. He suspected that the guards at the city gates took to the siesta, as the gates were closed during this time for fear of a surprise attack.

5. Gaspar de San Agustin, "Letter on the Filipinos," in E. H. Blair, A. Robertson (eds.), *The Philippine Islands 1493–1898*, vol. XL, 1690–1691. Arthur H. Clark, Cleveland, Ohio, undated.

6. *Ibid.*, p. 211.

7. *Ibid.*, p. 199.

8. *Ibid.*, pp. 294–295.

9. *Ibid.*, p. 214, note.

10. *Ibid.*, p. 215, note.

11. Feodor Jagor, "Travels in the Philippines", in Austin Craig (ed.), *The Former Philippines thru Foreign Eyes*, pp. 26–27. Philippine Education Co., Manila, 1916.

12. *Ibid.*, p. 35.

13. *Ibid.*, p. 36. Also quoted in Introduction p. 8 in this book.

14. *Ibid.*, p. 40.

15. Fr. Jaoquin Martinez de Zuniga, *An Historical View of the Philippine Islands*, p. 7. Tr. J. Maver. Filipiniana Book Guild. Manila, 1966.

16. Sinibaldo de Mas, *Report on the Condition of the Philippines in 1842*, p. 133. (Tr. from the Spanish by Carlos Botor.) Historical Conservation Society, Manila, 1963. Also quoted in Introduction p. 26, this book.

17. *Ibid.*, p. 160.

18. *Ibid.*, pp. 160–161.

19. *Ibid.*, p. 133.

20. *Ibid.*, pp. 159–160.

21. *Ibid.*, p. 156.

22. *Ibid.*, p. 163.

23. *Ibid.*, p. 192.

24. Robert MacMicking, *Recollections of Manila and the Philippines*, p. 94. Filipiniana Book Guild, Manila, 1957. The book covered the years 1848–1850.

25. *Ibid.*, p. 95.

26. *Ibid.*, pp. 99–100.

27. Sir John Bowring, *A Visit to the Philippine Islands*, pp. 93–94. Smith, Elder, London, 1859.

28. *Ibid.*, pp. 138–139.

29. *Ibid.*, pp. 140–141.

CHAPTER 4

The Image of the Javanese from the 18th to the 20th Century

As in the case of the Malays and the Filipinos, judgement on the lazy Javanese became more forceful and numerous as Dutch colonial control of the island grew. By the beginning of the 19th century, particularly after the introduction of the culture system by van den Bosch, the idea of the lazy Javanese figured more prominently in the controversy between the liberal and conservative factions in Dutch circles; however the question was first raised at the end of the 18th century.[1] Even during this period opinion differed, but the myth of the lazy Javanese won the day. The Dutch East India Company's system of forced delivery and later van den Bosch's system of forced cultivation, required a moral justification and the myth of the lazy Javanese furnished this. Earlier Dutch records on Java (17th–early 18th century) made very little reference to laziness. During that time the Dutch did not directly regulate the labour of the Javanese. After the system of forced cultivation of cash crops was introduced, notably in 1830 by van den Bosch, negative judgements on Javanese character became more frequent. Van den Bosch himself considered the Javanese as a nation barely comparable in intellectual development with Dutch children of 12 or 13 years.[2]

The image of the lazy Javanese subsequently lingered in the minds of others. Thus in 1904 the economic historian Clive Day, commenting on the situation at the end of the 19th century, suggested the following: "The class of natives who had neither land nor a trade to support them and who served others for hire was not large in numbers and was absorbed to a considerable extent in the internal organization of the village. The scale of living of the average cultivator would appear hopelessly low if measured by western standards: the total personal property of a family, including house, furniture, clothing, and implements, might be worth only a few dollars, say five or ten, in our currency. Where wants are small, however, a low scale of life may satisfy, and in fact among the Javanese the lower the scale of life the more likely they are to rest content with it so long as they are not absolutely starving. In practice it has been found impossible to secure the services of the native population by any appeal to an ambition to better themselves and raise their standard. Nothing less than immediate material enjoyment will stir them from their indolent routine. As a result, it is the universal practice among employers to offer a large part of the wages for any period in advance; if the native takes the bait, he can be held to labor (in theory, at least) until he has worked out the debt that he has incurred. The system of advances to secure the services of laborers is described as universal down to the present time. Employers and officials deplore it, but recognize its necessity; even the government makes advances when it requires the services of wage laborers."[3]

The theme of the lazy Javanese in Dutch colonial circles functioned as a major constituent of the colonial ideology. In the case of the Philippines and Malaysia, the theme of the lazy native, as we shall show later, functioned as an ideological foundation in the overall ideology of Western Imperialism. In Java, however, it was more than this. The theme became entangled in the ideological conflict of two contending groups within the Dutch colonial circles, the conservative and the liberal. The period from the end of the 18th century to 1830, the introduction of the culture system, was characterized by a conflict of opinions on how the government of the Netherlands Indies should be run. How should the colony be run to the greatest advantage of Holland which was then in need of great financial assistance arising from the outcome of the war? Both the liberal and conservatives agreed on promoting the interests of Holland but they differed on the method of economic exploitation. In 1830, the conservatives won the battle with the introduction of the culture system by the Governor-General van den Bosch.

A Dutch scholar gave the following description of the culture-system and its reasons: "This halting between two opinions, so characteristic of the colonial administration during the first thirty years of the 19th century, was brought summarily to an end when the urgent need for money induced to a decision on conservative lines, resulting in the application of the so-called culture system. Owing to the continual deficits which the Government of the Indies experienced after the fall of the East Indian Company and in connection with the tremendous expenses incurred in the last Java war (1825–1830), a sum of no less than 38 million guilders had been borrowed by the mother country for the colonies. In Holland itself, the financial situation was also serious as a result of the after effects of the Napoleonic rule and of bad financial management. For this reason, a policy which promised an immediate replenishment of the public funds, even if this were accomplished at the expense of the welfare of the native population in the Indies, was welcomed. It is obvious that the designer of this scheme, meant to fill the empty treasury, had in mind the enhancement of the productivity of the soil of the Indies by an extensive cultivation of crops suitable for the European market. As a means to this end, however, he rejected the suggestion of encouraging private agricultural enterprise owing to the difficulty of competing with the cheap labour of the slave colonies in America, which marketed the same products. His original recommendation was to draw up voluntary contracts between the government and the village inhabitants whereby the latter was to agree to plant a maximum of 1/5th of its rice fields with commercial crops for the benefit of the government. This cultivation—to be carried out under the supervision of European officials and the management of the native headmen—was not to occupy more time than was necessary for their own rice cultivation over the same area. On the other hand the government was to take all risk for its account, allow exemption from land revenue, while the appraisement of all produce supplied over and above the amount exempted was to be paid to the producers."[4]

The culture system in practice led to several abuses. The first 20 years were characterized by increasing extortion of the native population by native officials charged with collecting the products. The condition that only 1/5th of the rice fields of a village should be used for cultivating the cash crops was rarely observed. The demand for compulsory labour, instead of 66 days per year, the normal original period, was extended to 240 days for certain government cultures. The culture system did not do away with the land revenue. This tax was levied in addition. "In addition to the intentional violation of practically all the fundamental principles of the system in the form in which its creator incorporated it in the Official Gazette (1834 No. 22) there were still other unfair and arbitrary practices. Of these may be mentioned not only the excessive use of forced unpaid labour for the construction of roads and bridges for the transportation of the produce, for the supply of building materials (wood, stone, tiles) and for the building of the necessary establishments, but also the use of forced unpaid labour for the growing of the crops demanded by the government. Another evil was the placing of all responsibility on the Javanese farmers, not only for crop failure but also for all natural and economic factors which adversely influenced the financial results. The scanty wages were not based on the services rendered but on the market value of the produce supplied and could therefore fall to nihil. This was all the more unfair since the people themselves had nothing to say regarding the choice of crops or the ground and were often forced, for years, to grow crops which were totally unsuited to the district so that they gave only a very poor yield. This condition was aggravated when the cultivation required greater attention and was laid out on remote sites."[5]   The detrimental influence of the culture system on Javanese society gave rise to the abolition of many of the compulsory cultivations in the 1860s. During this period the upholders of the culture system based their defence on two main arguments. One was that without the culture system millions of government profit could not have been sent to Holland. The other was that the Javanese was not capable of free labour. Labour in Java had always been forced.[6] The upholders of the culture system appealed to Javanese history. The liberals appealed to human nature and principles of justice. The liberals were sympathetic to the introduction of industry, European capital and managerial labour. They required free labour. Hence their opposition to the culture system. There was also a genuine concern for the fate of the Javanese. To see this in its historical setting, it will be necessary to refer to the famous critic of Dutch colonial policy at that time, Dirk van Hogendorp.

In 1791 Hogendorp recommended a series of reforms to a high commission established to look into the affairs of the Dutch East Indies. He strongly urged the abolition of compulsory labour, slavery and forced deliveries in kind, the introduction of free trade and free labour, and certain legal redresses to the indigenous population. Van Hogendorp anticipated Raffles in suggesting fixed taxation and the rcognition of individual ground property or hereditary land tenure. He was also vehemently opposed to corruption. In Java he was persecuted by the colonial administration. He then fled to Holland to seek justice and to attack the colonial administration of the Dutch East Indies. In his own words, "All the incomes of the Governor, the supreme chiefs, the residents and other servants of the Company in Java, cannot be otherwise considered than theft, robbery, plunder and monopoly".[7]

Around the turn of the 19th century, the liberal movement in Europe had become a force to reckon with. The memory of the

French Revolution was still fresh. The Enlightenment was beginning to affect the colonial outlook. As it was not possible for the opponents of such liberal and enlightened reformers as van Hogendorp to deny the principles of social justice invoked by them in their denunciation of the colonial set-up, so these gentlemen had to employ pragmatic arguments. The Governor General J. Siberg, in a refutation against van Hogendorp from Batavia dated May 19, 1802, offered 6 main arguments why the distribution of land and the abolition of forced delivery should not be carried out. (1) The Javanese was too lazy and too sluggish to acquire more than what he required for subsistence. (2) By the system of forced delivery he was compelled to produce more, to labour. (3) Should he make more profit in a liberal capitalist system, he would abandon work until his profit was exhausted. (4) As a result the distributed land would fall into desertion and ruin. (5) Consequently therefrom these lands would be sold to Chinese or European buyers, at miserable prices. These buyers might turn into little princes who would eventually exploit them. (6) If van Hogendorp's plan was introduced what were the means to compel the Javanese rulers to accept them? Their vested interests would be endangered by this plan.[8]

The suggested reform of van Hogendorp aroused very strong opposition from the colonial regime. But there was also some support. W. H. van Ijsseldijk in an official letter of August 31, 1802, recognised the prevailing abuses and adverse conditions. He supported the reform envisaged by van Hogendorp but he preferred it to be restricted to those directly under the jurisdiction of the Dutch East India Company. He was mainly concerned with the abolition of forced labour, the introduction of free trade, and the elimination of abuses. It is remarkable that Ijsseldijk made no reference to the lazy Javanese.[9] On the other hand, H. W. Muntinghe, in his advice to Raffles, May 27, 1812, noted the indolence of the Javanese, though the causes, he suggested, were not hereditary but environmental.[10] He was not completely in favour of the abolition of forced labour, though he agreed that the previous condition in Java was objectionable. His political philosophy, his conception of reform, was based on the principle that "every colony exists, or must exist for the benefit of the mother country".[11]

As indicated earlier; during the 19th century, particularly the 1860s, there was a continuous criticism against the culture system and forced labour (herendienst). There was such a thing as a "colonial opposition". The question of forced labour and the indolence of the natives figured prominently in the debates. As noted earlier, those for reform rejected the theory of the indolence of the natives and the efficiency of forced labour. Those for the status quo thought otherwise. At one time it was suggested by a minister of colonies that the Javanese preferred forced labour to free labour.[12] It was refuted by a writer who revealed the whole contextual background of the issue. The significance of the issue of forced labour and forced cultivation of cash crops was further revealed by the punitive steps taken by the Dutch colonial government against native dignitaries. In 1791 two Radens (members of the Javanese aristocracy) were banished for a year to Edam for neglecting the coffee cultivation. In 1706 one of the Javanese chiefs was, for a period banished to Onrust island on the ground of "laziness"! (not successful enough in compelling the population in his area to produce sufficient quantity of the prescribed crops). In 1747 the regent of Tjiblagoeng was punished for his "sluggishness". In 1788 a patih was threatened to be sent to Batavia "zorda hij weder den iuijaart speelt" (the moment he again plays the lazy one). The regents were also threatened with banishment to Ceylon and the Cape. One of the Soemedang chiefs was lashed by rotan and condemned to 5 years of forced labour in 1805 for neglecting the Dutch plantation. In 1800 a chief in Krawang was chained at the feet. In Krawang several village and supervisors were punished by chain on account of "laziness".[13]

The well-known novelist and critic of the culture system, Edward Douwes Dekker, whose book "Max Havelaar" was published in 1860 and whose pseudonym was Multatuli, had written extensively on the problem of forced labour. Like other liberal reformers and opponents of the Dutch colonial system, Douwes Dekker opposed the theme of the lazy native. It was the general situation, the oppression and ill-treatment of the native population, that led them to apathy in their forced undertaking. As Douwes Dekker put it, the Dutch colonial government said that it wanted coffee, the Javanese did not answer and it did not have coffee. He was then forced to plant without payment for his service. The apathic reaction of the Javanese towards forced labour was a silent protest against the Dutch government's policy to compel them to cultivate cash crops.[14] The recourse to force was made because of the unwillingness of the European population in the colonies to work as estate labourers. Whatever the reasons, the European community in the colonies did not include manual labourers. Muntinghe claimed that Europeans of any description were unfit to cultivate the ground in a tropical climate.[15] It was this unwillingness of the European population which made the colonial government rely on the labour of unwilling natives, and it was this unwillingness which was viewed as indolence. As Muntinghe observed, the indolence of the natives was one of the principal objections to the introduction of free trade and free cultivation in Java.[16]

How the myth of the indolent natives figured in the ideological struggle of the period in Java is clear. Its proponents were much more numerous and powerful than the liberal opposition such as van Hogendorp, Douwes Dekker, and others. The period when the myth was widely propagated and debated started around the beginning of the 19th century. It was created to justify forced deliveries and forced labour. Later in the 20th century it continued to function as the capitalist argument to maintain low wages. It will not be necessary here to cite numerous references in the different publications of the 19th and early 20th centuries, which revealed quite clearly how the idea of the lazy natives functioned in the ideological structure of European imperialism. They are too many instances to record them all but there is still one problem to solve. Could it not be that the validity of our thesis is restricted to Java and Dutch colonialism? Raffles attempted to abolish forced labour. How is it that despite this difference of outlook, Raffles and many others retained the image of the lazy natives? The answer to this is clear. Basically the British were confronted with the same problem, the native population remaining outside the network of British colonial capitalism, mining and planting of cash crops.

We must be very careful not to confuse the actual situation in Malaya and Singapore under British rule and the personal views of Raffles on certain issues like forced labour. We must also be careful not to misjudge the effectiveness of British legislation. Monopoly and forced labour existed under British rule but in a different guise. We may call it indirect forced labour and indirect monopoly. The indirect monopoly lies in British control of import and export, and cash crop cultivation, since the early part of the 19th century. Economic studies of Malaysia and Singapore do not usually supply an ethnic breakdown of investment and control as far as the European group is concerned. However from the names of the dominant companies, from the 19th century onwards, we get a glimpse of their nationalities. Records available in England provided the data we need. At the outbreak of the First World War (1914–1918), the total world investment in the Straits Settlements was approximately US $200 millions of which 150 millions came from the United Kingdom. The investments of France, Germany, and U.S.A. were negligible. On the eve of the Second World War (1942–1945), the United Kingdom's investment in Malaya was about US $ 400 millions out of US $ 700 of the world investments in Malaya.[17] British control of the Malayan economy was much greater in the earlier decades.[18] When Raffles spoke against monopoly, he had in mind the monopoly of a non-British company, or a non-British government. He was in favour of the dominant control of a country's economy by the British as a whole, though not any particular British company. His political philosophy bears witness to this.[19]

That Raffles employed a double standard in terms of government and company monopoly was clear. We have only to take the treaties which he imposed upon the Javanese princes. In his treaty (1811) with the Sultan of Mataram, Raffles demanded the transfer of the territories of the edible birdsnests to the British government, as well as the sole control and management of imposts upon trade, in return for a fixed annual grant to the Sultan. The Sultan was also requested to ignore other earlier treaties with European powers compelling him to sell commodities at forced and inadequate prices.[20] This was to enable the trade to flow into British hands. Such a policy was basic to his political philosophy. In his letter to Lord Minto, from Malacca (1811), Raffles condemned the harsh monopoly imposed by the Dutch on the Malay States but in principle he was in favour of monopoly by the British government provided it was not against the development of internal commerce and industry.[21] But nevertheless Raffles rejected the principle of equal opportunity. His trade policy was by no means liberal. It was imperial, in the interest of England.[22]

NOTES

1. F. de Haan, *Priangan,* vol. 4. Kolff/Nijhoff, Batavia /'s-Gravenhage, 1912. See pp. 725–729, "Ordeal over den Inlander" (Judgement over the native).
2. J. van den Bosch, *"Memorie van den Commissaris-Generaal J. van den Bosch,"* p. 373. *BTLVNI,* vol. 7, no. 11, 1864 (Amsterdam).
3. Clive Day, *The Dutch in Java,* pp. 355–356. Oxford University Press, London, 1966. (Reprinted from 1904 American edition.)
4. G. H. van der Kolff, "European Influence on Native Agriculture", pp. 107–108, in B. Schrieke (ed.), *The Effect of Western Influence on Native Civilisations in the Malay Archipelago.* Kolff, Batavia, 1929.
5. *Ibid.,* p. 110.
6. G. Gonggrijp, *Schets eener Economische Geschiedenis van Nederlandsch-Indie,* pp. 149–150. Bohn, Haarlem, 1928.

7. E. du Perron—de Roos, *"Correspondentie van Dirk van Hogendorp met Zijn Broeder Gijsbert Karel,"* p. 264. *BTLVNI,* vol. 102, 1943. The translation is mine.

8. "Korte Vertoog van den Gouv. Gen. Siberg, omtrent het Bericht van D. van Hogendorp", in J. K. J. de Jonge (ed.), *De Opkomst van het Nederlandsch Gezag over Java,* deel XIII, p. 40. Nijhoff, The Hague, 1888.

9. *Ibid.,* pp. 109–112.

10. H. R. C. Wright, "Muntinghe's advice to Raffles on the land question in Java", *BTLVNI,* deel 108, p. 231. The Hague, 1952.

11. H. W. Muntinghe, "Rapport van H. W. Muntinghe, van July 28, 1813", *Tijdschrift voor Nederlandsch Indie,* pp. 267–278, deel 2. Zalt-Bommel, 1864.

12. This was based on the report of the Resident of Surabaya, brought out in the ministerial speech of March, 1868. See *TNI,* pp. 332–333, 1868, *op. cit.*

13. On this subject and for further data, see F. de Haan, *Priangan,* vol. 3, pp. 630–633. Kolff, Batavia, 1912. See also pp. 538, 706; vol. 1, pp. 160–162; vol. 4, p. 296.

14. See Multatuli (Douwes Dekker), *Over Vryen Arbeid in Nederlandsch Indie.* (Publisher not known); and also Multatuli, *Nog-eens Vrye-Arbeid.* Cohen, Amsterdam, 1914.

15. H. R. C. Wright, *op. cit.,* p. 234. There is also an ideological root here. Though in favour of reforms, Muntinghe believed that the burden of cultivation should be laid on the Javanese. The reason, unfitness of the Europeans to till the soil in the tropics. One wonders why if the Europeans were fit to become administrators, physicians, managers, bakers, housewives, prostitutes, soldiers and so forth, they were not fit to till the soil. The life of the Dutch soldiers was much more severe and exacting compared to the estate labourers, if we consider toil and diseases as the criteria.

16. That the issue of indolence figures prominently in the ideological struggle between the liberal opposition and the colonial government, is apparent from the political discussions of the 1860s and later. The industriousness of the Javanese was a proposition to be established. See the instance, "Een Voorbeeld van Javaansche Luiheid", in *TNI,* part 3, 1869.

17. W. Woodruff, *Impact of Western Man,* pp. 154–160. See tables IV, 3 and 4. Macmillan, New York, 1966. The rounding was to the nearest 50 millions.

18. J. J. Puthucheary's useful study, *Ownership and Control in the Malayan Economy.* Eastern University Press, Singapore 1960; did not give the ethnic background for the European group, but only for the Asian. Statistical data on nationality groupings appears to be absent in the Malaysian records. It is obvious that the majority was British. For further interest, see Lim Chong-Yah, *Economic Development of Modern Malaya.* Oxford University Press, Kuala Lumpur, 1967; and G. C. Allen, A. G. Donnithorne, *Western Enterpise in Indonesia and Malaya.* Allen and Unwin, London, 1957.

19. M. L. van Deventer, *Het Nederlandsch Gezag over Java,* pp. 318–319. Nijhoff, The Hague. 1891.

20. See his letter to Thomas Murdoch, on the need to rule and direct the economic development of the tropics, *Memoir,* vol. 2, *op. cit.,* pp. 160–168.

21. James Brooke, The Rajah of Sarawak, and governor of Labuan, was also an advocate of British monopoly. See his *Narrative of Events in Borneo and Celebes,* vol. 1, p. 339. John Murray, London, 1848.

22. T. S. Raffles, *Memoirs,* vol. II, pp. 54–109. His vulgar denunciation of the Chinese and the Arabs made Raffles one of the great founders of racial prejudice in this part of the world. See Syed Hussein Alatas, *Thomas Stamford Raffles—Schemer or Reformer?,* Angus and Robertson, Singapore /Sydney, 1971.

CHAPTER 5

The Image of Indolence and the Corresponding Reality

In the preceding chapters we have described the image of the natives, Malays, Javanese and Filipinos, held by foreign European observers during the colonial period. The dominant image was of the indolent native. We have shown in the case of Java how the theme of the indolent native was linked to the ideological struggle of the conservative and the liberal in the 19th century. It is the thesis of this book that the image of the indolent native was the product of colonial domination generally in the 19th century when the domination of the colonies reached a high peak and when colonial capitalist exploitation required extensive control of the area. The image of the native had a function in the exploitation complex of colonial times. This was the time when the capitalist conception of labour gained supremacy. Any type of labour which did not conform to this conception was rejected as a deviation. A community which did not enthusiastically and willingly adopt this conception of labour was regarded as indolent.

To illustrate the above, let us first discuss whether the natives were actually indolent. We shall first define what indolence is, what is the 19th century capitalist conception of labour, and what are the characteristics in the attitude of the native community interpreted as indolence by the foreign observers who represented the rising bourgeois capitalist trend. We shall define indolence first, then we shall establish that native society was not indolent, and finally we shall explain why it was characterized as indolent. In our discussion at this juncture we shall exclude the Philippines. The theme of indolence amongst the Filipinos will be treated separately in connection with Rizal's discourse on the subject. There are also specific problems relating to the Philippines, arising from the Hispanization and Christianization of the Philippines. These made a separate treatment of the subject necessary. Spanish colonialism in the Philippines, from the point of view of modern capitalism, was backward. The colonial policy of the Spaniard differed radically from the Dutch and the British; unlike the Spaniards in the Philippines, the Dutch and the British left the religion and culture of the natives to the natives themselves. [1]

The foreign observers judging the natives never bothered to define what indolence is. Rizal, in his famous discourse on the indolence of the Filipinos, defined indolence as "little love for work, lack of activity". [2] Indolence is a relative concept, characterized by the absence, rather than the presence of certain elements.

It is the absence of the will and energy to work in a situation which demands it as in the case of a man having to earn a living. The constituent elements of the concept are thus the following: (a) no love for work, (b) no will for work, (c) no energy or enthusiasm manifested during an undertaking, (d) no concern for the outcome of the undertaking, (e) no concern for the gain from the undertaking, and (f) no concern for the necessity which impels the undertaking.

Operationally defined indolence can take many forms. Let us take one instance I know from first hand experience. It concerns the head of a family of 5. The head of the family, a man in his early forties was retrenched from his place of work. Thereafter he refused to work, spending his time sleeping during the day, driving around or visiting friends. He occasionally did some part-time work, a few hours a week. He had a small income barely sufficient for household necessities. We might claim, therefore that, this man is indolent. There is a need for him to earn more for his family. He shows no concern for the consequences of his refusing to work. He shows no concern either for the gain that may accrue as a result of his work. If a fisherman manifests those traits, he can then be called indolent. The same with farmers and other classes of the population. A person is classified as indolent if he habitually and regularly assumes that attitude. A short spell of unemployment which is outside the control of the individual is not indolence; similarly a shop assistant standing behind the counter or lounging around in the shop if he has no customers, cannot be described as indolent.

Indolence is thus characterized by the evasive response to cir-cumstances which require toil and effort. A man who chooses his work while he can is not indolent. He is indolent if he avoids any type of work. Judging by the above operational definition by no stretch of imagination can it be established that the Malays, the Filipinos and the Javanese are indolent. The bulk of the Malays, the Javanese and the Filipinos work regularly every day. If they did not they would not have survived. Foreigners have observed that millions of Javanese, Malays, and Filipinos toil. They plant, they fish, they build houses, they look after their farms, in short they are occupied every day. How was it then that the image of the lazy native developed? The clue is present in a remark made by Windstedt. He said, "Because he is an independent farmer with no need to work for hire, the Malay has got an undeserved reputation for idleness, which his Asiatic competitors take care to foster."[3] It was this unwillingness to become a tool in the production system of colonial capitalism which earned the Malays a reputation of being indolent. This was one factor in the creation of the image of the indolent Malay.

Another was the fact that the Malays did not come into a close functional contact with the Europeans who were predominantly concentrated in the urban areas. The Europeans there had very little experience of Malays serving them. The Malays were not their pillars of comfort. In the bars, in the rest houses, in the hotels, in the shops, Malays did not serve the Europeans. The most which they did was driving and gardening. Malays were also not involved in construction labour, in road building, in clerical estate work, in short in the modern private capitalist sector of the economy. Colonial capitalism, as a thorough going system, was not confined to strictly economic areas. It embraced the entire system of administration, the school, and all other connected activities. Thus if the government built a railway, those labourers building the railway, and those running it, entered the network of colonial capitalism. The Malays entered this network indirectly in the civil service. They served a state administration manipulated by colonial capitalism. Since this did not bring the Malays into direct and regular contact with the European colonial community, their services were not appreciated. The Malays did not function in the total life pattern of colonial capitalism.

An indication of this may be found in an observation by Thomson, a traveller in the region. He said the following about Penang: "It is indeed to Chinamen that the foreign resident is indebted for almost all his comforts, and for the profusion of luxuries which surrounded his wonderfully European-looking home on this distant island. At the fiat of his master, Ahong, the Chinese butler, daily spreads the table with substantial fare, with choice fruits and pleasant flowers—the attributes of that lavish hospitality which is the pride of our merchants in that quarter of the globe."[4] His approval of the Chinese was subject to the Chinese being restrained by British law. He said: "In Penang, where there are few, or almost no competitors in the various occupations in which the Chinese engage, and where their vices break out in a milder form, the difficulty presses more lightly. There the Chinese, when properly restrained, are the most useful and most indispensable members of society. True, they smoke opium, they lie without restraint, and whenever opportunity offers are dishonest, cunning, and treacherous; but for all that, those of them who have risen to positions of trust forsake their vices altogether, or—what is more probable—conceal them with Chinese artfulness."[5]

In contrast to the description of how the Chinese, at times considered to be cunning, dishonest and treacherous, supplied the needs of the European community, Thomson professed little knowledge of Malay activities and yet he judged the following: "There is a large Malay population on the island, greater than the Chinese. It is, however, a much more difficult task to point out how they are all occupied, as they do not practise any trades or professions, and there are no merchants among them. Some are employed on plantations catching beetles, pruning the trees, and tilling the soil; but on the whole, the Malays do as little work as possible; some own small gardens, and rear fruit; others are sailors, and have sea-going prahus, in which Chinese trade. But I do not recollect ever seeing a single genuine Malay merchant. There are Malay campongs (villages) scattered over the island, made up of a few rude bamboo huts, and two or three clusters of fruit-trees. But many of these settlements are by the sea shore, and there they dwell, fishing a little, sleeping a great deal, but always, awake or asleep, as I believe, chewing a mixture of betelnut, lime, and siri, which distends the mouth, reddens the lips, and encases the teeth with a crust of solid black."[6] Of the Malays in Province Wellesley, he wrote the following: "There are many Malays in Province Wellesley, but they do not work on the plantations, and indeed it is almost impossible to say how one-twentieth part of the Malay population occupies itself. As Mahometans they practise circumcision, and recite frequent prayers. The rest of their lives they seem to spend in rearing large families to follow their fathers' example, and to wait lazily for such subsistence as the bounty of nature may provide. The male Malay, in his own country, is a sort of gentleman, who keeps aloof from trade, whose pride is in his ever-ready kris, with its finely polished handle, and its pointed poisoned blade."[7]

The above is the ordinary, somewhat sensational, characterization of the Malays which was current during the period. The judgement on their indolence was entirely unfounded. There was no actual research done on the subject and the observers did not live or mix with Malays. But the image nevertheless developed. The root cause of this image was the Malays' reaction to cash crop agriculture and to working in colonial capitalist estates and plantations. They avoided the most exploitative kind of labour in 19th century colonial capitalist undertakings. Malay labour however in the capitalist sector like mining was not entirely absent. A British author who was himself involved in mining praised Malay labour. "As a general rule," he said, "Malays are not employed in actual mining; but there is a notable exception in the case of the Bundi tin mine, Tringganu, where Javanese Malays are employed on machine drills, in very hard and tough granite, and are giving every satisfaction, being much more careful of their machines than the Chinese with whom they are competing. Another instance in Malaya, although not on the Peninsula, is the coal mine of Labuan, Borneo, where they did most of the shaft-sinking in the early days—not merely shallow pits, but true shafts, under European management."[8]

Malays were also excellent supervisors, pump-men, plat-men, and brace-men. They were also very good engine drivers. "As engine-drivers, controlling hoisting-engines and locomotives, the Malay, especially the Javanese Malay, is at his best. During about 15 years at Raub, with at no time less than five winding shafts in operation under Malay drivers, there was never a mishap due to their carelessness. And the Pahang Automobile Service has found that it could safely substitute Malays on its motor-cars, for skilled Europeans at five times the salary, though the Pahang road is one of the most difficult in the world for motoring. Many Malay motor-car drivers can now be seen in the crowded streets of Singapore."[9] Other works the Malays were good at were the following: "For jungle-clearing, all river work, and survey and prospecting work generally, the Malay is indispensable, being an adept at woodcraft, a highly skilled boatman, and a born swimmer; of indomitable pluck, full of resource, and capable of extra-ordinary effort and endurance at need. And if he be disposed to idleness when he can afford it, he is never a drunkard (thanks to his excellent religion—Mohammedanism); he never begs; he is always clean and spruce in his dress, and dignified and courteous in his manner; and, in a word, he is as great a contrast to the Australian "sundowner" and "larrikin"—who cumber and foul the parks of Sydney and Melbourne, burn barns, and scare women and children—as it is possible to imagine."[10] But what was the thing the Malays were not good at, according to the view of 19th century upholders of European colonial capitalism? The same observer gave us the clue. He said: "But for the drudgery of mining—the hard, uninteresting, monotonous, never-ending toil with hammer and drill, pick and shovel, or *changkol* and basket—there has been until lately only one race worth considering, and that is the patient, plodding, thrifty, industrious Chinaman."[11]

The Chinese were considered industrious because they supplied the lowest form of labour. The Malays, despite their positive contribution to the kind of labour noted by the author, were considered indolent, not because they were really indolent, according to definition, but because they avoided the type of slave labour which the Chinese and the Indians were compelled to do owing to their immigrant status. The system, which will be described later, trapped them into the worst type of mining and estate labour. Here was the sociological and ideological origin of the image of the indolent Malays. Malays too planted rubber in small holdings and they went into mining.[12] Our author also praised the Malays in yet another field. "The Malays are expert trappers, and they monopolize the rewards paid by the Government for destruction of vermin. In 1904, about $5,000 was thus disbursed, the bag including 45 tigers, 20 leopards, and 13 panthers, besides 989 snakes, 1,130 crocodiles, and 1,732 crocodile eggs."[13] But despite all this, this is what he said about the communities: "From a labour point of view, there are practically three races, the Malays (including Javanese), the Chinese, and the Tamils (who are generally known as Klings). By nature, the Malay is an idler, the Chinaman is a thief, and the Kling is a drunkard, yet each, in his special class of work, is both cheap and efficient, when properly supervised."[14]

Of the Chinese coolies whom the author praised as industrious, he was candid enough to express the following opinions: "Without cruelty or tyranny; without any of the senseless brutality of the white miner towards the negro, which has brought lots of trouble in Rhodesia; without perpetual blows and foul language; the Chinese coolie must be made to realize that he is not on an equality with Europeans. He is the mule among the nations—capable of the hardest task under the most trying conditions; tolerant of every kind of weather and ill usage; eating little and drinking less; stubborn and callous; unlovable and useful in the highest degree. But never, under any conceivable circumstances, to be trusted or made a friend of."[15] He further continued: "In the whole philosophy of a

Chinese coolie, there is not a particle of fellow-feeling—every man is fighting for himself alone. He has no more sympathy than the lower animals, and kindness is much less appreciated by him than by them. Unless forcibly compelled he will refuse to aid in rescuing a mate from death even though he be himself liable to death or injury from the same cause every hour he is at work. To such a people unity of action for good or evil is impossible. I would far rather manage a thousand Chinese coolies than ten natives of Southern Italy. The former will never commit a vengeful murder, or raise a hand against authority, without having suffered very great injustice, though they think nothing of knocking a sleeping mate or helpless woman on the head, for the sake of a dollar or two." [16]

It is clear from the study of the philosophy of colonial capitalism, that for a labourer to qualify as industrious, he has to be "the mule among the nations—capable of the hardest task under the most trying conditions; tolerant of every kind of weather and ill usage; eating little and drinking less; stubborn and callous; unlovable and useful in the highest degree." Pre-occupation with other types of labour that fall outside the category of "the mule among the nations", is qualified as idle or indolent. To be a chattel of colonial agrarian capitalism is a requirement to be considered as industrious. The upholders of the system expected from the labourers what they abhorred doing themselves. They neither ate nor drink a little. They were not the mule but the queen bee among the nations. The "hard, uninteresting, monotonous, never-ending toil with hammer and drill, pick and shovel" they expected everybody else to do and like it. The conceptual association between industriousness and oppressive capitalist labour is thus clear. One would look in vain for any operational proof of Malay indolence. Nothing concrete and empirical has been brought forward to illustrate the concept of Malay indolence. If we apply our definition of "little love for work, lack of activity" to the Malays as a whole, this has never been the case. However if we apply the definition to the Malay attitude towards colonial capitalist plantation activity, it fits. Amongst the Malays there was little love for work in colonial European plantations.

A glimmer of the association between coolie labour and industriousness is apparent in Windstedt's description in his publication of colonial days. He said: "The Malay has a reputation for great indolence. A moist tropical climate, malaria, a soil that tickled laughs with crops, the sumptuary laws of his chiefs, which made fine houses and fine clothes dangerous for the peasant—all these have contributed to his choice of a quiet, unambitious life. But the reputation for laziness is not entirely deserved. He has jumped in fifty years out of the pastoral age into an age of steamships, railways and motor traffic, out of a patriarchal age into a crowd of alien wage-earners and capitalists. He is adapting himself to the change, but not more quickly than the struggle for existence demands. He would rather paddle all the way on a river or work in the mire of rice-fields than become a clock-driven slave of the workshop and office. But he is diligent where his interest is aroused."[17] What is this mysterious quality, "indolence"? Windstedt said the Malay "is diligent where his interest is aroused". Is that not the same for all people? If the Malays preferred to be independent cultivators, did this make them indolent? Did not the Europeans in the colonies avoid manual labour? Did they not avoid coolie labour? Why were they not called indolent? It is clear through available records that industriousness meant working at sub-human level in colonial capitalist setting.

The mystery of indolence is further evinced in a book by an English lady, who had done a great deal of mission work and who spent 5 weeks in Malaya in 1879. In her opinion the Malays were tolerably industrious as boatmen, fishermen, and policemen. The Indians "make themselves generally useful as their mediocre abilities allow". They were a harmless people "but they quarrel loudly and vociferously, and their vocabulary of abuse is said to be inexhaustible".[18] The Malays were said to be "symbolized to people's mind in general by the dagger called a *kris*, and by the peculiar form of frenzy which has given rise to the phrase 'running amuck'".[19] The Malays led strange and uneventful lives. "The men are not inclined to much effort except in fishing or hunting, and, where they possessed rice land, in ploughing for rice."[20] Their manner was cool and aloof and both males and females were decidedly ugly.[21] In a visit to a Malay house in Malacca our lady author judged the women as follows: "The women were lounging about the houses, some cleaning fish, others pounding rice; but they do not care for work, and the little money which they need for buying clothes they can make by selling mats or jungle fruits."[22] We may ask the author what is meant by work here? Is cleaning fish and pounding rice not work? Work here means wage earning outside the home. Are making mats and selling fruits not work? It is clear that work here means that activity introduced by colonial capitalism. If the ladies became coolies or servants of British planters or firm officials, she would then have considered them as working.

Assuming that the Malays whom the foreign observers came across were mostly fishermen and rice-farmers, or independent small-holders who did not exhibit an acquisitive greed for money, should they have been classified as indolent? If this is the case the most indolent people should be the European missionaries who laboured without the obsession of making money. So were the European civil servants whose desire for gain was much more restrained than the planters and the business men. Another author who was quite sympathetic to the Malays, nevertheless judged them not to be industrious. The reason is clear, the Malays' lack of interest in working according to the norms of colonial capitalism. He said: "With many virtues, the Malays of the present day are not industrious. It has been claimed for the Dyaks of Borneo, that they are all gentlemen, because they never accumulate the fruits of their labour; they will work, it is said, for the day's, or it may be the week's support; but, when they have attained the required means and laid toil aside, the payment of no consideration will induce them to break in upon their leisure or enjoyment—they are above everything but the immediate pressure of want. According to this theory, which I do not dispute, the Malays are essentially gentlemen too; they have no acquisitiveness, and if they can satisfy the wants of the moment they are happy—they lay great store by the proverb that sufficient for the day is the evil thereof. In a less genial clime, and with a more selfish people, the philosophy would be a poor one; but here, where nature is so kind, and where generosity is a native characteristic, it is sound enough." [23]

The above picture of the Malays working only to satisfy the wants of the moment is a vulgar distortion. It is true of only a section of Malay labourers, like some in European estates. The Malays had a reputation of being unable to work for a sustained period. This was true only in a colonial capitalist plantation. The foreign observers themselves noticed that the Malays were capable of prolonged sustained work in other areas, like the civil service, the police, driving, gardening, grooming, keeping horses, etc. They were only incapable, or to be more accurate, unwilling to work in the plantations owned by others. The unwillingness of the Malays to work as estate coolies was interpreted as an ethnic shortcoming. Here is an instance. "A vital factor in the cultivation of rubber and coconuts in Malaya is labour. The indigenous population of Malays is neither sufficient in number nor suited in many respects for employment on the larger estates; the Malay hates permanent routine work. On European estates the labour force is composed almost entirely of Tamil, Chinese and Javanese immigrants."[24] The same author went on to describe Malay agriculture. "The local Malay agriculturist is either a rice-planter or a small-holder owning a few acres, on which fruit trees, coconuts and rubber grow in confusion, generally untended, together with such catch-crops as vegetables, ground-nuts, pineapples, bananas and so on, where the shade produced by the permanent crops is not too great. As a rice-planter, the Malay is fairly successful within the limits of his agriculture knowledge."[25]

If the Malays hated permanent routine work, they would not have survived as human beings. They avoided permanent routine work of the exploitative type in other peoples' mines and plantations. Any observer could see how neatly the paddy fields were tended. So was the orchard at home. All these required sustained and permanent labour. The fact the Malays took to other routine employment outside the plantation and estates was ignored by our author. What was a perfectly healthy, normal and human reaction was regarded as a strange shortcoming. Malay labourers were averse to leaving their family and village. In some instances, in tin mining the wages for Malays were lower than for the Chinese.[26] This discriminatory practice still exists in some places in Malaysia today.

The accusation of indolence against the Malays was not due to actual indolence but to their refusal to work as plantation labourers. This attitude of the Malays offered a serious problem to colonial British planters in their competition with Chinese planters who acquired Chinese labour from China by deceitful means. The British planters in the 1880s and 1890s were faced by labour shortage owing to the refusal of the Malays to work in their plantations. The Sungei Ujong Report of 1882 pleaded for Tamil labour as against Malay labour. It said: "Nothing is wanted but Tamil labour. A great deal has been done by the planters here towards utilizing Malay labour, and large numbers of coolies come from the adjacent small estates to procure work both at Pantai and Rantau. But this labour is too expensive, and is very uncertain, as frequently at a time when the planter wants as much labour as he can get, he finds himself without a man to do the necessary work on the estate, the whole of his labour force having gone off to squander their small savings in their own country. As soon as this end has been accomplished, the men will return again, but in the meantime the mischief has been done."[27]

Similarly in Perak, the annual report of 1889 pointed out that a Malay "absolutely refuses to hire himself out as a labourer on any terms that a planter could accept. The mines absorb the attention of the Chinese, who prefer failure there to steady work and wages on an estate, and the planter's only chance of a labour force on which he can rely depends upon the natives of Southern India, whom he must import into the State on certain conditions for a term of months".[28] During her stay in Taiping in February, 1879, our lady author Isabella Bird was visited by a British Ceylon planter who was getting into difficulties with the labour on his coffee plantation beyond Perak. Bird commented: "This difficulty about labour will possibly have to be solved by the introduction of coolies from India, for the Malays won't work except for themselves; and the Chinese not only prefer the excitement of mining and the evening hubbub of the mining towns, but in lonely places they are not always very manageable by people unused to them."[29] It is clear that the sociological origin of the myth of the lazy Malays was based on their refusal to supply plantation labour and their non-involvement in the colonially-controlled urban capitalist economic activity. The same was true of the Javanese in Java. They did not respond enthusiastically to cash crop cultivation; they had to be forced. Hence they were also accused of indolence. In Europe and America, in 19th century, and after, there were many people who worked in different places for short periods. These people were not accused of indolence. It was the initial reaction of the planters to the Malay attitude which generated the image of the lazy Malay, and this image subsequently influenced others. Once disseminated its historical root was soon forgotten, and it became a dominant theory. It invaded the minds of journalists, school-teachers, visiting authors like Isabella Bird, civil-servants, merchants, businessmen, and numerous others.

The Malays, like many other peoples in history, were not idlers. Their activities in farming, industry, trade, commerce, war, and government are recorded in history. Only after the arrival of the Portuguese did the Malay merchant class decline.

The Indians and Chinese immigrants were ensnared in the colonial capitalist system of production; the bulk of them remained coolies. Only a handful of them like Yap Ah Loi became successful capitalists. The immigrant coolies were left in their illiterate, backward state. They were used merely as a tool, "a mule among the nations". The Malay refusal at the time to be exploited as "a mule among the nations", was a rational and sound response. They attended to their own work in their own areas of interest. The accusation of indolence was merely a veiled resentment against Malay unwillingness to become a tool for enriching colonial planters.

NOTES

1. On this aspect of Spanish conquest see J. L. Phelan, *The Hispanization of the Philippines,* University of Wisconsin Press, Madison, 1959.
2. Jose Rizal, "The Indolence of the Filipinos", in E. Alzona (tr. and ed.), *Selected Essays and Letters of Jose Rizal,* p. 182, Rangel and Sons, Manila, 1964.
3. Sir Richard Windstedt, *Malaya and Its History,* p. 17, *op. cit.* See p. 50 of this book.
4. J. Thomson, *The Straits of Malacca, Indo-China and China,* p. 17. Low, Marston and Searle, London, 1875.
5. *Ibid.,* pp. 16–17.
6. *Ibid.,* pp. 18–19.
7. *Ibid.,* p. 33.
8. C. G. Warnford-Lock, *Mining in Malaya for Gold and Tin,* pp. 31–32. Crowther and Goodman, London, 1907.
9. *Ibid.,* p. 32.
10. *Ibid.,* p. 32.
11. *Ibid.,* pp. 32–33.
12. There was a definite Malay interest in mining before the expansion of Chinese interest in mining. Malay mining dated back to the pre-Portuguese period. In Kinta alone, in the early 1890s there were some 350 private Malay mines. See J. B. Scrivenor, "Mining", p. 186, in R. O. Windstedt (ed.), *Malaya.* Constable, London, 1923.
13. C. G. Warnford-Lock, *op. cit.,* p. 3.
14. *Ibid.,* p. 31. The labour point of view was the colonial capitalist one, cheap and efficient.
15. *Ibid.,* p. 38.
16. *Ibid.,* pp. 39–40.
17. R. O. Windstedt (ed.), *Malaya,* pp. 89–90, *op. cit.* Windstedt suggested that English education would spoil the Malays.
18. Isabella L. Bird, *The Golden Chersonese,* pp. 115–116. Oxford University Press, Kuala Lumpur, 1967. (Reprinted from 1883 edition.) Her observations referred to those in Singapore.
19. *Ibid.,* p. 137.
20. *Ibid.,* p. 138.
21. *Ibid.,* p. 138. She visited one Malay family and this was sufficient apparently for her to form opinions on the Malays.
22. *Ibid.,* pp. 138–139.
23. John Cameron, *Our Tropical Possessions in Malayan India,* pp. 133–134. Smith, Elder, London, 1865.
24. B. J. Eaton, "Agriculture", p. 198, in R. O. Windstedt (ed.), *Malaya.*
25. *Ibid.,* p. 199.
26. T. T. Newbold, *Political and Statistical Account of the British Settlements in the Straits of Malacca,* vol. 2, p. 97. John Murray London, 1839.
27. *Straits Settlements Gazettes 1883,* p. 1180. Also quoted in R. N. Jackson, *Immigrant Labour and the Development of Malaya,* pp. 92–93. Government Printing Press, Federation of Malaya, 1961.

28.   *Straits Settlements Gazette 1890,* p. 1474. Cited by R. N. Jackson, *ibid.,* p. 95.
29.   Isabella L. Bird, *op. cit.,* p. 357.

CHAPTER 6

Colonial Capitalism and its Attitude Towards Labour in the 19th and Early 20th Century

In 1846, Karl Marx and Friedrich Engels wrote a joint work which provided an important clue to the understanding of history. For our theme this is specially relevant. They observed the following: "The ideas of the ruling class are in every epoch the ruling ideas: i.e. the class, which is the ruling material force of society, is at the same time its ruling intellectual force. The class which has the means of material production at its disposal, has control at the same time over the means of mental production, so that thereby, generally speaking, the ideas of those who lack the means of mental production are subject to it."[1] They further continued: "The individuals composing the ruling class possess among other things consciousness, and therefore think. In so far, therefore, as they rule as a class and determine the extent and compass of an epoch, it is self-evident that they do this in their whole range, hence among other things rule also as thinkers, as producers of ideas, and regulate the production and distribution of the ideas of their age: thus their ideas are the ruling ideas of the epoch."[2]

As the plantation-based colonial capitalism was the dominant ideology of the ruling power in the 19th century, their ideas on the natives and the different communities, their concept of indolence and their classification of labour into useful and meaningless, became the dominant ideas of the day. In the Philippines, in Indonesia and in Malaysia, the natives had been accused of indolence. The general common sociological origin of the accusation was the natives' response to plantation labour. In Indonesia, labour was directly forced upon the natives during the period of the culture system. In the Philippines, the Spaniard had also relied on forced labour. In Malaysia, although directly there was no forced labour, indirectly there was. The system of forced labour in the Philippines and Indonesia allowed the Dutch and Spanish colonial government to dispense with immigrant labour. In Java during colonial times there was no Chinese or Indian labour, although there were Chinese and Indian merchants. There was some Chinese plantation labour in Sumatra.

The colonial capitalist ideas of development were largely based on unlimited greed for profit and the subordination of all other interests to this. Both the Chinese and British capitalists in 19th century strongly exhibited these traits. Human life and health were considered of secondary importance judging from the type and manner of abuses which took place; so much so that even the colonial government deemed it necessary to legislate against certain abuses. They were mainly connected with the recruitment and the subsequent employment of indentured labour from China and India. The capitalist enrichment in Malaya was achieved at the expense of these indentured labourers. At the time when the Chinese coolies were praised as industrious, they found themselves exploited in a situation which they could not avoid. A number of legislative measures were taken, the last one in 1912 abolishing indentured labour. In 1823, Raffles published the following ordinance: "As it frequently happens that free labourers and others are brought from China and elsewhere as passengers who have not the means of paying for their passage, and under the expectation that individuals resident in Singapore will advance the amount of it on condition of receiving the services of the parties for a limited period in compensation therof—such arrangements are not deemed objectionable provided the parties are landed as free persons, but in all cases the amount of passage money or otherwise is limited to twenty dollars, and the period of service by an adult in compensation thereof shall in no case exceed two years, and every engagement shall be entered into with the free consent of the parties in presence of a Magistrate, and duly registered."[3]

Raffles's ordinance was not concerned with what happened before arrival in Singapore, with the conditions of work during the two years, and with what happened after the two years. Some immigrants had sufficient means to pay for their own passage. However the demand for labour was so great that a credit-ticket system came into being. Coolie brokers in South China, Hong Kong and Singapore arranged for the shipment of batches of coolies to Penang and Singapore. On arrival the brokers found employment for the immigrant coolies. These brokers were particularly unscrupulous. The employers paid them according to the market price for each labourer. The labourers imported under this system were called "piglets" and the people in charge of their lodging houses were called "heads of piglets" (Chu Tsai Thau).[4] They were lured from their villages in South China by stories of prosperity to be gained, or they would be lured to the city, involved in gambling where they lost their money, and then the recruiter or the lodging house keeper would cajole or compel them to emigrate in order to pay their gambling debts. The wages offered overseas were higher but they were rarely obtained in full by the labourers. The means of recruitment were inhuman even by 19th century standards. "The coolies were, in fact, treated like cattle or pigs, and there are well authenticated cases of hundreds of coolies dying during the voyage or being drowned like rats without a chance of escape when ships sank. The more serious of these abuses took place not on the short runs to Malaya but on the longer crossings of the Pacific. The surprising fact is that, despite the inhumanity with which the trade was conducted, more and still more coolies could be found to swallow the bait. Chinese authorities at the China ports did, indeed, prohibit the traffic because of the abominable abuses which were connected with it. It is on record that in 1888, a coolie broker at Swatow was decapitated for having deceived coolies into emigrating. But though sharp warnings such as this acted from time to time as checks on emigration, the business was so lucrative and the field for corruption so wide that emigration under the same old system continued, and no effective action was taken in China to ameliorate the hard lot of the unfortunate emigrant under the Credit-ticket system."[5]

Neither was any effective action taken in Singapore or in the Straits Settlements. Raffles's ordinance did not include an effective machinery to enforce it, except the magistracy.[6] After leaving the hands of the brokers, the coolies passed into the hands of the estate contractors. It was here that the characteristic evil of the system perpetuated itself. Both the European and the Chinese enterprises were guilty of it. The following description explains the system: "For example the usual system of employment on the sugar plantations in Province Wellesley whether European or Chinese-owned was the 'rumah ketchil' system. Under this system, the estate owner divided up his estate into sections each of which was in charge of a Chinese contractor. The owner arranged for the purchase of coolies and then handed them over to the contractors debiting their expenses to the contractors' account. The contractors took complete charge of the coolies, provided a house (the rumah ketchil) and made all arrangements for wages, food, etc. The coolies were not allowed to leave the rumah ketchil except when at work on the estate under supervision, and there was widespread ill-treatment. Coolies were beaten, badly fed, and locked in at night to prevent their escape. In general no medical treatment was provided and disease was rife. The contractors supplied the coolies with chandu at high prices and encouraged its use to increase their own profits. They, or their kepalas, ran 'crooked' gambling and thus relieved the coolie of what little balance of wages he might have. In actual fact the coolie did not receive any cash wages. His wages were credited to his account, and his chandu, gambling debts and other purchases were debited to his account. He was invariably in debt. Similar conditions existed wherever coolies engaged under the credit-ticket system were employed." [7]

The above system had operated for more than half a century, supplying labour for European and Chinese capitalist enterprises. The abuses inherent in the system remained unchecked with the connivance of the colonial authority. In 1871, Chinese merchants and citizens petitioned the Governor concerning the disappearance of newly-arrived labourers. In 1873, a further petition was received by the Governor from the local Chinese begging for an ordinance prohibiting the disgraceful kidnapping of new arrivals, the appointment of inspecting officers, and the establishment of depots for registration and lodging. "In 1873 a Bill was introduced to regulate the system of immigration. It was vigorously opposed by the unofficial members of Council who considered that the evils had been exaggerated and that nothing should be done to interfere with the importation of free [sic] labour because if immigration were cut off or discouraged 'enterprises of great moment that are now developing must wither and collapse'. The Bill passed into law as Ordinance X of 1873 but was never brought into force." [8] Succeeding ordinances, like this one, to improve the system of recruitment, especially the fate of the labourers after arrival, remained on the whole as paper measures. In 1890, the Protector of Chinese noted that no examination depots had been established and instead private depots licensed by government were established. A commission established in 1890 noted several of the familiar abuses, including the fact that coolies were forced to go to Sumatra against their will.

In Penang, the Protector of Chinese there noted some of the serious abuses. Some labourers were working in a Chinese estate under compulsion. Some having fulfilled their contract 3 or 4 years earlier, were kept continuously in debt, and compelled to work there. One man worked against his will for 9 years and still remained in debt. They could not get off the island because the watchmen of the ferry would stop them and no boatman would ordinarily take them as passenger. The circumstances surrounding their arrival were worthy of notice. European boats were used to ship them to the Straits Settlements unlike the Chinese boats used during an earlier period. The coolies were disembarked and confined for 10 days at most to the depots where there was no opportunity for exercise. The depot-keepers brought them from the ships, guarded them in the depots, and eventually obtained their employment on payment. They were treated like livestock. There was a consensus among observers during that period that the depot-keepers as a whole were totally unscrupulous. Scenes of disorder, almost amounting to riots, sometimes occurred aboard ships on arrival. Rowdies from the shore snatched ear-rings and bangles from women passengers, and incited the "unpaid passengers" to run away. [9]

The 1890 Report of the Commission to enquire into the state of labour in the Straits Settlements, which was submitted to the government in 1891, included information on terms of contract in ordinary use for new arrivals to the Straits Settlements. For agricultural work in the Straits Settlement and the Malay States, working days were 360 in a year. The wage was $30 per year, about $8\frac{1}{2}$ cents per day. Of this, $19.50 was deducted for passage from China. Food and some clothes were provided by the employer. If the labourer at the end of his first year was in debt and was retained, the wages were $3 a month with food. The interesting part of the contract was the anticipation of the debt. There was some slight variation in wages and passage fees for the mine labourers in Perak and Pahang. The European estates adopted the Chinese system of contract labour. The estates paid the contractor-headman and he in turn paid his labourers. "The ordinary method of employing Chinese on European estates is as follows. The coolies are procured through the agency of a headman. The usual contract with the employer is signed at the Protectorate, but it has no practical meaning, for the men are never paid direct by the manager, nor, in many cases, are their names known to him. All that the employer does is to sign the contracts and pay the necessary expenses to the headman who obtains them. The work which they afterwards do is paid for at contract rates through the headman, whose accounts with his coolies are never examined. Thus the control of the coolies is thrown entirely into the hands of the headman, who has them completely in his power. The lines or kongsi-houses in which they live are generally dotted about the estates at long distances from the main buildings and from each other, and are practically free from supervision. This state of things is calculated to favour ill-treatment on the part of the Tyndals (headmen), and such practices undoubtedly exist. Moreover, we have not seen or heard of a single estate employing a European who speaks Chinese, so that except through the headmen, or perhaps a Chinese clerk, there is no channel by which the employer can question his coolies or they can make their complaints." [10]

Some of the instances of cruelty on the estates are worth mentioning. In Penang, a coolie was starved to death in a little shed of a hospital in the stable yard of the employer's house, fifty yards from a police-station. The Commission had no doubt that both in the Chinese and European estates, the labourers were not infrequently beaten by the headmen. As a rule they were well fed as long as they were able to work, but the Commission was not so sure about the sick and the unfit. The Commission gave scant attention to labour in the tin mines. This was because during that time, European activity in mining was negligible. It was the accepted idea that mining in Malaya was not a profitable undertaking for Europeans. Hence the colonial capitalist government was not much interested in the problem of mining labour. While there was no acute shortage of labour for mining, for the European estates there was a problem. The 1880s was the period of European capital expansion in the agricultural sector. Late in 1912 indentured labour was abolished owing to the frequency of abscondment, in other words it created a problem for the European plantations. The growing number of free labour and the abuses in the estates encouraged indentured labourers to run away after the expiry of their term.

In some estates labourers were locked in between 6p.m. and 6a.m. These were in remote places. The Commission gave details of non-treatment of sick and diseased labourers, of illegal charges debited to the coolies, accounts, and of the supply of opium to coolies at high prices in advance of their wage, in a cruel and ferocious manner. [11] The health hazard to which the coolies were exposed could be judged from a case in 1873. The mentri of Larut who drew $200,000 a year from his mines, stated that the annual immigration of Chinese labour to Larut was about 2,000 to 3,000 coolies. About 10%–20% died from fever when clearing new jungles. When the mines were first opened 50% died. In 1857, at the opening of the tin mines in Ampang at Kuala Lumpur, there was 87 coolies in the first batch. After 2 months, due to the ravages of fever and tiger, only 18 were left. [12] The most remarkable case of cruelty noted by another Commission of 1910 concerned an estate on the Kurau river. Three men were sentenced to rigorous imprisonment and the owner fined $50 for delay in sending a sick sinkheh (an arrival from China serving his first year) to hospital. He was admitted to hospital at 6p.m. and died at 6a.m. the next morning. "Diagnosis of cause of death on post mortem was dysentery. Enquiries on 25th February had elicited the fact that this *sinkheh* was made to eat human excrement on the day before he was sent to hospital in addition to a long course of cruelty, because he was too ill to go to bathe. The headman compelled this cooly to eat human excrement. He rubbed the excrement on the cooly's teeth. This *Kong Thau* was one of the three headmen who was sentenced to imprisonment for voluntarily causing hurt to another *sinkheh* as above stated." [13] No further proceedings were taken in connection with this incident as the medical officer said that the excrement forced upon the victim could not be proved to be infectious. In another estate in the Krian area the labourers were terrorized by the headman who was eventually convicted. He raped the labourers. Homosexuality was not uncommon in these estates.

Another group of indentured immigrant labour were the Indians from South India. They were recruited mainly to serve European estates. Until the year 1857, Indian migration to Penang was spontaneous, in native vessels. Because of overcrowding, the Indian government passed laws regulating the traffic in 1857 and 1859, specifying the amount of deck space for each passenger and the load. The effect of this was to increase the expenses and decrease the number of emigrants whose fares were advanced by the owners of the vessels. The employers then sent agents to India for recruitment. Labour became an even greater export commodity. The result was similar to the Chinese case, indentured labour perpetually subjected to debt bondage, with all the attendant abuses. Although there were differences in details owing to cultural factors, basically the pattern of exploitation was the same. In 1873 some estates in Province Wellesley shamefully neglected their Indian labour. The sick were sent to government hospital in time to die. [14]

The institutional legal framework of the time (1876) was embodied in the *Indian Immigrant Protection Ordinance*, cheerfully accepted by the planters of Province Wellesley. It was a conspicuous bias on the part of the Colonial Government that in the several commissions which were formed, representatives of labour were not appointed while planters were. The ordinance stipulated an agreed number of years for the payment of the passage and other sums advanced by the employer to be worked out. The monthly wage was calculated at 12¢ a day in a first-class gang and 10¢ a day in a second-class gang. The maximum deduction by the employer was $1 a month. A labourer who absented himself, neglected or refused to labour, forfeited 50¢ for each day. If this happened for more than 7 days, the employer could request him to be sentenced to rigorous imprisonment for 14 days. For desertion he could be sentenced to one month's rigorous imprisonment for the first offence, two and three for the second and third. A conviction did not release the labourer from his obligation. [15] The dice were loaded heavily against the labourers. While it was possible to prove infringement of the law by the labourers, it was always difficult to prove likewise in the case of employers.　Cases of cruelties were unearthed periodically every few years, 5 or 10 or even more, when commissions of enquiry were set up. For at least a century abuses and cruelties against labourers continued. Concerned government servants complained of the lack of personnel to protect labour effectively. Many of these legislations were good only on paper, as far as the protection of labour was concerned.

The condition of Indian labour was discussed in 1879. A European planter suggested that the $3.60 per month earned by the Indian coolie was ample. Rice cost him $1.20 a month. He had thus $1.40 to save, according to this planter. Accommodation was free; fuel he could gather; when sick he got free food and medicine. But the Principal Medical Officer of the Straits Settlements who had visited the estates reported a different picture. The officer said this was not a true description of the situation. At the end of the month the coolie had probably nothing to save. "He gets victimised right and left by the older hands on the estate and by the Tindals, becomes entangled in debt and is beset with troubles on all sides, and any planter will tell you who sees to paying his coolies himself that as a matter of fact this $1.40, as a rule, is not in his possession for five minutes before it is pounced upon by his creditors, and openly so, before the very eyes of the paymaster himself. The managers of Estates should guard against these Tindals imposing upon the newly arrived coolies in the way they do. Drinking arrack among them, too, leads no doubt to a heap of misery and sickness, but I think if their food is better seen to, this practice will be less resorted to. It is their feeling of wretchedness which leads them to it." [16] The result of the above situation was that a labourer rarely got himself free after 3 years. The Labour Commission Report of 1890 noted that "the average man does not, and will not, do more than twenty days work in a month."[17] The legal contract required the labourer to work for 36 months, 6 days a week, 9 hours a day. The advances from the employer, the days spent in prison or attending courts, absent from work, sick leave in excess of 30 days, all these entangled the labourer to his estate. "Only a small minority of the labourers were in fact released at the end of three years."[18]

Many of the government reports put the blame for the abuses on the local supervisors, the headman, rather than the European owners. It is unthinkable that Europeans owners were not aware of abuses which had lasted a century. Most of them were simply disinterested in the fate of their labourers. They were aware of the debt bondage; they were aware of opium smoking in the estates; then they were aware of toddy drinking and gambling. The colonial government of the period derived enormous revenue from these items. While interest was shown by government in the individual health of estate labourers, there was hardly any interest to eliminate the root cause of the ill-health, opium smoking and toddy drinking, which were merely accepted by the government. A graphic description was given in 1879 by Isabella Bird during a visit to a Chinese village in Seremban. "In the middle of the village there is a large, covered, but open-sided building like a market, which is crowded all day — and all night too — by hundreds of these poor, half-naked creatures standing round the gaming tables, silent, eager, excited, staking every cent they earn on the turn of the dice, living on the excitement of their gains—a truly sad spectacle. Probably we were the first European ladies who had ever walked through the gambling-house, but the gamblers were too intent even to turn their heads. There also they are always drinking tea. Some idea of the profits made by the men who 'farm' the gambling licences may be gained from the fact that the revenue derived by the Government from the gambling 'farms' is over £900 a year."[19]

Gambling, opium smoking and toddy drinking were the three addictions approved by the colonial government despite individual protests of humanitarian characters during the period some of whom were civil servants. These three addictions served colonial capitalism in the sense that they tied the workers to the employers for a longer period than stipulated in the agreement. They depleted whatever meagre saving the workers had theoretically at the end of the month. The debt grew with the consumption of opium and toddy. In addition these were sources of revenue. The majority of the new arrivals from China did not smoke opium. *The Straits Settlements and Federated Malay States Opium Committee Report 1908*, suggested that the majority of Chinese labourers learned to smoke opium after arrival in Malaya. The initiation centres were mainly the brothels. Some believed that opium was good for health and the sexual act. A European miner and planter who was a medical man, referring to the year 1904 or thereabout, defended opium smoking when he was a managing director of a large mine in Kinta. Fifty per cent of his over 2,000 coolies smoked opium. Some of the benefits of opium smoking were mentioned. It warded off malaria and it was believed to have a beneficial effect on the tuberculosis of the lung. This planter said: "I do not think this country could have been opened up without the opium pipe. They use it as a stimulant when tired, they can go without food for a longer period, they say it prevents diarrhoea and dysentery. That is the Chinese coolies' firm conviction, and they dare not go into the interior without the opium pipe."[20]

It was the conditions of labour which drove the coolies to opium smoking. A Chinese tin miner and planter, himself an opium smoker, told the Committee of 1924 the following: "The average mining coolie takes to opium more for the sake of preserving his life than for playing with it. In the Federated Malay States there is primary jungle, primitive work and an unmodified climate. Seventy per cent of woodcutters are opium smokers. Without opium I doubt whether they could stand the conditions."[21] The upholders of colonial capitalism suggested a further virtue of opium smokers. They were law abiding. They feared they would not get opium in prison. An old towkay summarized it in the following: "I put the four well-known evils in this order — womanising is the worst, gambling comes next, drinking next and, last of all, opium smoking. The womaniser's disease is visited upon his children and family; the gambler squanders his father's inheritance; the drunkard acts and behaves recklessly; on the other hand, the opium smoker is steady. He thinks carefully before he acts."[22] This was an attempt to defend the use of opium when it served the purpose of colonial capitalism, to relieve the intolerable condition of labour and to enrich the dealers in opium as well as the colonial government. It was the bait to attract and tie down the Chinese coolies. A large part of the revenue of British Malaya came from opium. Between 1896 and 1906, the lowest was 43·3 per cent, and the highest in 1904, 59·1 per cent.[23] From January 1, 1910 the British Government nationalized and monopolized the manufacture, sale and distribution of opium. The annual reports, or Blue Books, for the Straits Settlements provided these figures:[24]

	Revenue S$	Expenditure S$	Opium Revenue S$	Percentage of revenue
1918	23,262,015	15,966,145	15,706,741	60
1919	34,108,465	34,901,233	17,511,229	51
1920	42,469,620	39,260,318	19,983,054	47
1921	39,545,735	35,430,899	15,236,538	38

The revenue of the other states of British Malaya was also substantially derived from the revenue of opium, from human misery and degradation. This was the clearest known instance in history of a policy being adopted and organized on a huge scale, without any moral scruple, in the interests of colonial rule and capitalism. The drugging of whole nations by British colonial rulers had persisted for more than a century, despite protests from several quarters, both within and outside the British community. The Dutch and Spaniards did likewise but were not as rapacious as the British in the 19th century and the first decades of the 20th century. In 1918, 46 per cent of the revenue of the State of Johore was from opium. It covered 72 per cent of the total expenditure. Thus for more than 100 years, the civil servants of British colonies and protectorates were paid partly from opium, from the proceeds of human misery and degradation. La Motte's remarks are worth quoting: "The crux of the opium trade lies in the Far East. For over a century opium has been used as a money-getter to swell the revenue of certain European countries with possessions in the Orient. Individuals have grown rich on the proceeds. Colonies have prospered. Labour, the cheap and plentiful labour of China, has been lured by opium to certain colonies where native labour is not obtainable; and however individuals were damaged by this policy of wanton disregard for their welfare, there were always more, by the million, to draw upon. Human life has been utterly disregarded. Considerations of public health, of building up a stable, sober community, have never entered in. Nothing is so cheap as human life in the Orient, nothing so easily replaceable. An opium has been called upon to waste this human life, by destroying its value and efficiency, in order that Europeans might prosper."[25]

For the Indian immigrant labour, toddy was the bait and bondage.

In addition to this, there was the problem of diseases such as diarrhoea, dysentery and malaria on the estates. A general picture of the condition was drawn from the report of an enquiry on toddy drinking in the estates of the coast districts of Selangor. There were 38 estates involved. The period was between 1911 and 1916. In 1916, the total labour force from these 38 estates was 48,408. Most of these workers were Indian. Of this number, 22,343 were admitted to hospitals during the year. 2,354 were admitted for diarrhoea and dysentery, and 9,786 for malaria. 20·2 per cent of the labour force suffered from malaria, not counting the victims from preceding years, admitted previously. In 1911, 10·1 per cent were admitted for malaria, out of a labour force of 41,879. The total deaths for 1916 from all diseases was 1,064. [26]

The use of drugs like opium by the Government to raise revenue encouraged the habit in other forms. In 1936, it was found impossible to abolish toddy in the rubber estates owing to a possible intrusion of a more dangerous drink, samsu. The result was that all agreed to retain toddy, at the expense of Indian labourers. Sastri, a member of the Indian Legislature, sent by the Indian government to enquire on Indian labour in Malaya, in 1936, noted the following: "It occurred to me that in a country like Malaya where surplus budgets appear to be the rule rather than the exception, and excise is not a major head of revenue, conditions were particularly favourable for a policy directed towards ultimate prohibition, and I endeavoured to find out how informed opinion stood on this question in so far as it affected Indian labour. A certain number of managers are inclined to regard toddy as a harmless indulgence if within limits, and as a means of keeping their labour contented and happy. Others, on the other hand, perhaps forming the majority, agree that toddy is by no means a necessity and would not object to a suppression of the toddy drinking habit. Without it, labourers would undoubtedly be in a position to save more money and their efficiency would at least not be impaired, while the managers themselves would be spared the trouble of supervising the shop and its accounts and settling the occasional disputes which arise from drunkenness. In practice, however, they are almost unanimous in declaring that this is only a counsel of perfection. There is available in Malaya a potent and highly deleterious spirit known as 'samsu' which is easily and cheaply distilled from rice. Practically throughout Malaya I was informed, not only by planters but also by Government officials, that illicit distillation of this spirit by Chinese is rampant. It appears that the apparatus required is so simple in construction and cheap to erect that effective control is a matter of the greatest difficulty. In Johore I was told that the most stringent penalties were enforced, but in spite of this, the evil appeared to be unchecked. 'Samsu' is said to be far more damaging physically and mentally than toddy, and most planters told me that they dare not abolish the toddy shop since the immediate result would be that their estates would be encircled with numbers of illicit stills brewing 'samsu'. The fear of 'samsu' also prevent them from attempting to reduce toddy consumption by raising its retail prices. The weight of evidence regarding the widespread illicit distillation of 'samsu' is so great that it is impossible to disregard it."[27]

The attitude of colonial capitalism towards labour in the 19th century and early 20th century serves to explain the Malay response towards labour in colonial economic enterprises. The conditions and circumstances of labour then were far from favourable. The Malays were better off in their villages and traditional occupations. They could avoid inhuman conditions of labour. They did not become willing tools of greedy planters and miners. For this they were accused of indolence, despite acknowledgement by those who accused them, that they did good work in some fields. But these fields of Malay labour did not directly serve colonial capitalism. For instance the Malays planted rice. But government revenue from rice was negligible compared to opium, rubber and tin. Hence the Malays were not considered very productive in the colonial capitalist sense. Activities which positively contributed to total social development were not valued accordingly owing to the restricted and distorted criteria used. Malay contributions to running the administration were ignored. The fact that the country belonged to the Malays was ignored. Labour in the padi field was not light, furthermore it had its own social merits, as Baumgarten observed. "An extensive paddy field has a beautiful appearance, and keeps the air in a pure state, for which reason it should be preferred to other kinds of culture; but if the planter has a mind to cultivate the swamp himself, he should not, I think, undertake paddy cultivation, as the labour is great and he will require a number of hands which will eventually cost him dear, if the grain should by any chance be destroyed."[28]

A clear instance of the association of industriousness with plantation labour is furnished by a writer of the period, Owen Rutter. He was full of praise of the upland Dusans. They were "the backbone of an estate labour force" working well under Europeans who understood their idiosyncracies.[29] It was not only the question of labour which was linked with the colonial capitalist ideology, the entire concept of humanity was derived from the interest of colonial capitalism. Gambling, opium, inhuman labour conditions, one-sided legislation, acquisition of tenancy rights belonging to the people, forced labour, were all in one way or another woven into the fabric of colonial ideology and given an aura of respectability. Those outside it were derided.

NOTES

1. Karl Marx and Friedrich Engels, *The German Ideology*, p. 39, ed. R. Pascal. Lawrence and Wishart, London, 1938.
2. *Ibid.*
3. Quoted in W. L. Blythe, "Historical Sketch of Chinese Labour in Malaya", p. 68. JMBRAS, vol. XX, pt. 1, June, 1947.
4. *Ibid.*, p. 69.
5. *Ibid.*, p. 70.
6. *Ibid.*, p. 71.
7. *Ibid.*, pp. 70–71.
8. *Ibid.*, pp. 74–75.
9. *Ibid.*, pp. 78–79.
10. From *Straits Settlements Labour Commission Report 1890*, quoted by Blythe, *ibid.*, pp. 80–81. The Commission recommended Government inspection of Chinese labour and the abolition of private depots to be replaced by government depots.
11. Quoted in Blythe, *ibid.*, p. 91.
12. *Ibid.*, p. 111.
13. *Federated Malay States Labour Commission Report 1910*, quoted in R. N. Jackson, *Immigrant Labour and the Development of Malaya*, p. 152. Government Printing Press, Kuala Lumpur, 1961.
14. R. H. Vetch, *Life of the Hon. Lieut-General Sir Andrew Clarke*, p. 126. John Murray, London, 1905.
15. R. N. Jackson, *op. cit.*, p. 62.
16. Quoted in R. N. Jackson, *ibid.*, pp. 63–64.
17. Quoted in R. N. Jackson, *ibid.*, pp. 68–69.
18. *Ibid.*, p. 69.
19. Isabella L. Bird, *The Golden Cheronese*, p. 189, *op. cit.*
20. *British Malaya Opium Committee Report 1924*—C.224, quoted in R. N. Jackson, *op. cit.*, p. 55.
21. *Ibid.*, C.194 of Report. R. N. Jackson, *ibid.*, p. 55.
22. *Ibid.*
23. Ellen N. La Motte, *The Opium Monopoly*, p. 24. Macmillan, New York, 1920.
24. Ellen N. La Motte, *The Ethics of Opium*, p. 53. Century, New York, 1924.
25. *Ibid.*, pp. 12–13. In England opium was forbidden by law at a time when it was promoted in Malaya.
26. *Proceedings and Reports of the Commission appointed to inquire into certain matters affecting the good Government of the State of Selangor in relation to the alleged misuse and abuse of toddy in the coast districts of Selangor*, pp. 323–324. Federated Malay States Government Press, Kuala Lumpur, 1917.

27. V. S. Srinivasi Sastri, *Report on the Conditions of Indian Labour in Malaya,* p. 11, para. 16. Government of India Press, New Delhi, 1937.
28. F. L. Baumgarten, "Agriculture in Malacca", pp. 716–717. *JIAEA,* vol. 3, 1849.
29. Owen Rutter, *British North Borneo,* p. 64. Constable, London, 1922.

CHAPTER 7

The Indolence of the Filipinos

The title of this chapter is in honour of Rizal's work on the subject bearing a similar title. His work was probably the first historical sociological analysis of the subject, published in *La Solidaridad*, in Madrid in five instalments, from July 15 to September 15, 1890. He was reacting to the writing of a Filipino doctor of law, Sancianco, who discussed the subject of indolence and refuted it. Rizal pleaded for a dispassionate treatment of the subject. The term indolence, he contended, had been abused and misused. This however did not disprove its existence. He believed there was something behind the much discussed indolence. As noted earlier, Rizal's definition of indolence is "little love for work, lack of activity". This, according to him, was a problem in the Philippines. "Analysing carefully then all the incidents and all the men we have known since our childhood and the life in our country, we believe that indolence exists there. The Filipinos who can stand beside the most active men of the world will doubtless not challenge this admission. It is true that they have to work and struggle hard against the climate, against nature, and against men; but we should not take the exception for the general rule and we should seek the welfare of our country by stating what we believe is true. We must confess that there indolence actually and positively exists: but instead of regarding it as the *cause* of the backwardness and disorder, we should regard it as the *effect* of disorder and backwardness, which fosters the growth of a *disastrous predisposition.*"[1]

The predisposition towards indolence was not confined to the Filipinos alone. It was exhibited by the Europeans in the tropics. A warm climate requires rest, just as a cold climate encourages work and action. For this reason, according to Rizal, the Spaniard was more indolent than the French, and the French more indolent than the German. Indolence was thus not a unique trait of the Filipinos. The Europeans in the tropics were even more indolent. "The very Europeans who accuse the peoples of the colonies of indolence (and I am no longer referring to the Spaniards but also to the Germans and Englishmen), how do they live in the tropical countries? Surrounded by many servants, never walking but riding, needing servants not only to remove their shoes but even to fan them! And nevertheless they live and eat better, work for themselves and to enrich themselves, with the hope of a future, free, respected, while the poor colonial, the *indolent* colonial, is poorly nourished and lives without hope, toils for others, and is forced and compelled to work! What? The white men will reply perhaps that they are not made to suffer the rigors of the tropical climate. A mistake! Man can live under any climate if he will only adapt himself to its requirements and conditions. What kills the European in the warm countries is the abuse of alcohol, the desire to live as in his own country under another sky and another sun. We the inhabitants of tropical countries, live well in northern Europe whenever we take the same precautions as the people there do. The Europeans can also live well in the torrid zone if they would only get rid of their prejudices." [2]

Severe work is not a good thing in the burning heat of the tropics. An hour's work in the burning sun is equivalent to a day's work in temperate climate. It is thus fair that the land yields a hundred fold. Look at the way people in Europe reacted to hot summer days. They abandoned work during the few days of summer, running to watering-places, sitting down at cafes, strolling about. Rizal compared the indolence of the Filipinos with the Spanish officials and priests in the Philippines. "Who is the indolent one in the offices in Manila? Is it the poor clerk who comes in at eight in the morning and leaves at one o'clock in the afternoon with only his parasol, and copies and writes and works by himself and for his chief, or is it his chief who comes in a carriage at ten o'clock, leaves before twelve, reads his newspaper while smoking with his feet stretched out on a chair or a table, or speaking ill of everything with his friends? Who is the indolent one, the *Indio* coadjutor, poorly paid and badly treated, who has to visit all the indigent sick living in the countryside, or the friar curate who gets fabulously rich, goes about in a carriage, eats and drinks well, and does not trouble himself unless he can collect excessive fees?" [3]

Rizal posed the same question about the Chinese in the Philippines. What hard work did they do? Almost all of them engaged in trading, in commerce. Rarely did they take up agriculture and those who did in other colonies retired after a number of years.

Rizal ended his discussion on what I term "physiological indolence" in the following manner: "We find then the tendency to indolence very natural and we have to admit it and bless it because we cannot alter natural laws, and because without it the race would have disappeared. Man is not a brute, he is not a machine. His aim is not merely to produce, despite the claim of some white Christians who wish to make of the colored Christian a kind of motive power somewhat more intelligent and less costly than steam. His purpose is not to satisfy the passions of another man. His object is to seek happiness for himself and his fellow men by following the road towards progress and perfection."[4]

So far he was referring to indolence as a physiological reaction to heat. In winter one loves to walk in the snow. Under the burning sun one loves to remain under a shade, not to walk about on the street. This phenomenon is true. A load of mental work, in the tropics, should be spread over a certain period of time rather than rigorously continued at a stretch. Thus if a man has to do four hours of intense mental labour in a day, it is best for him to spread it throughout the day, some in the morning, some in the late evening. The same is true of physical labour. In a cold climate it is possible to do it at a stretch. I am referring to this as a work pattern, not as single sporadic instances. However it is only an adjustment that is required. This aspect of Rizal's concept of indolence, strictly speaking does not fall under his definition. There may be much love for work but adjusted to the climate in the manner of performance. However Rizal referred to something more. He said: "The evil is not that a more or less latent indolence exists, but that it is fostered and magnified. Among men, as well as among nations, there exist not only aptitudes but also tendencies toward good and evil. To foster the good ones and aid them, as well as to correct the bad ones and repress them would be the duty of society or of governments, if less noble thought did not absorb their attention. The evil is that indolence in the Philippines is a magnified indolence, a snowball indolence, if we may be permitted the expression, an evil which increases in direct proportion to the square of the periods of time, an effect of misgovernment and backwardness, as we said and not a cause of them. Others will think otherwise, especially those who have a hand in the misgovernment, but it does not matter; we have affirmed one thing and we are going to prove it."[5]

As he considered the indolence of the Filipinos an effect rather than the root cause of their backwardness Rizal did not consider it to be hereditary. It was the social and historical experience of the Filipinos under Spanish domination which created the phenomenon of indolence. He recounted the illuminating past of the Filipinos. Before the coming of the Europeans the Filipinos carried on an active trade with China. A 13th century Chinese record noted the honesty of the traders of Luzon. Pigafetta, who came with Magellan in 1521, arriving at Samar, was impressed by the courtesy and kindness of the inhabitants. He mentioned vessels and utensils of pure gold found in Butuan, where the people engaged in mining. They wore silk dresses, daggers with long gold hilts and scabbards of carved wood, gold teeth, and a host of other things. Rice, millet, oranges, lemons, and Indian corn were grown. Cebu had trade relation with Siam. The warriors of Luzon took part in the struggle against Acheh in Sumatra, in 1539. The sea of the islands bore everywhere commerce, industry and agriculture by the oars of hundreds of boats. Wealth abounded in the islands. "All the histories of those first years, in short, abound in long accounts of the industry and agriculture of the people—mines, gold placers, looms, cultivated farms, barter, ship-building, poultry- and stock-raising, silk- and cotton-weaving, distilleries, manufacture of arms, pearl-fisheries, the civet industry, horn and leather industry, etc. All these could be found at every step and considering the time and conditions of the Islands, they proved that there was life, there was activity, there was movement."[6]

Rizal documented his observations from well known earlier sources such as Morga, Chirino, Colin, Argensola and others. The question he raised was what made the active and pagan Filipino into a lazy and indolent Christian as alleged by contemporary writers? How did the Filipinos abandon their former industry, their trade, their fishing, their enterprise, to the point of completely forgetting them? It was due to a combination of circumstances, some independent of the will and efforts of men, some due to ignorance and stupidity. The Spanish conquest and the resulting Spanish rule brought about the conditions leading to the decline of the Filipinos. "First came the wars, internal disturbances which the new order naturally brought about. It was necessary to subject the people either by cajolery or by force; there were fights, there were deaths; those who have submitted peacefully seemed to repent of it; insurrections were suspected and some occurred; naturally there were executions and many skilled workers perished. To these disorders add the invasion of Li Ma Hong, add the continuous wars to which the inhabitants of the Philippines were dragged to maintain the honor of Spain, to extend the sway of her flag in

Borneo, in the Moluccas, and Indochina. To repel the Dutch foe, costly wars; futile expeditions in which it was known that thousands and thousands of Filipinos archers and rowers were sent but nothing was said if they never returned to their homes. Like the tribute that at one time Greece sent to the Minotaur of Crete, the Filipino youth who joined the expedition bade their country farewell forever. Before them, in the horizon, was the stormy sea, the endless wars, the hazardous expeditions."[7]

Rizal then quoted San Agustin's remarks on the depopulation of whole areas where the natives were the best sailors and most skilful rowers. In the island of Panay, in a little over half a century, 50,000 families were reduced to 14,000 taxpayers. It was from this area that the governors got most of the crews for the vessels which they sent out. Added to this were the frightful devastations of piratical attacks from the south. The piratical excursions from the south further reduced the population of the Philippines. According to Rizal, their motive was to weaken Spanish rule by devastating the areas which were helping the Spaniards or were under Spanish rule. This in turn resulted in the Spaniards organizing their defence against the pirates. They also wanted to get rid of their troublesome neighbours, the Dutch. They needed new and large ships. For this the Filipinos were again used. The ships were so large that it became a problem to find the necessary timber. The masts of a galleon took 6,000 Filipinos three months to haul seven leagues across rough mountains. San Agustin observed in 1690 that there was an uprising in a province owing to continuous cutting of timber for the shipyards which hindered the inhabitants from cultivating their very fertile plains.

There was then the exploitation by the *encomenderos*, those Spaniards holding large tracts of land with a right to levy taxes and tributes. Some sold Filipinos into slavery, to pay the taxes levied on them. Some Filipinos were hanged. Some fled into the mountains leaving their wives and children behind. There were cases of women, who were crushed to death by their heavy burdens, who slept in the fields and gave birth, who nursed their children there and died bitten by poisonous insects. "Is it strange then that the inhabitants of the Philippines should be dispirited when in the face of so many calamities they could not tell if they would ever see sprout the seed they have planted, if their farms would be their graves, or if their crop would feed their executioner? What is strange when we see the pious but impotent friars of that time advise their poor parishioners, in order to free them from the tyranny of the *encomenderos*, to stop work in the mines, abandon their industries, to destroy their looms, pointing to them heaven as their sole hope, preparing them for death as their only consolation."[8]

Rizal noted the various exploitations and oppressions resulting from Spanish rule. The cases and circumstances adduced by Rizal are historically well documented and those familiar with Philippine history required no further illustrations. The important thing to note is his recourse to these methods of exploitation to explain the most important single factor generating what he called indolence, notably the lack of motivation to work. "Man works for a purpose; remove the purpose and you reduce him to inaction. The most industrious man in the world will fold his arms the moment he learns that it is folly to be so, that his work will be the cause of his trouble, that because of it he will be the object of vexations at home and the greed of the pirates from outside. It seems that these thoughts never crossed the minds of those who cry out against the indolence of the Filipinos."[9] The permanent institution and group instrumental in erasing the motivation for work were the *encomendia* and the *encomenderos*. "The miserly return that the Filipino gets from his labor would in the end discourage him. Through the historians we learn that the *encomenderos*, after reducing many to slavery and compelling them to work for their benefit, made the rest sell them their products at an insignificant price or for nothing or cheated them with false measures."[10] San Agustin noted an area in Panay where people preferred to live in poverty rather than to acquire gold, to avoid troubles from the provincial governors. The rapacity of the *encomenderos* lasted a long time. Although the earlier breed of *encomenderos* had become extinct, the vices remained.

Rizal noted another factor which destroyed the motivation of the Filipinos. "The great difficulty that every enterprise encounters with the administration also contributes not a little to kill every commercial or industrial movement. All the Filipinos and all those in the Philippines who have wished to engage in business know how many documents, how many comings and goings, how many stamped papers, and how much patience are necessary to secure from the government a permit for an enterprise. One must count on the good will of this one, on the influence of that one, on a good bribe to another so that he would not pigeonhole the application, a gift to the one further on so that he may pass it on to his chief. One must pray to God to give him good humour and time to look it over; to give another enough talent to see its expediency; to one further away sufficient stupidity not to scent a revolutionary purpose behind the enterprise; and may they not spend their time taking baths, hunting, or playing cards with the Reverend Friars in their convents or in their country houses. And above all, much patience, a great knowledge of how to get along, plenty of money, much politics, many bows, complete resignation. How strange it is that the Philippines should remain poor despite its very fertile soil when History tells us that the most flourishing countries today date their development and well-being from the day they got their liberty and civil rights? The most commercial and most industrious countries have been the freest countries. France, England, and the United States prove this. Hong Kong, which is not worth the most insignificant island of the Philippines, has more commercial activity than all our islands put together because it is free and is well governed."[11]

The rulers gave the bad example of despising manual labour. "The pernicious influence of the rulers, that of surrounding themselves with servants and despising physical or manual labor as unworthy of the nobility and aristocratic pride of the heroes of so many centuries; those lordly manners that the Filipinos have translated into *Tila ka Kastila* (You're like a Spaniard); and the desire of the ruled to be the equal of the rulers, if not entirely, at least in manners—all these naturally produced aversion to activity and hatred or fear of work."[12] This and all the factors previously cited caused any motivation to disappear. There was also the encouragement of gambling by the Spaniards. The cost of frequent religious functions; the curtailment of individual liberty; the fear of being accused as a rebel; the entire social system, with its corruption and iniquities, removed any motivation to excel, or to become rich. Wealth attracted the predatory eyes of officials and intriguers. Furthermore such activities were not encouraged. The government's apathy towards commerce and agriculture partly fostered indolence. "There is no encouragement at all either for the manufacturer or the farmer; the government gives no aid either when the harvest is poor, when the locusts lay waste the fields, or when a typhoon destroys in its path the wealth of the land; nor does it bother to seek a market for the products of its colonies. Why should it do so when these same products are burdened with imposts and duties and have no free entry in the ports of the mother country, nor is their consumption there encouraged? While we see all the walls of London covered with advertisements of the products of its colonies, while the English make heroic efforts to substitute

Ceylon tea for Chinese, they themselves starting the sacrifice of their taste and stomach, in Spain, with the exception of tobacco, nothing from the Philippines is known—neither its sugar, coffee, hemp, fine textile, nor its Ilocano blankets." [13]

In addition to the lack of material inducement was the lack of moral support by the government for aspiring Filipinos. There was a case of a Filipino chemist who won a competitive position. After his success the post was abolished! In such a situation "one who is not lazy must needs be a fool or at least an imbecile". [14] The education of the Filipinos under the Spanish regime was brutalizing and depressing. During his primary education the Filipino was told not to part from his carabao, that it was evil to know Spanish, that he should have no further ambition. "Thus, while they try to make of the Filipino a kind of animal, they expect from him divine actions. And we say divine actions because he must be a God who does not become indolent under that climate and the circumstances already mentioned. Deprive a man then of his dignity, and you not only deprive him of his moral stamina but also you render him useless even to those who want to make use of him. Every being in creation has his spur, his main-spring; man's is his self-respect; take it away from him and he becomes a corpse; and he who seeks activity in a corpse will find only worms." [15]

Rizal also referred to the religious practices of the Catholic Church under the Spaniards in the Philippines. "They have dazzled him with tinsel, with strings of multi-colored glass beads, with noisy rattles, shining mirrors and other trinkets, and in exchange he has given his gold, his conscience, and even his liberty. He changed his religion for the rituals of another religion, the convictions and usages dictated by his climate and his necessities for other usages and other convictions which have grown under another sky and different inspiration. His spirit, disposed to everything which seems to be good, then was transformed according to the taste of the nation that imposed upon him its God and its laws; and as the trader with whom he dealt did not bring along the useful iron implements, the hoes to till the fields, but stamped papers, crucifixes, bulls and prayer-books; as he did not have for an ideal and prototype the tanned and muscular laborer but the aristocratic lord, carried in a soft litter, the result was that the imitative people became clerks, devout, prayer-loving, acquired ideas of luxurious and ostentatious living without improving correspondingly their means of subsistence." [16]

On the whole Rizal's appeal to historical and sociological factors to explain the absence of motivation amongst the people is sound. His thesis that the character of Filipino society had undergone a tremendous change owing to Spanish rule is equally sound. Historical and contemporary scholarship bears that out. But we differ from Rizal on the extent of indolence in the Philippines and on whether the phenomenon which he alludes to can be called indolence. An absence of the will to work conditioned by circumstances can hardly be called indolence. During the last war we had many prisoners of war held by the Japanese, British soldiers, who were not enthusiastic about working for the Japanese. Their reaction could hardly be called "indolence". While we are not denying that there were indolent Filipinos, members of the upper and middle-classes, conforming to our definition of indolence, it seems hardly appropriate to consider the larger section of Filipino society as indolent just because they were reacting to circumstances and conditions which suppressed motivation and enthusiasm for vigorous effort. The continuous rebellions against the Spaniards, the war with the south, finally the Philippine Revolution itself, the activity of the Katipunan, the stirring of the masses which Rizal himself witnessed before he was shot to death by the Spaniards, in other words the burning spirit of resistance which had never died since the Spanish conquest, clearly indicated that indolence, in Rizal's sense, had not entirely crippled Filipino society.

Rizal's appraisal on the extent of indolence is further weakened by another limitation. He had not extensively travelled throughout the length and breadth of the Philippines. The changes wrought by Spanish rules contributing to indolence mainly affected the urban centres. The Spaniards never had a complete control over all the villages of the Philippine Islands. But Rizal is to be credited for raising it as a problem and for attempting to explain it. He had succeeded at least in showing that the problem was more serious in the Philippines than anywhere else. However there is one major weakness in his treatment. He accepted the phenomenon and explained it historically and sociologically. The facts he cited were sound. His reasoning was sound. But he neglected the Spanish contribution in exaggerating the significance of the theme. Rizal was not aware of the sociology of knowledge. The fact that a conflict of interests conditioned the emergence of the theme escaped Rizal's notice. This factor was the conflict between Spaniards themselves, similar to the conflict between Dutch groups around the theme of the lazy Javanese. We shall return to this very soon but before this a reference is warranted to an earlier work on the Filipinos, much along the lines developed by Rizal but with different philosophical undertones.

An Englishman, who did not give his name, wrote a book on the Philippine Islands.[17] He made use of basically the same arguments as Rizal had. He considered the Spaniard to be Indolent, oppressive, and unjust. He traced the effect of the system on the general development of the Filipino society. Observations on the negative qualities of the Filipinos were based on those at Manila, who by necessity and the examples of the Spaniards, developed those negative qualities.[18] He found the Filipinos of the provinces in general mild, industrious, hospitable, kind, and ingenious. But for 300 years they had been oppressed. The country itself had been greatly favoured by nature and yet it remained an undeveloped forest. This state of affairs was attributed to the indolence of the Spaniards and the Filipinos. "The cause," the author explained, "lies deeper, man is not naturally indolent. When he has supplied his necessities, he seeks for superfluities—if he can enjoy them in security and peace;—if not—if the iron grip of despotism (no matter in what shape, or through what form it is felt), is ready to snatch his earnings from him, without affording him any equivalent—then indeed he becomes indolent, that is, he merely provides for the wants of today. This apathy is perpetuated through numerous generations till it becomes national habit, and then we falsely call it nature. It cannot be too often repeated, that from the poles to the equator, man is the creature of his civil institutions, and is active in proportion to the freedom he enjoys."[19] It is interesting that we find here a rare, clear, formulation of the capitalist concept of indolence, the mere provision for the needs of today. This is not physiological inactivity, but the absence of motivation to work for tomorrow.

He described the exploitation of the population by the *alcaldes mayores*, and referred to Comyn as his source. On the subject of the clergy he suggested there were 250 Spanish priests in the islands and between 800 to 1,000 Filipino priests. The majority of them according to him were of unseemly conduct. Seldom a week passed, or at most a month, without some of them being brought before the ecclesiastical tribunals. The cause of their misconduct was their insufficient training, and their exclusion from higher ecclesiastical positions. "A keen and deadly jealousy subsists between these and the Spanish ecclesiastics, or rather a hatred on the one side, and a contempt on the other. The Indian clergy accuse these last of a neglect of their ecclesiastical duties, of vast accumulations of property in lands etc. which, say they, 'belong to us the Indians'. The Spaniards in return treat them with silent contempt, continuing to enjoy the best benefices, and living at their ease in the convents. From what has been said, it will be easily seen, 'that much may be said on both sides'; but these recriminations have the bad effect of debasing both parties in the eyes of the natives, and are the germs of a discord which may one day involve these countries in all the horrors of religious dissentions."[20]

It was this underlying conflict between the Spanish and the Filipino clergy which had led to the arguments based on the theme of Filipino indolence. Most of those who had written on the Philippines had been priests. The underlying cause of San Agustin's denunciation of the Filipinos was his motive to degrade the Filipino clergy.[21] This question had further significant ramifications. It was not only a conflict between two groups of rival priests. It was a matter of survival for the Spanish regime. A clear expression of this was given by the Captain General and Governor of the Philippines, Don Pedro Sarrio, in his letter to the King of Spain, of December 22, 1707. The first reason why he preferred the Spanish priest was the improved state of affairs which they established in the towns and parishes. The second reason was most revealing. It was the dominant trend of Spanish thinking on the subject. Don Pedro Sarrio said: "My second motive for not separating the regulars from their parishes is that even supposing that the Indios and Chinese mestizos possess all the aptitude and necessary qualifications, it would never be convenient to the State and to Your Majesty's royal service, to place all the parishes in their hands. The experience of over two hundred years teaches us that in all wars, seditions and uprisings, the regulars as parish priests have had a large share in the pacification of the restless. It can be assured that in every European minister, Your Majesty has a sentinel who observes all the actions and movements of the Indios in order to notify this government of every happening. On the contrary, since almost all of the Spaniards live in Manila and its environs, if all the parishes were in the hands of the clergy, either natives or Chinese mestizos, the government would lack the means thru which it would certainly receive the needed news and information. Being priests does not denude them of the fact that they belong to a conquered people nor of the natural affection towards their own countrymen and equals. Although the benevolence of law makes the yoke of conquest light, a little meditation by some would at some moment make it appear a heavy burden. Even if the native clergy do not positively encourage revolt there always will remain the suspicion that they are remiss in putting out any spark of rebellion right at the beginning and communicating to their superiors the information conducive to applying a timely remedy. Of this, we have a recent example in the incident last February in the province of Bataan, where it is certain that two parish priests knew that the province was restless and that a mutiny was being readied against the administration of the tobacco monopoly where an assistant inspector and seventeen guards perished and yet they failed to notify either the archbishop or this government. In case of an enemy invasion, like that of the English in the year 62, the Spaniards would not enjoy the corresponding safety of flight to some province nor the means of sending messages to remote parts if there should be no European whosoever in the intervening towns who can be made use of." [22]

That was the dominant view of the role of Spanish clergy in the Philippines. The attack on the Filipino character in ecclesiastical writings was actually an attempt to subject the Filipino priests to the dominance of the Spanish ecclesiastical authorities in the Philippines. They were defending their position against a pro-Filipino trend in the Church, weak though it was. "This hostile attitude of the Spanish regulars rested on a selfish desire to preserve their privileges as well as upon genuine scruples of conscience. A numerous Filipino clergy obviously would have undermined the dominant position of the Spanish regulars." [23] The debate on this problem was most pronounced during the second half of the 18th century right up to the 19th century. That the conflict between the Filipino priests and the Spanish priests had political and other ramifications is clear. The underlying motivation was the control of the parishes with their attendant political powers and social prestige. [24] There was another dimension to this controversy suggested by Majul. The majority of the candidates for priesthood came from the *principalia* class, the principal citizens of the towns, the privileged Filipino class. In 1872, the Cavite Mutiny broke out and three native priests were executed in connection with it. The struggle for control of Philippine affairs was started decades earlier. There was an indirect struggle of the *principalia* via the native priesthood. "In an important sense, the secularization controversy, in so far as it represented an attempt of native priests to increase their share of parishes and in their attendant political and social benefits, was a function of the *principalia's* general struggle for a more active share in the control of the social life of the colony. The execution of the three priests in order to be understood in its true significance must be viewed with this background."[25]

Rizal did not consider all these factors in his analysis of the indolence of the Filipinos. The theme was magnified beyond proportion because it was a product of an ideological conflict which started about one and a half centuries earlier. Aside from genuine cases of indolence found among a section of the Filipinos, the majority were not indolent, as some witnesses testified. Those who refused to produce a surplus acted in this way owing to the exploitative social system which erased motivation for productive work. More than anything else the theme of the indolence of the Filipinos was brought into prominence as an outcome of the ideological conflict between the Spanish friars and native Filipino priests, preceded by a conflict of opinion between Spanish priests on the question of the Filipino priesthood. As the dominant group in the Philippines up to the time when Rizal wrote were the Spanish friars, their ideas became prevalent. The really indolent group, the Spanish ruling class in the Philippines, was never subject to the same type of scrutiny. It was the Filipinos who toiled, sweated and died for the Spaniards. The refusal of a slave to work with enthusiasm is natural. But the desire of a man to let others do his work for him by force is true indolence.

NOTES

1. Jose Rizal, "The Indolence of the Filipinos", in E. Alzona (tr. ed.), *Selected Essays and Letters of Jose Rizal,* pp. 182–183. Rangel and Sons, Manila, 1964.
2. *Ibid.,* pp. 183–184.
3. *Ibid.,* pp. 184–185.
4. *Ibid.,* p. 185.
5. *Ibid.,* pp. 185–186.
6. *Ibid.,* p. 190.
7. *Ibid.,* pp. 192–193.
8. *Ibid.,* p. 196.
9. *Ibid.,* p. 196.
10. *Ibid.,* p. 200.
11. *Ibid.,* pp. 201–202.
12. *Ibid.,* pp. 202–203.
13. *Ibid.,* pp. 205–206.
14. *Ibid.,* p. 207.
15. *Ibid.,* p. 209.
16. *Ibid.,* pp. 213–214.

17. *Remarks on the Philippine Islands and on their capital Manila, 1819–1822.*
     By an Englishman W. Thacker, St. Andrew's Library, Calcutta, 1828. This is
     reproduced, with edition, in E. H. Blair, J. H. Robertson (eds.), *The Philippine
     Islands 1493–1898,* vol. L1—1801–1840, pp. 73–181, *op. cit.* All quotations
     used here are from this source.
18. E. H. Blair, J. H. Robertson, *ibid.,* p. 89.
19. *Ibid.,* p. 91.
20. *Ibid.,* p. 117.
21. San Agustin described what would occur if the Filipino priests were to take
     the place of the Spanish clergy. "For the Indian who is ordained does not
     become a priest because it is the calling that conduces to the most perfect
     estate, but because of the great and almost infinite advantage that comes to
     him with the new estate that he chooses. How much it differs from being a
     father cura, to be a *baguntao* or sexton! From paying tribute, to being paid a
     stipend! From going to the [compulsory] cutting of timber, to being served in
     it! From rowing in a banca, to be rowed in it! That does not count with a
     Spaniard, who, if he becomes a cleric, often gives up an office as alcalde-mayor,
     captain, or general, with many other comforts in his native place, while his
     house is exalted above all the nation of the Indians. Let one contrast this with
     the vanity with which one who has been freed from the oar, or from an axe in
     the cutting of timber, will give his hand to be kissed! What a burden for the
     village will be the father, and mother, sister and nieces ranked as ladies, when
     many other better women are pounding rice! For if the Indian is insolent and
     intolerable with but little power, what will he be with so much superiority?"
     Gaspar de San Agustin, "Letter on the Filipinos", pp. 270–271, in E. H. Blair,
     J. A. Robertson (eds.), *The Philippine Islands 1493–1898,* vol. XL—1690–
     1691, *op. cit.*
22. Sinibaldo de Mas, *Report on the Condition of the Philippines in 1842,* III,
     pp. 144–145, *op. cit.*
23. J. L. Phelan, *op. cit.,* pp. 84–85.
24. Cesar A. Majul, "Social Background of Revolution", p. 8. *Asian Studies,*
     vol. IX, no. 1, April, 1971.
25. Cesar A. Majul, *ibid.,* p. 9.

CHAPTER 8

The Colonial Image and the Study of National Character

Before we proceed further, we may assess the evidence which we have come across in the previous chapters. The negative image of the people subjugated by Western colonial powers, which dominated the colonial ideology, was drawn on the basis of cursory observations, sometimes with strong built-in prejudices, or misunderstandings and faulty methodologies. The general negative image was not the result of scholarship. Those who proclaimed the people of the area indolent, dull, treacherous, and childish, were generally not scholars. They were monks, civil servants, planters, sailors, soldiers, popular travel writers, and tourists. They generated the image of the natives. Subsequently a few scholars became influenced, such as Clive Day. It appears that their shortcomings originated in five major sources. They are (a) faulty generalization, (b) interpretation of events out of their meaningful context, (c) lack of empathy, (d) prejudice born out of fanaticism, conceit and arrogance, and (e) the unconscious dominance of certain categories of Western colonial capitalist thought. The sum total of their labour can be described in a popular word, insult. Their judgements on the whole can be considered as insulting to the people concerned. The European powers forced themselves upon the people of the area and thereafter insulted them in their writing and in their action in addition to exploiting them. It was only after the first decades of the 20th century that attempts were made to introduce certain beneficial influences from the West, as a result of the liberal and humanitarian trends which existed in Western Europe. As late as 1924 the British and the Dutch were feeding opium to the population of Malaya and Indonesia. The virtues which they subsequently introduced have to be weighed against the vices. This requires a special treatment which will not be attempted here.

The modern and scientific studies of national character are recent developments relating to problems of culture and personality generated by the war situation. The concern with national character as such has a long history stretching back to antiquity. However, in the post-1939 world political situation, the study of national character assumed a new significance, in particular under the influence of anthropologists like Ruth Benedict, G. Gorer, Margaret Mead, G. Bateson, Ralph Linton, and psychoanalysts like Abram Kardiner, to mention only a few prominent contributors. At this juncture we may introduce a broad description of national character study by citing Margaret Mead. "National character studies, like all culture and personality studies, are focused on the way human beings embody the culture they have been reared in or to which they have immigrated. These studies attempt to delineate how the innate properties of human beings, the idiosyncratic elements in each human being, and the general and individual patterns of human maturation are integrated within a shared social tradition in such a way that certain regularities appear in the behavior of all members of the culture which can be described as a culturally regular character."[1]

One of the most impressive studies of national character in the past was accomplished by Abdul Rahman Ibn Khaldun, the North African Muslim historian and sociologist, during the second half of the 14th century. His study dealt with the national character of the Arabs and the Berbers. There were several important conclusions drawn by Ibn Khaldun one of which was the difficulty of the Arabs to form a stable government due to factors inherent in their culture and mentality.[2] Following the First World War, a study of Englishmen, Frenchmen and Spaniards was made by Salvador de Madariaga, published in 1928. The aim of the national character study is to know to what extent the characters of different nations are conditioned by their cultures. Here it would be desirable for us to make the distinction between the culture of a particular nation and its national character.[3] The culture of a nation in the words of Tylor, would refer to "that complex whole which includes knowledge, belief, art, morals, law, customs, and any other capabilities and habits acquired by man as member of society".[4] Culture is a way of living, a mode of ordering life as expressed by a particular group in society.

During recent decades the concept of culture has been subjected to sustained analysis so that an adequate description of culture would require volumes. However, it is sufficient for our present purpose to refer to an approximate concensus on the definition of culture which was formulated as follows: "Culture consists in patterned ways of thinking, feeling, and reacting, acquired and transmitted mainly by symbols, constituting the distinctive achievements of human groups, including their embodiment in artifacts; the essential core of culture consists of traditional (i.e., historically derived and selected) ideas and especially their attached values."[5] The study of national character, as distinguished from other studies of culture, selects as its central theme the behaviour and modes of reaction of national groups towards specific situations and problems or towards other nations. The aim is not only to enquire into the cultural conditioning of those behaviours and reactions as a form of explanation, but also to predict the line of future behaviour and reactions towards specific problems.[6] In the study of national character, attention is devoted to such factors as the child rearing practices of particular cultures, the values these cultures uphold, the interests they strive for, the sentiments and temperaments cultivated by them, etc. The basic assumptions and the method employed depend on the focus of interest. It must be pointed out here that as far as Malaysia, Indonesia and the Philippines are concerned, or for that matter Southeast Asia, national character study is practically a virgin field. With the absence of developed culture and personality study of the inhabitants it is difficult to launch a national character study on an adequate footing. Hence the prevailing opinions on the character of the Malays, the Javanese and the Filipinos, are at best superficial attempts. The many publications on the Malays, the Javanese and the Filipinos have not been directly suited to psychological and sociological analysis. Though themes like magic, culture, religion, customs, superstition, running amok, aggressiveness, piracy, loyalty, etc. have been touched upon, they have rarely been sociologically and psychologically studied on a proper basis. Burma is somewhat exceptional. There have been some studies on Burmese religion, adult life, character formation, belief in determinism, attitudes to crime and punishment, towards money, gambling, forgery, violence and cruelty; theatricality, male vanity, female dominance, preceded by a historical background of Burma. There are also some studies on Thailand and Bali.

The writings of the foreign authors we have identified are not scientifically based, and in addition they are extremely one sided. They have formed a totally unbalanced picture of the character of the communities. As an illustration we may take their writings on the Malays, which are basically the same, with some minor differences, as their writings on the Javanese and Filipinos. In the case of the Javanese, the difference is the stress on their attitude towards labour. In the case of the Filipinos their imitativeness. For the rest the picture drawn is basically the same. The picture drawn of the Malays by foreign writers during the colonial period concluded that the Malays are easy-going; that they are sensitive to insult; that they are prone to violent outbursts; that they are good imitators, lacking originality in thought and culture; that they are fond of idleness; but loyal to their chiefs and kings; that they are polite; that they are morally lax; but that they lack incentive or initiative for acquiring wealth; and that they are treacherous and wily. These traits have been suggested by different authors in the course of approximately 4 centuries.

On the whole, the foreign portrayal of Malay character has exclusively emphasized traits which were considered negative by the observer. Judged by modern scientific standard, the portrayal is unsound and naive. It reveals the observer more than the observed. The method and the basic assumptions employed in the study were crude and amateurish. The study of Malay character was not that of disciplines relevant to it. Thus Clifford who was not a psychologist and who was apparently not even familiar with the psychology of his day, felt no hesitation in declaring that the Malay as a nation was a potential victim of a pathological disorder of the mind. The key disciplines in national character study such as history, anthropology, psychoanalysis, and sociology, have never been applied by the scholar administrators and travellers. Their conclusions on Malay character do not qualify as scientific hypotheses. Nevertheless the ideas expressed are of interest to us. Their writings have created an image of the Malays, or to use a technical term, a stereotype, which has influenced a great many people in Malaysia and Singapore. They have been the most persistent and widespread sources of communal misunderstanding. It is not only on the "lazy Malay" that they dwelt, but also on the "venal" Chinese and the "cringing and cheating" Indian. From the point of view of scientific objectivity the stereotypes were inaccurate conclusions derived from unsound methods. From the point of view of modern religious or humanitarian philosophy by which national ends and values are defined, these stereotypes were dangerous, since in Malaysia they have influenced practical politics.

The scientific refutation of these stereotypes requires that they should be analysed in greater depth. Hence we proceed along the lines of the sociology of knowledge. The question to be raised is the validity of this image of the Malays. In the sociological sense of the word, an ideology, as we have shown at the beginning of this book, is not just any system of knowledge and belief. An ideology is a style of thought of a ruling group anxious to maintain its domination. The basic categories which form one's view of social reality, the vision of the past and future, especially the conception of human nature and human freedom, are bound up with the thinker's basic political stand and group identification. Even where the observer is careful to control his personal bias, his social and historical background conditions his way of thought.

The image of the Malays formed by the European observers can be traced to the historical position of the individual authors. In the accounts of the earlier explorer there was a great deal of interest in the flora and fauna of the region, in the trade and custom of the inhabitants. The spice trade was the centre of attraction. Judgements on the local inhabitants depended on whether the local inhabitants were friendly or not to the European visitor. Thus Bowrey, during his visit to Kedah (about 1677) was highly appreciative of the country and inhabitants. He noted the prosperity of Kedah, praised the Sultan of Kedah as a most just, honest, and courteous ruler, a great peacemaker, and a friend of the English. [7] On the other hand he disliked the Chuliar Indians, "a subtle and roguish people" who travelled to all countries and kingdoms of Asia. An incident when some Siamese and Malays rose against the Chuliars placed in a high position by a Malay raja, resulting in the killing of 70 or 75 of them, was welcomed by Bowrey. As a matter of fact he hoped that a similar fate awaited them in Banten, Acheh, Kedah, Johore, Siam and "many other places they are crept into".

Raffles's praise for the Bugis of Celebes is well known. The reasons, clearly expressed by Raffles, were their esteem for the English, and their martial qualities which could assist the British in empire building. In Raffles's opinion the Bugis were the most bold, adventurous and enterprising of the eastern nations, and they were extremely fond of military life. They were loyal and courageous. For the above reasons they had been employed, as the Swiss in Europe, in the armies of Siam, Camboja, and other countries, and also as guards of their princes. [8] British commercial and political interests were the criteria upon which Raffles based his judgements. He described the Americans as "another class of commercial interlopers, who would require our vigilant attention, for whenever they went they spread the sale of firearms, a commodity of the highest demand. Such a commercial adventure would jeopardise British political and commercial interest". [9]

To judge from available sources, the image of the Malays became more negative during the 19th century. This is understandable in view of the fact that British contact with the Malays increased rapidly and the idea of intervening in the affairs of the Malay states was gaining ground. The twin gospel, commercial benefit for the mother country and civilization for the natives, which includes Western Christianity, became the reigning ideology. As European contact with the area had always been accompanied by resistance and counter-attack, a conflict situation arose from the 16th right throughout the 17th, 18th and 19th centuries. The stereotypes of the foe or serious competitor were part of this situation. Functionally they served to justify conquest and domination. When Raffles and many of the British administrators of the 19th century arrived on the scene, the Malays and others in the region had passed through more than three centuries of political, economic, social and military onslaught by predatory European powers who took them by surprise when they first arrived. Many of the negative traits described by the 19th century observers were the creation of the Europeans of the earlier centuries.

Let us first consider the image of the lazy Malay. It struck us as odd that a people who, in the words of Raffles, "is so indolent, that when he has rice, nothing will induce him to work", could be continuously engaged in war and piracy against formidable opponents. The history of the Malays from the 16th century onwards was full of internal as well as external conflicts. As a matter of fact the Malays were the most harassed people. No region in South East Asia had been attacked and occupied by so many forces from so many parts of the world. The Portuguese, the Dutch, the Siamese, had all attacked and occupied certain parts of the Malay Peninsula. We may also mention the attack of Acheh and the Bugis raids. If the Malays were that lazy they would have lost their independence long ago. The fact that the British succeeded in occupying Malaya through diplomacy, while those using force failed, was partly the result of the activity and alertness of the Malays.

As I noted earlier, the image of the indolent Malay nation has no sound scientific basis. It arose because the Malays avoided colonial capitalist plantation labour. There is no doubt that a proportion of Malays were lazy, but these were usually from the upper classes. Similarly there were Malays who were cunning and treacherous but their cunning and treachery were linked to their profession and situation. What can be expected of them if their life and livelihood depended on successes against opponents who were equally cunning and treacherous? The cunning and treachery of those Malays in conflict with the Dutch and Portuguese was part of the situational response towards groups who were themselves cunning and trea-cherous.

Raffles himself, after approximately seventeen years of sojourn and travel in this part of the world, could not shake off the habit of generalization. The highest consciousness he ever attained was expressed in a letter to the Duchess of Somerset, June 12, 1821, seventeen years after his arrival, in Penang, in September, 1805. He wrote the following: "It is very certain that on the first discovery of what we term savage nations, philosophers went beyond all reason and truth in favour of uncivilized happiness; but it is no less certain, that of late years, the tide of prejudice has run equally strong in the opposite direction; and it is now the fashion to consider all who have not received the impression of European arms and laws, and the lights of Revelation, as devoid of every feeling and principle which can constitute happiness, or produce moral good. The truth, most probably, as is generally the case, lies between the two extremes, and there is, no doubt, much difference according to the circumstances under which the people may have been placed. We find, in some of the islands of the South Seas, people who are habitually mischievous, given to thieving, lazy, and intractable; in others, we find the very opposite qualities; and philosophers, speculating upon the first data that are afforded, without full and general information, are led into error."[10]

It is apparent from the above that Raffles was still thinking of characterizing whole groups though not the whole region and ethnic collectivity. There was however no consideration that those negative traits which he rejected were linked in the sense in which Abdul Rahman Ibn Khaldun suggested.[11] The truth is that those factors were found in all communities and classes in varying degrees depending on sociological and historical backgrounds. Though it may be possible to argue about the theory of national character, it is hardly possible to delineate such a character in terms such as indolence, wiliness, treacherousness, predatoriness, and so forth. Even in terms of small primitive communities, other characteristics are used to delineate national character. If we were to relate it to class, occupational and situational structure we would obtain a different picture. Thus Vaughan, writing in 1857, attempted to correct certain false impressions of the Malays, cherished by the majority of Europeans in his day. He was conscious of not generali-zing the impressions which he had gathered from the seaport towns to cover the whole country. He considered truthfulness a prominent feature of the Malays, and also the absence of obscenity in their language when they were angry. They made excellent naval crew. Conflicts which occurred between European and Malay sailors were often caused by misunderstandings. As he put it, "European officers accustomed to the abuse of Indian sailors and ignorant of the Malayan prejudices on his head, behave towards them as they are wont to do to the Bengalies or other natives, and abuse and strike them indiscriminately. The consequence is, the deadliest passions of the Malay are aroused and in revenge they wreak a fearful retribution on their oppressors. It is probable that a crew of Englishmen would resort to the same course, if similar treatment were pursued towards them. On the other hand, when the Malay is treated as a man and not a brute, he proves docile, faithful and industrious, and without exception superior to any eastern sailor afloat".[12]

Neither culturally nor religiously has laziness (malas) been approved by the Malays. We shall discuss this later. Anyone having first hand knowledge of Malay fishermen and padi planters will realize how absurd the contention is. The Europeans who observed the Malays in the port towns had no idea of what was happening in the interior, of the padi planters who started work at dawn and returned home at dusk, of the fishermen who sailed at night and attended to his boat and net in the day time; or of the gotong royong (mutual help) labour in the village. Raffles knew only the Malays in the port towns. That the Malays he knew did not show the aggressive capitalist spirit is, however, a different story. There was then no Malay middle class whose livelihood depended on commerce. The bulk of the Malays were fishermen and padi planters. In the Europe of his time, commerce and empire building were the most esteemed activity by both aristocrats and capitalists whose spirit infused the East India Company. Hence a group which was not equally moved by this spirit was considered to be lazy. Industriousness was equated with acquisitiveness.

To assess the reliability of such images we have extended our area of study. These images were actually part of the general European image of the Orient. As we have shown, not only the British, but also the Dutch and the Spaniard upheld the same image of those under their domination. It was the product of an enthnocentric and arrogant outlook. The snobbery, the conceit, and the naivity of this outlook were further characterized by a lack of inhibition and refinement in their modes of expression. Raffles called Islam a robber-religion.[13] Sir William Norris, when delivering the sentence on a trial of a Malay convicted of amok killing, in Penang, July 13, 1846, seized it as an opportunity to hurl invectives against Islam, on the grounds that only Malays committed amok, and that they were Muslims, who "alone of all mankind, can ever attach to such base cowardly and brutal murders, notions which none but the devil himself, the father of lies, could ever have inspired."[14] Gonggrijp, in an article to the *Bataviaasch Handelsblad*, July 17, 1911, mentioned how it was necessary for him to light a cigar first before talking to a group of Javanese, in the hope that the cigar odour would drown the stench from their clothes.[15] The myth of the lazy and semi-civilized Javanese has been as widely circulated as that of the lazy Malay.

As noted earlier, the image of the Malays resembles that of the Filipinos and the Javanese. These images had been circulated among countless thousands of minds in the course of more than four centuries by hundreds of books and continuous verbal communications. It is astonishing that no serious effort has been made to study the roots and implications of such images. From the survey which we have accomplished the following conclusions may be drawn: that the image of the Malays has been part of a similar and wider image of the whole region, which was exclusively created by the Europeans of the colonial period. Furthermore, this image was based on hasty generalizations rather than on a sound methodology and rigid scholarship. It was partly generated by cultural misunderstanding or lack of empathy, but mainly it was ideological, a justification of colonial domination.

In order to explain the above in a more analytic and staisfactory manner let us first start with the question of cultural misunderstanding and lack of empathy. It is an acknowledged fact that in behavioural studies this understanding of outward appearances is crucial to the explanation and interpretation of the culture. Similarly, unless we apprehend the innermost depth of a culture, we are bound to obtain a distorted interpretation of the behaviour in question. Ideally the author should attempt to put himself in the position of the participant reacting within a particular cultural context. We should attempt to sense his emotional and logical motivations as he experiences them. We may then appraise and interpret the behaviour within a wider framework of reference.

This process of emphatic understanding (verstehen), is not always accomplished. Thee basic conditions have to be met. The first is the attitude of objectivity in the comprehensive sense of the word. The second is knowledge of the necessary sciences to explain the behaviour. The third is knowledge of the factual and concrete data pertaining and related to the behaviour in question. Let us cite the following illustration: "Like all Orientals, the Javanese has a secret that we have not: the secret of true repose. Unlike the Europeans, he feels no need to fill up his free time with entertainments (though he greatly enjoys them when they come his way), for he knows as well how to idle as he does how to work. He does neither the one nor the other at high speed as we do, and consequently knows nothing of the 'nerves' that drive us feverishly to perpetual motion. He works so hard, so steadily, and so long, that when he does stop, his one desire is to rest, and he asked no more than to be allowed to do nothing. It is this complete relaxation of his that leads European visitors so ludicrously astray in their superficial judgment of the 'lazy native'." [16]

In the above illustration all the conditions are present. The behaviour is interpreted within its proper context. The moment we adopt the correct method and acquire the necessary data, we will get a different picture. The Javanese, Malays and Filipinos generally worked hard but their work pattern was different from European workers. The majority did not have what was then a regular Western pattern of work, such as that of a mine labourer or factory worker. They did not have fixed hours of work. The best instance I can think of was what I saw myself before the Second World War and during the Second World War in West Java. There was a group of vendors called *tukang arang*, or charcoal sellers. Coal was sold in grocery shops or by the *tukang arang*. Each of these vendors would carry on his shoulder two large baskets of coal hanging on a bamboo rod placed on the shoulder of the vendor. It required special strength to carry the load. At dawn, these vendors would leave their homes in the villages, miles away from the town. The transporting of heavy baskets of coal on the shoulder for miles at a stretch required more than average physical exertion. When he reached the town, the coal seller would go from house to house until he found a buyer at a suitable price. I also frequently saw these vendors at sunset, with faces drooping in despair, their coal unsold. If one of the vendors was in luck by noon he would have sold his ware. After this he would relax, go to native food stall, have his meals or smoke his native cigarette, and then go home. If a Dutch colonial like Gonggrijp had seen him smoking and chatting at the stall, he would have condemned him as indolent. The facts surrounding his labour would not have been understood, nor the meaning of his rest perceived, and his presence during European normal working hours outside the place of work at odd times would have been misinterpreted.

It was said that such a *tukang arang* had no spirit to acquire more. Why should he not sell more? The explanation lies in the production system which was not mechanized. The charcoal was prepared by small traditional production units, there was no accumulated surplus since whatever was ready was immediately sold. It would have required an abnormal human effort for our *tukang arang* to have gone back to his village and to have carried the heavy load again on his shoulders for miles and arrive in the town by the late afternoon; he would have worked himself to death. Hence he was satisfied with one sale a day, his full load. There were thousands of people employed in such unmechanized occupations in Indonesia before the war. In such a society a tremendous amount of physical labour is expended compared with a mechanized society. Leaving aside the question of productivity in terms of capitalist norms, the accusation of indolence in a society which expended enormous physical labour is, to say the least, the most brazen distortion.

The distortion arises either from prejudice or from the influence of capitalist thinking. As an illustration we shall use the following judgement on the Javanese: "On seeing a Javanese expending a great amount of physical effort, in a temperature constantly above eighty degrees, to dig the countless ditches needed in order to plant sugar-cane in the fields, and all for a mere pittance, one is inclined to compare him to a busy bee. One obtains the same impression even more emphatically on seeing a Native go on long journeys for the sake of a small financial gain. On the other hand, on seeing how a Native can relax for days at a stretch without any apparent qualms, passing the entire time in a half-waking, half-dreaming state without the least urge to do even the slightest work, whenever the exceptional case presents itself that he is not short of money, and so lacks an immediate inducement to work, one finds him a lazy creature with all one's heart. The Javanese lacks the inward urge towards regular work that is generally manifest in northern European nations. But his conditions of life usually prevent him from cultivating his inclinations, hence the peculiar oscillation between great exertion and great indolence." [17]

The factor which qualified the Javanese as indolent was his inclination "to relax for days at a stretch without any apparent qualms". His previous hard work was ignored. On the other hand, if European labourers relax and do nothing for a longer stretch, it is not considered as indolence; it is a healthy holiday regulated according to time and taken at the convenience of the factory. Hence in his appraisal of the meaning of rest, Schmalhausen was employing capitalist categories of thought. Any rest or abstention from work outside the Western colonial capitalist norm was regarded as indolence and a waste of time. As regards his judgement that the Javanese lacked the urge for regular work, this was also a distortion. The Javanese employed in the colonial administration worked regularly. The Javanese soldiers in the Dutch army worked regularly. What about the *tukang delman* in West Java and other parts of the island? A *delman* in West Java is a horse carriage on two wheels used as public transport. They were the taxis of the towns within a radius of 10 to 15 miles before the war. Every day for years, as a matter of course even for a life-time, many drivers left their village houses at dawn and returned around 10p.m. in the evening. What could have been more regular than this? But this activity was outside the capitalist system of production proper. Hence it was ignored.

What Schmalhausen had in mind was a regular worker in a Dutch plantation or a town factory operating in the colonial capitalist system. Regular work existed in a traditional society. No society could survive without regular work. The vegetable farmers, market sellers, soldiers, government servants, village school teachers, *tukang arangs* and hundreds of other vendors, stall hawkers, and *tukang delmans* had all been employed in regular work. They could not conceivably have escaped the notice of the Dutch colonials. The fact is that Schmalhausen and others of similar views, had the modern Western proletariat in mind: hence the talk about their indolence and inability to work regularly. The truth is that many Javanese were not attracted by plantation and factory labour. Historically speaking all over the world capitalism had recruited its sources of cheap labour on the basis of oppression and injustice. In Europe it was the serfs who ran away to the town, victims of exploitation. In Malaya, labour was supplied by means of deceptive recruitment and thereafter workers were corrupted by opium and gambling and remained bound to the place of work. In Java and the Philippines during the 19th century where there was no sizeable immigrant labour force, the population was forced to work. With the abolition of forced labour, opium was distributed and manufactured by the Dutch Government. By the 1920s it manufactured and sold the opium directly.

We may note other instances of interpretation out of context from the Philippines. One was a complaint of San Agustin against

Filipino dogs and children in his letter of 1720. He said: "It is a thing to be wondered at that even the dogs have another disposition, and have a particular aversion toward Spaniards. When they see Spaniards, they choke themselves with barking. And when the children see a father they cry immediately, and thus from their cradle they begin to hold every white face in horror." [18] This was an interpretation out of context. Sinibaldo de Mas commented on this: "If our father had traveled, he would have known that dogs bark at anyone whose clothes are unfamiliar to them. In regard to their horror of white faces, he at least exaggerates. It is not at all strange that a child should cry at an object being presented to him that he has never had in his ken before. I have seen many children burst into sobs at the sight of my eye-glasses. It is a fact that some of them have just as little as possible to do with us, either for contempt, embarrassment, or antipathy; but there are a very great number who profess affection for us." [19]

San Agustin also complained of the workmen who asked their pay in advance and then left the work but kept the pay. "This," said Delgado, a contemporary of San Agustin, "is peculiar only to some workmen, and not to all the nations of these islands, and the same thing happens also in our own country among cobblers, tailors, and other deceitful and tricky workmen". [20] On asking for advance de Mas gave this explanation: "There is no tailor, cobbler, or workman of any kind, who does not begin by begging money when any work is ordered. If he is a carpenter, he needs the money in order to buy lumber; if a laundryman, to buy soap. This is not for lack of confidence in receiving their pay, for the same thing happens with those who have the best credit, with the cura of the village, and even with the captain-general himself. It consists, firstly, in the fact that the majority have no money, because of their dissipation; and secondly, because they are sure that after they have received a part of their price, their customer will not go to another house, and that he will wait for the workman as long as he wishes (which is usually as long as what he has collected lasts), and that then the customer will have to take the work in the way in which it is delivered to him." [21]

Another instance is Morga's judgement that the Filipinos were hostile to manual labour, in connection with the modification of the tribute system to the *encomenderos*. They were allowed to pay in money also instead of exclusively in kind. This modification was urged by the religious group, seeing that the *encomenderos* exploited the population, by fixing an arbitrary value to the tribute which they sold at a much higher price, introduced false measures, and forced certain lucrative products only as acceptable tributes. According to Morga, as a result of this modification they paid less attention to agricultural labour. "For, since they naturally dislike to work, they do not sow, spin, dig gold, rear fowls, or raise other food supplies, as they did before, when they had to pay the tribute in those articles. They easily obtain, without so much work, the peso of money which is the amount of their tribute. Consequently it follows that the natives have less capital and wealth, which was formerly very well provided and well-supplied with all products, is now suffering want and deprivation of them. The owners of the encomiendas, both those of his Majesty and those of private persons who possess them, have sustained considerable loss and reduction in the value of the encomiendas." [22]

The disinclination of the Filipinos to cultivate was interpreted out of context. It was attributed to their nature then. But Rizal stressed the following contextual explanation: "This is not exact, because they worked more and they had more industries where there were no *encomenderos,* that is, when they were heathens, as Morga himself asserts (Pp. 229, 358, etc.). What happened—and this is what the Spaniards do not understand, in spite of the fact that it shines through the events and some historians have indicated at it—was that the Indios, seeing that they were vexed and exploited by their *encomenderos* on account of the products of their industry, and not considering themselves beasts of burden or the like, they began to break their looms, abandon the mines, the fields, etc. believing that their rulers would leave them alone on seeing them poor, wretched, and unexploitable. Thus they degenerated and the industries and agriculture so flourishing before the coming of the Spaniards were lost, as is proven by their own accounts relating incessantly the abundance of the supply of foodstuffs, gold placers, textiles, blankets, etc. Contributing not a little towards this was the depopulation of the Islands as a consequence of the wars, expeditions, insurrections, cutting of timber, shipbuilding, etc. that destroyed or kept busy farm and industrial laborers. Even in our own days we hear often in the huts the sad but puerile desire of the hapless who hoped for the day when there shall not be in the Philippines a single cent so that they might be liberated from all plagues." [23]

The unwillingness of some Filipinos noted by Morga to exert themselves in agriculture is thus brought into proper context by Rizal. An observer who adopted a contextual approach was the

Dutch rear admiral Stavorinus. His understanding of the problem was rare for the period. He was in Java in 1777, and discussed the indolence of the Javanese. He attributed it to the result of an oppressive system carried out by the Dutch East India Company and the native rulers. Java, he said, could only develop and prosper by a change of circumstances, "by ceasing to depress and impoverish the natives by constant injustice and continual extortion, and by avoiding, in future, every species of war", which would eventually depopulate the country further and bring ruin to the Company.[24] It was the excessive demands of the Dutch East India Company, through their vassals, the native rulers, which stifled the spirit of industry. The Javanese, like the rest of mankind would have liked the freedom to command and dispose of their own property. "But now, deprived of the most distant prospect, and not encouraged by any hope of bettering their situation, they sit down sullenly contented, as it were, with the little that is left to them, by their despotic and avaricious masters; who, by this unwise, as well as unfeeling, conduct, extinguish every spark of industry, and plunge their subjects into the gloom of hopeless inactivity."[25]

Stavorinus rejected the climatic explanation of the lack of enthusiasm for production. He pointed to the Chinese in Java who operated under the same climate but were nevertheless endowed with enthusiasm. His reason was their position in the colonial system. "But they are comparatively unshackled, and are free masters of what they can earn by trade, or procure by agriculture, beyond the pecuniary or other assessments levied upon them by the government. This encourages them readily to undertake the most laborious occupations, and diligently to persevere in them, while they feel a rational hope of obtaining, in proper time, the reward due to their exertions."[26] The position of the Javanese as an object of colonial exploitation, the uncertainty surrounding his right of possession, made him satisfied with little. From this and similar observations by Rizal and others, the phenomenon characterized as indolence among a section of the native population, may in actual fact be interpreted as a silent protest. It was a form of strike, secret, collective, and steady. That was their only means of resistance; indeed it was a camouflaged resistance at that. The Javanese were brought to Malaya for the European estates, beginning at the end of the 19th century. The British authorities were full of praise for them. They were less liable to contract diseases; they were well treated by their employers. A Javanese labourer was inclined to resent ill-treatment and it was "not possible to make a slave of him".[27] In addition to the above reasons, they were not subjected to opium, gambling and toddy. In a different setting the Javanese was not classified as indolent.

The interpretation out of context had caused several negative traits to be woven into the image of the native. Bowring, who praised Filipino kindness and hospitality to visitors, a rare positive trait as compared to the negative he noted, expressed a characteristic uncouthness and absence of refinement when he said that the Filipino was more a quadruped than a biped.[28] Such characterization of the native population in negative and unspeakable terms was common in the colonial period. They cannot be taken seriously. They had to be exposed and debunked. They had woven an image of the native devoid of decency, humanness, realism, and honesty. The image of the native under colonial domination is the most unprovoked prejudice entertained by a dominant group towards the subject people. The Malays gave up their land and political power to the British. They were displaced from mining. They accepted the situation where the wealth of the country was drained to England and to other countries. They become the poor in their own country. They had to share their country with a sizeable immigrant population who were brought down in the interest of colonial capitalism. Yet despite their acceptance of all these they were accused of indolence, treachery, amok running, etc.

The Dutch converted Java into a plantation of cash crops. The Javanese who laboured and sweated for them were called dull, indolent and childish. The Spaniards in the Philippines depended entirely on the Filipinos for their income and livelihood, and for fighting their wars against other nations. Yet the Filipinos were accused of indolence and decadence. The ingratitude, insolence, crudeness and fanaticism that gave birth to these images were somewhat out of the ordinary in the sense that they did not emerge as a result of a conflict situation, a provocation of long standing. Insult after insult was hurled upon people who led ordinary lives, working, minding their own business, accepting their colonized status, serving European colonial capitalist interest to the point of accepting forced labour, inoffensive to the colonial power, unabusive to the European community, and on the whole behaving like many other civilized communities, both in Europe and elsewhere. It was clear that the origin of the images lies in the need to justify domination or a particular policy, as the Dutch controversy on Javanese labour shows. The causes were ideological conflict and rationalization. Though the images are by no means a reliable portrayal of national character, yet these images, as we shall see in the next chapter, have still a considerable influence after the independence of the colonies.

NOTES

1. Margaret Mead, "National Character", in A. L. Kroeber, ed. *Anthropology Today*, p. 642. University of Chicago Press, Chicago, 1953.
2. Ibn Khaldun, *The Muqaddimah.*Tr. ed., F. Rosenthal, vols. 1–3. Routledge and Kegan Paul, London, 1958.
3. Margaret Mead, *op. cit.*, p. 657. This distinction is duly noted by Mead, together with the view that a national character study is derivative of the culture and personality study.
4. M. J. Herskovits, *Cultural Anthropology*. A. A. Knopf, New York, 1955. Quoted in p. 306.
5. C. Kluckhohn, "The Study of Culture", in D. Lerner and H. D. Lasswell (eds.), *The Policy Sciences*, p. 86. Stanford University Press, California, 1951. Quoted from A. L. Kroeber, C. Kluckhon, *The Concept of Culture: A Critical Review of Definitions*. Papers of the Peabody Museum, vol. XLI, 1950. (Harvard University.)
6. See further, M. Mead, "The Study of national character," in *The Policy Sciences, op. cit.*
7. Thomas Bowrey, *A Geographical Account of Countries round the Bay of Bengal, 1669 to 1679*, pp. 265, 267. R. C. Temple (ed.), Hakluyt Society, Cambridge, 1905. On the reason for his dislike for the Chuliars he wrote, "They are like wise a very great hinderance to us, for, wherever these rascals be, we cannot sell goods to a native of the country, but they creep in along with them, and tell them in private what our goods cost upon the coast, in Surat, or Bengal, or elsewhere, which doth many Christians a great prejudice." (P.258.)
8. T. S. Raffles, *Memoir*, vol. 1, p. 67, *op. cit.* (His letter to Lord Minto, Malacca, June 10, 1811.) (See also Syed Hussein Alatas, *Thomas Stamford Raffles—Schemer or Reformer) op. cit.*
9. *Ibid.*, p. 86.
10. T. S. Raffles, *Memoir*, vol. 2, p. 193, *op. cit.*
11. City merchants are more prone to dishonesty than peasants owing to their way of earning a living. Bravery is developed more in nomadic societies than in sedentary societies. Ibn Khaldun's approach is modern though he lived in the 14–15th century. See Ibn Khaldun, The *Muqaddimah*, vols. 1–3, *op. cit.*
12. J. D. Vaughan, "Notes on the Malays of Pinang and Province Wellesley," *JIAEA*, p. 125, New Series, vol. 11, no. 2, 1857.
13. *Memoir*, p. 94, vol. 1, *op. cit.* He mistakenly thought that Islam preached the massacre and plundering of unbelievers. The bigoted attack on Islam was due as much to political factors as to religious bias.
14. Sir William Norris, "Malay Amok referred to Mohomedanism", *JIAEA*, pp. 460–463, vol. III, 1849. The sentence ended with the following: "Your body will then be handed over to the surgeons for dissection, and your mangled limbs, will be cast into the sea, thrown into a ditch, or scattered on the earth at the discretion of the Sheriff. And may God Almighty have mercy on your miserable soul." (P. 463.) One wonders whether in such an instance a British murderer would be deprived of a decent burial according to his religion. Sir William's sentence on the disposal of the corpse was in flagrant violation of the Islamic teaching that requires all dead to be buried in a decent and religious manner.

15. G. L. Gonggrijp, *Brieven van Opheffer*, p. 71. Leiter-Nypels, Maastricht, 1944. This book has gone into several editions.
16. H. W. Ponder, *Javanese Panorama*, p. 17. Seeley, Service, London. The book must have been written before the Second World War. It was printed in 1942, but no date of publication was given.
17. H. E. B. Schmalhausen, *Over Java en de Javanen*, Amsterdam, 1909. Quoted in G. Gonggrijp, "Value Curves and the Lowest Level of the Indies Economy", in W. F. Wertheim and Others (eds.). *Indonesian Economics*, p. 104. W. Van Hoeve, the Hague, 1961.
18. Gasper de San Agustin, "Letter on the Filipinos", *op. cit.*, p. 249.
19. *Ibid.*, p. 249, footnote.
20. *Ibid.*, p. 198, footnote.
21. *Ibid.*, p. 198, footnote.
22. Antonio de Morga, *History of the Philippine Islands*, vol. 1, pp. 159–160. E. H. Blair, J. A. Robertson (trs. eds.). A. H. Clark, Cleveland, Ohio, 1907. (Klaus Reprint, New York, 1970.)
23. Antonio de Morga, *Historical Events of the Philippine Islands*, Jose Rizal (ed.), p. 317. Jose Rizal National Centennial Commission, Manila, 1962. References to pages in the quotation refers to this work. It is translated into English by E. Alzona. Other translations and editions of Morga's *Sucesos de las Islas Filipinas*, are by Blair and Robertson, and J. S. Cummins. See Bibliography.
24. J. S. Stavorinus, *Voyages to the East-Indies*, vol. III, pp. 362–363. S. H. Wilcocke (tr.). Robinson, Pater-Noster-Row, London, 1798.
25. *Ibid.*, pp. 369–370.
26. *Ibid.*, p. 370.
27. R. N. Jackson, *Immigrant Labour and the Development of Malaya*, p. 128, *op. cit.*
28. John Bowring, *A Visit to the Philippine Islands*, p. 140, *op. cit.* See p. 59, note 29, of this book.

CHAPTER 9

The Malay Concept of Industry and Indolence

European colonial writers, the amateur scholar administrators, loved to dwell on the sensational incidents of native life as part of their general attempt to portray the character of native society. Piracy, injustice, disorder, warfare, tyranny, which existed during the period were exaggerated in order to justify colonial rule which was alleged to have brought about the very opposite situation. Hundreds of sensational incidents were publicised. One such instance is Swettenham's account of the case of Raja Alang, who lived in a house by the path between Kuala Kangsar and Larut. One day, a Malay from Patani with his wife and two children walked past the front of his house. Raja Alang was in the house within full view of the Malay traveller. As the traveller passed Raja Alang's house, he raised his trousers to avoid the mud. Raja Alang considered this behaviour disrespectful to him. He called the man and demanded a fine of a hundred dollars, which the traveller could obviously not pay. As a consequence, Raja Alang detained him, his wife and two children in his house. They were given no food for a couple of days. Raja Alang threatened to sell the wife and children to raise the fine. The following morning, at dawn, the Malay from Patani ran amok, killing nine people and wounding three. His wife and Raja Alang were wounded while his two children were killed.[1]

Swettenham, who became the British Governor of the Straits Settlements and High Commissioner for the Malay States in 1901, quoted some sensational incidents in his earlier writing on the Malays. For instance he described the Malay youth, among others, as one who ran away with his neighbour's wife.[2] How many Malay youths dared do that? The few who did that should not be taken to characterize the nature of Malay youth in general.

Apart from the sensational the amateur colonial scholar was inclined to make unfounded judgements on native society, its history, culture and religion. An instance is Raffles's allegation that Islam was a dividing agent in the homogeneity of the Malay ethnic configuration. He considered the ancient Malays to be one nation, speaking one language, preserving their character and customs in all the maritime states embracing the Philippines, Sumatra, and Western New Guinea.[3] The coming of Hinduism and Islam led to further diversification according to Raffles. This led to an absence of a well defined and uniform system of law. If Raffles had been a serious scholar he would have discovered that the ethnic, linguistic, political and religious diversification of the Malay world had started long before the Islamization of the area. On the contrary, Islam brought about tremendous unification, politically as well as legally. In Indonesia, Malaysia and the Philippines, Islam has acted as a unifying agent in a region which had already diversified.[4] In fact it was Islam which first introduced a common system of law. Raffles's judgement on Islam was based on his ignorance of the facts and a marked antipathy towards it. Between the 16th and 19th centuries, Islam was the only formidable foe of Western Imperialism which had a political appeal transcending the geographical and ethnic diversities. The Dutch, the Portuguese and the Spaniards all engaged in warfare against several Muslim states in the area.

Another preoccupation of colonial European scholars was the parading of vices among native rulers. There were several tyrants in the area but so were there among the European rulers. Dutch colonial historians never omitted to mention the Susuhunan of Mataram, Amangkurat I, who when he succeeded his father in 1646, condemned the commander of his father's bodyguard and his whole family to death. At the death of a beloved concubine, to give expression to his grief, he made one hundred women die of hunger in an enclosure above the grave of the concubine.[5] Marsden mentioned the cruelty of Iskander Muda, Sultan of Acheh who died in 1636, and who imprisoned his own mother who was suspected of conspiracy, and had her tortured. He put to death his nephew, son of the king of Johore, and his near relations, a son of the king of Pahang and a son of the king of Banten.[6] These incidents are on record. But what the European colonial scholars failed to do was to draw a balanced picture of native rulers as a whole, and also a similar picture of their own colonial rulers (governors, residents, alcalde mayors). The tyranny, oppression and iniquities of some of these officials were suppressed from discussion while those of the native rulers were highly publicized. The cruelty of some of the *encomenderos* in the Philippines was well known.[7] The history of the area was distorted by colonial historians, at times consciously and at other times unconsciously. Events were given a tendentious interpretation. For instance, Furnivall echoed the general European view derived from colonial historical writing, that the Dutch East India Company "only with reluctance and in order to control the trade did it extend its rule."[8] Furnivall was aware that the Dutch under Coen conquered Jacatra. But the gradual extension of their dominion was interpreted as a necessary evil and done reluctantly.[9]

In the minutes of the Dutch parliament (Staten-Generaal) of November 29, 1609, in assuming sovereignty over Dutch possessions in the East Indies, and forming the Council of the Indies (Raad van Indie) to advise the Governor-General, reference was made to "our territory already there or those which will come later".[10] The Governor-General was given the power to employ any means necessary to promote Dutch interest. It would be naive to believe that territorial conquest was not within the imagination of the Dutch government at the time when such an undertaking was the order of the day among European powers. The phasing of the policy and the timing were left to necessity, but not the intention. Hence it is a distortion to explain the birth of Dutch colonialism in Indonesia as a phenomenon to which the Dutch were reluctantly drawn in. The colonial actors in the history of the period were all enthusiastic about expansion; they certainly showed no signs of reluctance.

There is a general tendency to distort which prevailed in the entire field of colonial historical scholarship or studies on politics, society, religion, and culture. Just as the other products of colonial scholarship influenced the indigenuous people, so did the image of the lazy native. Rizal conceded that there was some truth in the accusation of indolence but attempted to explain it as a result of Spanish rule. On the other hand Mabini considered the idea of the indolent Filipino as humbug.[11] In discussing the image which the indigenous people had of themselves we must bear in mind that some 20th century converts to this aspect of the colonial ideology are present among the indigenous people. An ideology is never confined to its originating group. It is also shared by those who are dominated by the system of which the ideology is the rationalization. During the time when slavery was current there were many slaves who believed in it. They shared the false consciousness inherent in the ideology.[12]

The picture of the indigenous society and its rulers created by colonial historians and observers was one of despotism, instability, anarchy, backwardness, and the absence of the rule of law. There is an element of truth in this but it does not represent the entire picture. Moreover, Western colonialism also introduced its own form of despotism, instability, anarchy, backwardness, and the absence of the rule of law. In indigenous society the rule of law was never entirely absent for the majority of the population, despite the occasional rule of mad despots or tyrants. So was it under European colonial rule. There had been cases of perverts giving full expression of their perversion at the expense of the local population. One such pervert was a certain Mr. Bean, a senior British officer who was brought to Malacca to take command of the Indian garrison troops. This incident took place during Farquhar's Residency in Malacca, probably after he destroyed the Fort, in 1807. Mr. Bean used to place two soldiers on guard at the door of his house. Their job was to snatch children passing along the road at night and thereafter confine them to a fenced compound. Those trying to escape were pursued by two dogs. After collecting, to be more accurate kidnapping, many children, Bean brought them out in pairs and forced them to box each other on the pain of being caned. Abdullah bin Abdul Kadir Munshi (1797–1854) mentioned this affair in his autobiography.

Mr. Bean took great delight in seeing the young boxers' bruised faces and noses. He leaped about and roared with laughter, and rewarded those who bled more than those who did not. Then he would call out another pair. "He spent every day thus, watching human blood flowing." [13] Soon his place became a boxing centre. Good people dared not allow their children to pass along that road. Soon he became wearied of children and he started paying for the services of adults. A number of poor people made some money boxing for Mr. Bean. After some time he got tired of this and took to cock-fighting. Several cocks perished every day. This he gave up soon and he went for the ducks, which he released in front of his house and then set two or three fierce dogs on them. "He used to take great delight in this exhibition which drew crowds to watch it. He would take his gun and shoot any duck which had escaped the dogs. All the ducks were killed, some savaged by the dogs, others hit by bullets, while Mr. Bean leapt about in his delight. A few days later he brought a number of monkeys which he let climb to the top of an angsena tree in front of his house. Then he shot them and they fell to the ground dead. Every day this senior officer behaved in this fashion, doing all sorts of wicked and unpleasant things endangering the lives of animals and causing men much pain. I do no know how much money he wasted in this futile manner. As long as he lived in the house no woman dared use the lanes round it for fear he would interfere with her." [14]

The sadism of this pervert encompassed a wide range from boys and monkeys to cocks and pigeons. Abdullah was generous and refined in his judgement of this Englishman's character and did not treat it as a generalization applying to all Englishmen, an attitude which the colonial ruling class of his time lacked. "I was surprised," he said, "that Mr. Farquhar who became Resident of Malacca at the time took no action over the doings of this official, for other races despised the things I have mentioned, which they held to be typical of the behaviour of all Englishmen, following the Malay proverb 'A single buffalo has mud on it and the whole herd is smeared.' Such deeds and behaviour remain long in the memories of other men, for one man tells another and the tale passes round until it becomes firmly rooted in peoples' minds." [15] He also noted the terrorizing behaviour of drunken English sailors, who chased people, and those who fell into the river and drowned were robbed of their money. They looted the stall in the market. "Anyone happening to meet an Englishman at once fled far away. Women could not walk about the streets if there was an English ship in the port. Even slaves, to say nothing of respectable people could not afford to be seen for fear of being assaulted. All those things I have mentioned made people afraid, and were aggravated by conduct like that of the officers I have already described, which caused more and more alarm." [16] Abdullah was sympathetic to the English, in particular Raffles. He was full of praise for British rule. This is probably the reason why British colonial scholars disseminated his work.

My point is that qualities such as indolence, cruelty, despotism, lawlessness, piracy, murder, and looting were present in the colonial ruling class as they were among the native ruling class. Just as we have had intriguing and murderous rajas, we have also had intriguing and murderous European colonial governors and rulers like the Dutch governor-general Valckenier and members of his *Council for the Indies*, including his successor van Imhoff. In October, 1740 the Chinese in Batavia were massacred and plundered for more than 10 days, including those in jail and in hospital. There was a threat to rebel by armed Chinese outside the gate. Those inside the town enclosure were massacred. It was mob hysteria. "Blood flowed in little streams throughout the streets; neither women nor children were spared, and even the defenceless Chinese in the jails and the hospital were slaughtered." [17] Though there were reasons for the Dutch to be apprehensive, the massacre was unprovoked. The Chinese outside the city of Batavia were equally afraid of the Dutch. They complained of oppression; whereas the Dutch complained they were bad elements bent on destroying their city. It is not intended to give a detailed and balanced picture of the event but merely to point out instances of barbarism committed by Europeans, with the assistance of their native henchmen during the colonial period.[18] Instances of cruelty committed by Europeans in the colonial period are legion. Nevertheless this does not justify a generalization. The Dutch, the Portuguese, the Spaniard, and the British community as a whole are not cruel and treacherous because some elements are. This simple and obvious logic is not applied to the communities in this region. If some were cruel, a whole nation was considered cruel. If some were lazy a whole nation was considered lazy.

Historically speaking, tyranny, oppression and exploitation were never the work of whole communities against each other. It has always been the dominant minority of a particular community imposing its will upon its own, or another community; or both, as in the colonial period. Thus the Dutch ruling class involved with the running of the Dutch East India Company in the beginning of the 17th century not only exploited the Javanese but also its own national. The ordinary Dutchman enlisting as soldier to the Company had to buy his own uniform, pay for his own hospital expenses, and he had also to bribe his captain. During ceremonies the Company lent him elegant uniforms but for the rest many had to walk around without shoes. It was only around the beginning of the 19th century that the European soldiers generally put on shoes. Since 1695 the supply for a soldier included shoes which he had to buy from the Company's store.[19] They were apparently sparingly used for going to Church and ceremonies, as the cost was deducted from the soldiers' meagre pay. Like the Chinese and Indian coolies earlier many of these soldiers were recruited by deception. Glowing stories of pearls and diamonds, which abounded in the Indies, were related to them; whereas in fact many died on the sea-voyage at sea due to diseases and bad accommodation.[20]

A life of leisure and little physical effort was reserved for the ruling class, both among the natives and the colonial rulers. Complaints of laziness amongst the Dutch, the Spaniard and the British colonial ruling classes against the indigenous population, as we have shown, had no factual basis. Native rulers never complained of the laziness of their subjects although some of them were as unscrupulous as the colonial *conquistadores*. The reason was that they were aware of the indigenous system of values which placed industriousness and labour in high esteem. Historical records stressing the value of labour and industriousness were rare to find since most of these values were orally transmitted, and since indolence had never been felt or perceived as a problem in the pre-colonial indigenous societies. Nevertheless there are some records discovered recently. One of them is the Malay *Undang-Undang Sungai Ujong*. This is a digest of customary law of Sungai Ujong, an area in the present state of Negeri Sembilan, whose inhabitants were from the Minangkabau community in Sumatra.

Out of 113 articles of the Digest, 7 stressed the value of labour and industriousness. Article 99 classified the roots of evil into: cock-fighting and gambling, drinking, smoking opium, and slothfulness, the avoidance of work.[21] The philosophical basis of this Digest, a synthesis between Islam and *adat,* customary law, goes back at least to the 16th century if not earlier. The text as is written probably dates back to the 18th century. What is beyond doubt is that the text was formulated in pre-colonial times. It expresses the indigenous philosophy of values and social life of the pre-colonial society. The basic conditions for clearing land cultivation were: great effort and care, strength, intense planting, keen watch, great economizing, careful purchasing, knowing what to consume, intelligence, knowing prices and values, and generosity to friends.[22] The basic conditions for a successful trader were similarly: knowing how to fix prices, and to evaluate properly; intelligence, economy, knowing how to dress, a capacity for great effort, being able to wait for a favourable wind, being able to remember negotiations, looking after profit and losses, selling when prices were high and buying when prices were low.[23] Industriousness was further stressed in acquiring knowledge, in practising a craft, in breeding animals and poultry.[24] The conditions for becoming a chief in the land were: refinement in speech, saying pleasant things to his friends, a willingness to spend, showing a greater industry, profundity of thought, and a great alertness.[25]

Basically the values upheld by the digest were those common to the Malay world. The Malays strongly disapprove of indolence (malas). In the Malay society it is a disgrace to be called a *pemalas,* one who is indolent. The condemnation of laziness was further found in Abdullah's *Hikayat,* which was partly autobiographical and partly a narration of events during the time. He started writing it in 1840. He noted the severe punishment meted out for laziness at his Islamic school[26]. Approximately two years earlier in 1838 he had the occasion to dwell further upon the indolence of some of the Malays in Pahang, Trengganu and Kelantan, in his account of his voyage to Kelantan. He condemned some of the Malay males who loitered in the streets displaying their weapons while their womenfolk were making a living. This according to him was not bravery. He who could subdue his passion for indolence was the brave one.[27]

Abdullah's view on the cause of indolence among a section of the male population in Pahang and Kelantan resembles that of Rizal half a century later. He invoked the environmental explanation, that is, the social system and its abuse by the ruling elites. The only difference is, that what Rizal attributed to the Spaniards, Abdullah attributed to the Malay rulers and their dependents (hamba raja). He noted that the men of Trengganu also spent their time in idleness. In Pahang, Kelantan and Trengganu, men lived in fear of their rulers and henchmen. The lawlessness of the ruling houses created idleness and killed the motivation to work and amass property. His reflection on the desolation and poverty of Pahang was meant to apply to Trengganu and Kelantan. Why had a once famous state sunk to a level of poverty and desolation? It had not been plundered by enemies or conquered by other countries. Neither was it due to piracy, for he had never heard of any great country losing its trade and wealth on account of piracy, or on account of the poverty of its soil. "Nor was it due merely to the laziness of the inhabitants, for there has never yet been a country anywhere in the world in which all the inhabitants were lazy: if any man who is willing to exert himself to seek fortune, knows that his enjoyment of such fortune will be undisturbed, then even if only half the population do work for their living with energy and loyalty, their country cannot fail to become great and prosperous."

"No, in my opinion, the reason for the poverty of Pahang is to be found in the fact that its inhabitants live in continual fear of the oppression and cruelty of the Rajas and other notables. Naturally they feel that it is useless to be energetic when it is certain that any profits they make will be grabbed by those higher up. And so they remain poor and miserable all their lives."[28] The reason was the oppression and cruelty of the Rajas and notables. The inhabitants felt it was useless to work hard and amass profits for these would merely be seized. Hence they preferred to remain poor and miserable.

Abdullah described the mechanism of oppression in detail. If a man acquired a fine house, a plantation or an estate of any size, a Raja was sure to get hold of it. He would demand a loan or a gift and if the man refused he would confiscate his property. The loan was never repaid. If he resisted, he and his whole family would be killed or fined. The young rajas were brought up on cock-fighting, opium-smoking, gambling, greed and indulgence towards their lusts. They remained unreformed until their fathers died and they were let loose like tigers on the people. A raja's celebrations for a marriage, circumcision for his son, or ear-boring of his daughter, was an occasion for opium smokers, gamblers, and cock-fighters to assemble. Many people were ruined, some became thieves and others were caught in stabbing affrays.[29] When the people were called upon to do work for the rajas, they were not paid. They had to bring their own food and tools. Abdullah was very shocked by the conditions he saw in the Malay states for the first time in his life. He grew up in Malacca and Singapore under the British. He was 42 years old when he first visited the Malay states. It was the law and order which existed under the British in Malacca and Singapore which made its inhabitants willing to work and seek profit. There was security of life and property.[30]

Abdullah's observation on indolence was restricted to the men, and not the women of the states he visited. Unlike his British contemporary he did not generalize. He was very conscious of the fact that the phenomenon of indolence he described was part of a pathological social system. It did not characterize the entire Malay community. He was conscious of the Malay Islamic system of values condemning indolence and injustice. Nonetheless Abdullah's attitude was partial because his was a captive mind in the world of colonialism. Before he left Kelantan, Abdullah pointed out the evils of opium-smoking to Tengku Temena, the local raja of Sabak, and the need to drop such an evil habit. He told the raja there were seven evils of opium-smoking: it was forbidden by Islam; it ruined the body; it exhausted money; it generated laziness; it wasted time; it ruined a good reputation; and it was despised by reputable people.[31] If opium-smoking was good, why was it avoided by reputable and wealthy Europeans? Abdullah was blind to the fact that the good and reputable Europeans, like his master Raffles, developed and exploited the opium trade on a scale hitherto unknown. They did not smoke it themselves but they traded in it and spread its use. They forbade it in their own country. Furthermore their drug was alcohol. In Malacca, on the eve of the English invasion of Java, Raffles presented two boxes of opium to his emissaries, Tengku Penglima Besar and Pengeran. Abdullah noted this in passing, without comment.[32] What happened to his earlier moral discourse to Tengku Temena? Was the reputable Englishmen who did not smoke opium but promoted its use and profited from it not equally guilty of the seven evils?

After 1843, when Abdullah had completed his first volume of his *Hikayat,* he reflected further on the conditions of the Malays. He was not optimistic. His reflection touched upon the problem of indolence. "I viewed with particular disfavour the lives led by the Malays and the circumstances of those with whom I had been acquainted. I had observed their conduct, behaviour and habits from my youth up to the present time and had found that, as time went on, so far from becoming more intelligent they became more and more stupid. I considered the matter carefully in my mind and came to the conclusion that there were several reasons for this state of affairs, but that the main one was the inhumanity and the repressive tyranny of the Malay rulers, especially towards their own subjects. The point had been reached at which their hearts had become like soil which no longer receives its nourishment, and wherein therefore nothing at all can grow. Industry, intelligence and learning cannot flourish among them and they are simply like trees in the jungle falling which ever way the wind blows. I noticed that they were always ruled by men of other races, small fry whose only value is to provide food for the big fry."[33] The Malay ruler despised his subject. When a man met his ruler, he was obliged to squat on the ground in mud and filth. The ruler seized the daughters and chattels of ordinary folk, without any fear of God and concern for the poor. His laws and punishment depended on his private whims. He condoned the wicked behaviour of his kith and kin, or his dependents, against the common people. He kept hundreds of debt-slaves who brought ruin on the common people, seizing their property and at times murdering them. The ruler made no attempt to protect his subjects.

The greatest defect of the Malay ruler and his society was the neglect of education. The ruler brought up his children with vices, and their example was followed. Ignorance, indolence, and the unwillingness to change immobilized Malay society, and literacy and the study of language were neglected. The extinction of the will to learn, to work hard, and to accumulate wealth, were attributed by Abdullah to the dominant ruling power. He summarized his views as follows: "As it is, under Malay rule ordinary folk cannot lift up their heads and enjoy themselves, and dare not show any originality for it is forbidden by the ruler. Wishing possibly to build themselves finely decorated houses of stone they are afraid to do so. They are afraid to wear fine clothing, shoes and umbrellas in case these are taboo. They are afraid even to keep fine clothing in their houses because it is said that such things are the perquisites only of royalty. Rich men especially live in perpetual fear and are fortunate if their only losses are their belongings. For indeed their very lives are in danger. Means are found whereby such men may be penalized and mulcted of their belongings. If a man is reluctant to lend any of his most cherished possessions, it is accounted a serious offence. And once he has given them up they are lost for ever; he will never see them again. A beautiful young girl in his house is like a raging poison, for it is quite certain that the ruler will take her as one of his wives with or without her guardian's permission. This practice more than any other arouses the hatred of the servants of Allah. I heard of one courageous man who refused to part with his daughter. The ruler ordered him to be murdered on some pretext, and then took the child away. All such acts as these are forbidden by Allah and His Prophet and incur the censure of mankind throughout the world." [34]

Abdullah felt free to condemn the Malay ruling power of his time because he was not living under them. He was perceptive of their influence and hoped for a change in Malay society. Abdullah was the first known Malay to be concerned with the modernization and progress of his community based on the indigenous Malay and Islamic values. The injustice of the Malay ruler and the decadent conditions which he created were to him a deviation from the true path.

The themes of work, education, and progress were subsequently revived by Islamic reformers around the turn of the 20th century, by people like Syed Sheikh Alhadi. Shaykh Mohd. Tahir bin Jalaluddin, Shaykh Mohd. Salim al-Kalali, and Haji Abbas bin Mohd. Taha. [35] Before the Second World War, Zainal Abidin bin Ahmad (ZABA) published some articles in the press on the issue of Malay progress. The theme of indolence did not become the subject of lengthy discourses as in the Philippines. However, in 1922, the Majlis Ugama Islam dan Istiadat Melayu Kelantan (the Council of Islam and Malay Custom, Kelantan) published a second edition of an interesting brochure entitled *Semangat Kehidupan*

(The Spirit of Living), composed by Haji Wan Mohammed bin Haji Wan Daud Patani. The Council approved its contents in January, 1918. It was meant for the religious schools under the Council's administration. The Secretary of the Council, in his foreword to the brochure, stressed the necessity to observe the message carried therein "so that we shall be raised to the level of nations that have attained maturity in the race for living at all ages."[36] There was a great deal of emphasis on labour, on hard work, and on the proper use of time and energy. Inaction was condemned. A man who did no work was considered a stone pillar. "Man's duty to work is because work is the best means of purifying him from weak and evil habits. Is not work the cause of bringing man towards a situation of trial and effort leading to a true existence?"[37]

Laziness, wasting time and unpunctuality were condemned. Patience and frugality were stressed in the execution of work, and the attainment of knowledge, together with careful scrutiny and investigation. Play and exercise were recommended as alternatives to labour. When a man was not working, he was advised to keep himself busy with either play or exercise, to ensure good health. The whole 46 page booklet, is an all round philosophy of labour, written in simple language. It was an attempt to establish the value of work and the evils of indolence. It was partly a reaction to the attitude of the ruling class towards labour. It was not a coincidence that such a booklet was written in Kelantan as a guide for the coming generations, bearing in mind the condition in Kelantan described by Abdullah. The content and spirit of the philosophy in the booklet were indigenous. It was an assertion of the Malay Islamic attitude towards labour. The Quran, the Prophet Mohammed and his faithful companions all stressed the value of hard work and serious effort. No one is to bear the burden of another. Man can have only what he strives for.[38] The theme of hard work, sacrifice, and a seriousness of purpose recurred in a contemporary work by the well-known Muslim leader, scholar and reformer, Shakib Arsalan, when he analysed the causes of the backwardness of the Muslims, in reply to questions submitted to him by the Imam of the Kingdom of Sambas in Indonesian Borneo, a Malay by the name of Sheikh Bashuni Imran.[39]

We have shown sufficiently that diligence and hard work pertain to the Malay system of values. This is also the case with the Javanese and Filipino system of values. Even though these values have not been literally expressed in written documents by all the societies in the area, nevertheless their language, myth, folklore and daily preoccupations explicitly or implicitly upheld the value of hard work. I have deliberately excluded here Islamic opinion on indolence which does not directly relate to the area. Muslim reformers like al-Afghani in the late 19th century had expressed in forceful terms the Islamic concept of progress which included a condemnation of indolence. The attitude of Malay indigenous society towards indolence is clear. We shall now turn our attention to a section of the present Malay elites in Malaysia who have succumbed to the colonial ideology in questioning the diligence of their community. Two recent works will be discussed. One is the publication of the dominant ruling Malay party, the United Malay National Organization, UMNO. The other is the work of a Malay physician, Mahathir bin Mohamad, written at a time when he was outside his party, which he has now rejoined. Both are the products of the colonial ideology. They are a reaction to the colonial thesis which apparently conditioned the response and attitude expressed in the publications. The image of the easy-going, unindustrious, lethargic Malay figures prominently in their works. Unlike Rizal's treatment of the indolence of the Filipinos, the two recent Malay works are not penetrating, analytic, or scientific. They resemble their progenitor, the ideology of colonial capitalism.

NOTES

1. Frank Swettenham, *Stories and Sketches by Sir Frank Swettenham*, p. 91. Oxford University Press, Kuala Lumpur, 1967. This is a selection from various books by Swettenham, selected and introduced by William R. Roff. The above incident occurred in November 1895.
2. *Ibid.*, p. 19. From his book *The Real Malay*. See p. 43 of this book, or bibliography.
3. T. S. Raffles, *Memoir*, p. 29, vol. 1, *op. cit.* See p. 38 of this book for the quotation from Raffles's book.
4. The records of earlier European visitors to the region indicated linguistic, political and legal diversification in areas untouched by Islam. A highly decentralized area as the pre-Spanish Philippines, was partly centralized by Islam so that it could offer effective resistance against Spanish rule. As Phelan observed, "In the case of the Moros the factor of transculturation seems decisive. The creed of Islam gave them a religious belief, one which had amply demonstrated over the centuries its dynamic capacity to resist and even, in several cases, to overwhelm Christianity. Since Spanish nationalism had been born in the *reconquista* crusade against the Moors, the conflict between the Spaniards and the Moros in Mindanao became another clash between the Cross and the Crescent. Such a war seemed just and understandable to both belligerents. Islam's sway over the southern Philippines gave the Moros a political means of organizing successful resistance, for Muslim cultural influence introduced the suprakinship unit of the state. The new institutions of the *rajah* and the sultanates were superimposed on the pre-Muslim kinship

units, which lost none of their vitality. Political-military authority was centralized sufficiently to organize effective resistance, but it never arrived at the point where the Spaniards could defeat and usurp it. What made the Moros unconquerable was the sound balance in their political-military organization between pre-Muslim decentralization and Muslim-sponsored centralization." J. L. Phelan, *op. cit.*, pp. 142–143.

5. F. W. Stapel, *Cornelis Janszoon Speelman*, p. 84. Nijhoff, 's-Gravenhage, 1936. But the Dutch supported Amangkurat against the rebel prince Taruna Jaya of Madura. They maintained friendship with Amangkurat.

6. William Marsden, *The History of Sumatra*, p. 446. Oxford University Press, London, 1966. (Reprinted from an 1811 publication.)

7. In 1573, seven years after the Spanish arrival in the Philippines, the Friar Diego de Herrera complained to the Spanish king, Philip II of the cruelty of the Spanish conquerors against the natives. Villages were burned and pillaged, not only on refusal to pay tribute, but on disagreement of the amount. Spaniards in remote areas committed murders. Captains, soldiers and other leaders tyrannized the natives. "There has been no punishment inflicted for all the above which is very well known and notorious to all people. Consequently, great dissoluteness has reigned, and I believe that there are very few whose skirts are clean of this vice." Fray Diego de Herrera, "Memoranda", p. 231, in *The Colonization and Conquest of the Philippines by Spain.* Filipiniana Book Guild, Manila, 1965. See also Herrera's letter of 1570 to Philip II, pp. 179–182. The index of this book is revealing. Spanish cruelties were described as "injustices" and "abuses". In 1573 the Friar Fransesco de Ortega in his letter to the Viceroy of New Spain, described how the Spaniards forced the native women to give up their necklaces and bracelets. "When these so evil abuses are inflicted upon them, some of them refuse to give the tribute or do not give as liberally as those who ask it desire. Others, on account of having to give this and of their fear at seeing a strange and new race of armed people, abandon their houses and flee to the tingues and mountains. When the Spaniards see this, they follow them, discharging their arquebuses at them and mercilessly killing as many as they can. Then they go back to the village and kill all the fowls and swine there and carry off all the rice which the poor wretches had for their support. After this and after they have robbed them of everything they have in their miserable houses, they set fire to them. In this way they burned and destroyed more than four thousand houses in this expedition to Ylocos, and killed more than five hundred Indians, they themselves confessing that they committed that exploit. Your Excellency may infer how desolate and ruined this will make the country, for those who have done the mischief say that it will not reach its former state within six years and others say not in a lifetime." pp. 214–215.

8. J. S. Furnivall, *Netherlands India*, p. 34. Cambridge University Press, London. 1939.

9. According to Furnivall the instruction to the first governor-general in 1609 did not suggest territorial expansion. *Ibid.*, p. 26.

10. J. K. L. de Jonge, *De Opkomst van het Nederlandsch Gezag in Oost-Indie* (1595–1610) vol. 3, pp. 130–131. Nijhoff, Muller,'s-Gravenhage. Amsterdam, 1865.

11. Apolinario Mabini, *The Philippine Revolution.* L. M. Guerrero (tr.), National Historical Commission, Manila, 1969. The translation is from a 1931 Spanish edition. Mabini said: "Since the *encomenderos*, to enrich themselves faster, required their serfs to pay tribute in kind according to the industry of each,

and since a serf had little left to meet his needs after having paid tribute, he had to give up the crafts he had learned from his forefathers or from the Chinese, Japanese, and other races which had traded with the Filipinos before the conquest, and make his living only from the natural fruits of the soil which were still sufficient for his needs, thanks to the low density of the population. So much for all that humbug about the indolence of the Filipinos." p. 19.

12. For further discussion on the problem of false consciousness, see Karl Mannheim, *Ideology and Utopia*, pp. 62–63, 66, 68, 84–87, *op. cit.* See also Karl Marx, *The German Ideology*, pp. 19–21, 39–40, *op. cit.* For an instructive and concise presentation of Marx's and Engels's views on false consciousness see the selection by David Caute, *Essential Writings of Karl Marx.* MacGibbon and Kee, London, 1967.

13. A. H. Hill, "The Hikayat Abdullah", p. 70. *JMBRAS*, vol. XXVIII, pt. 3, June, 1955. This is an annotated translation into English, and a reproduction of the Malay text in Rumi (Latin script), of Abdullah's autobiography.

14. *Ibid.*, p. 71.

15. *Ibid.*, pp. 71–72.

16. *Ibid.*, p. 71.

17. J. K. J. de Jonge, *op. cit.*, vol. 9, p. LXIII (1877). The translation is mine. The background to this massacre was a growing hostility and mutual suspicion arising, among others, from dangerous rumours. The historical antecedents were rather complicated. Nevertheless even the Dutch government felt subsequently uneasy about this. Valckenier was later arrested and put on trial but more as a result of his conflict with some members of the Council over his authority, than because of the massacre. His accusers were equally responsible.

18. The barbarism of some Spanish commanders during the Philippine Revolution is well known. In 1897 the Spanish general, Monet, put everybody including women and children to the sword at Zambales. In San Fernando, La Union, three Filipino priests were tortured with hot iron rods applied to their body, to force them to confess that they were Freemasons. See Teodoro A. Agoncillo, *Malolos*, p. 10. University of the Philippines, Quezon City, 1960.

19. D. de Iongh, *Het Krijgswezen onder de Oostindische Compagnie*, p. 83. Stockum en Zoon, 's-Gravenhage, 1950. This is a book on the army of the East India Company. See further ch. V, "De Europeesche Troepen" (The European Troops), pp. 79–101.

20. *Ibid.*, pp. 79–80.

21. Sir Richard Windstedt, P. E. de Josselin de Jong, "A Digest of the Customary Law of Sungai Ujong", p. 68 (Malay text). *JMBRAS*, vol. XXVII, part 3, July, 1954. For the English translation see p. 35. Both the Malay text *Undang-Undang Sungai Ujong*, and the English translation are included.

22. *Ibid.*, p. 69, art. 102 (Malay text). The translation is mine. The English translation contains several inaccuracies.

23. *Ibid.*, p. 69, art. 104 (Malay text). The translation is mine.

24. *Ibid.*, p. 69, arts. 103, 105; p. 71, art. 110.

25. *Ibid.*, p. 71, art. 112 (Malay text). The translation is mine.

26. A. H. Hill, "The Hikayat Abdullah", *op. cit.* Of this Abdullah said: "There was a punishment for pupils who were lazy in their studies. Smoke was generated in a heap of dry coconut fibre and the child made to stand astride it. Sometimes dry pepper was put in the fire. The reek of the smoke was most irritating and caused a copious discharge from eyes and nose." p. 46.

27. R. Brons Middel, *Kesah Pelajaran Abdoellah bin Abdelkadir Moensji dari Singapoera sampai ka Negeri Kalantan*, p. 43. Brill, Leiden, 1893. This is a transliteration from the Jawi (Malay in Arabic script) into Rumi (Malay in

Latin script) in the Indonesian Malay spelling. See also A. E. Coope, *The Voyage of Abdullah*, p. 22. Malaya Publishing House, Singapore, 1949. This is an English translation with notes and appendices.

28. A. E. Coope, *The Voyage of Abdullah*, p. 15, *ibid.*
29. R. Brons Middel, *Kesah Pelajaran Abdoellah*, p. 124, *op. cit.*
30. Much of the social injustice generated by British colonial capitalism in Malaya took place after Abdullah's death. His shock on seeing the condition of the Malay states made Abdullah a fervent enthusiast of British rule to the extent that he was not conscious of the British responsibility for the misery and cruelty occurring in Singapore. In his *Hikayat* he gave a graphic account of the cruelty of the slave trade occurring in British Singapore. "The man who owned these slaves behaved like a beast, shameless and without fear of Allah. The younger girls hung round him while he behaved in a manner which it would be improper for me to describe in this book. For anyone who wished to buy these slave-girls he would open their clothing with all manner of gestures of which I am ashamed to write. The slave dealers behaved in the most savage manner, devoid of any spark of feeling, for I noticed that when the little children of the slaves cried they kicked them head over heels and struck their mothers with a cane, raising ugly weals on their bodies. To the young girls, who were in great demand, they gave a piece of cloth to wear, but they paid no attention to the aged and the sick. The greatest iniquity of all that I noticed was the selling of a woman to one man and of her child to another. The mother wept and the child screamed and screamed when she saw her mother being taken away. My feelings were so outraged by this scene that, had I been someone in authority, I would most certainly have punished the wicked man responsible for it. Furthermore those in charge of male slaves tied them round the waist like monkeys, one to each rope, made fast to the side of the boat. They relieved nature where they stood and the smell on the boat made one hold one's nose." *The Hikayat Abdullah*, p. 162, *op. cit.* Hundreds of Chinese came to purchase the slaves, who were mostly from Bali and Celebes. Abdullah reported what he saw to Raffles who said that the business was also found in Europe and that the English would one day put a stop to this evil. But the point is he did nothing in Singapore to make the transaction at least human, while the system was yet upheld. Raffles could have prevented the separation of mothers and children, and all the inhuman treatments, at least in Singapore. He was very good at uttering pious wishes. Abdullah failed to see the responsibility of the British for allowing the situation to prevail.
31. *Kesah Pelajaran Abdoellah*, p. 97, *op. cit.* *The Voyage of Abdullah*, p. 54, *op. cit.*
32. "The Hikayat Abdullah", p. 80, *op. cit.*
33. *Ibid.*, p. 269.
34. *Ibid.*, p. 271.
35. For a historical account of the reform and educational efforts of the Malays towards modernization, see W. R. Roff, *The Origins of Malay Nationalism*. University of Malaya Press/Yale University Press, Kuala Lumpur/New Haven, 1967.
36. *Semangat Penghidupan*, p. III. Majlis Ugama Islam dan Istiadat Melayu, Kelantan, Kota Bahru, 1922 (in Malay Arabic script).
37. *Ibid.*, p. 4. The translation is mine.
38. Abdullah Yusut Ali, *The Holy Quran*, Sura LIII, 38—41, vol. 2. Published by Khalil Al-Rawaf, New York, 1946. This is this text, translation, and commentary of the Quran in English considered as reliable by Muslims. There are numerous verses of the Quran emphasising work and righteousness.

39.   Shakib Arsalan, *Our Decline and its Causes.* M. A. Shakoor (tr.), Muhammad Ashraf, Lahore, 1952. A Malay translation of Shakib Arsalan's analysis in Arabic, originally printed by the well-known Islamic publication, Al-Manar in Cairo, around 1930, appeared in 1954. See Al-Amier Sjakieb Arsalan, *Mengapa Kaum Muslimin Mundur dan Mengapa Kaum Selain Mereka Madju?* H. Moenawar Chalil (tr.). Bulan Bintang, Djakarta, 1967. (Third edition.)

CHAPTER 10

Mental Revolution and the Indolence of the Malays

In 1971, the dominant ruling Malay party in Malaysia, the United Malay National Organization (UMNO) published a book in Malay called *Revolusi Mental* (Mental Revolution). It was the labour of fourteen authors, three with doctorates, seven with degrees, one with a diploma degree and three had no degrees. The chief compiler was Inche Senu bin Abdul Rahman, the Secretary-General of the Party, a former Minister of Information, and a former ambassador to Indonesia. Needless to say, he got the title of the book from the term coined by Sukarno. Aside from the commonly known valid and simple ideas, the concept of mental revolution remains vague. A mental revolution is defined as a change in the attitude, values and social philosophy of a given society.[1] The aim of the mental revolution is "to change the way of thought, view and attitude of society's members in order to adjust to the requirements of the age and drive them towards further effort to acquire progress in all fields of life".[2] What is of interest to us here is the view of the authors of the community to be changed by the mental revolution. We shall avoid a discussion on the inaccuracies found in the book, its lack of intellectual depth, its ridiculous conclusions in some instances, its simple outlook on the development process, its contradictory statements, and its attitude of ignoring previous works and opinions on the same problem by Malays themselves in the course of approximately a century.

The Malay society in Malaysia, according to the book, is generally characterized by the following attitudes: the Malays are not honest to themselves, and they do not see their own faults. Hence the causes of their backwardness are suggested to be colonialism, exploitation by other communities, the capitalist system, religion, and a number of other causes. The Malays on the whole lack the courage to fight for the truth. The unresisted oppression which occurred frequently in Malay history is quoted as evidence of this. On the whole, the Malays know how to take on responsibility but there are many Malays who do not possess this quality. Malays are prepared to make sacrifices under good leadership. They are law abiding, and as long as their religion is not offended and they are not insulted, they are tolerant of other communities. The Malays emphasize the general welfare but they are fatalists, and this is a major cause of their backwardness. "This is an attitude that makes the Malays less keen on making effort, and if they desire to make effort, they easily admit defeat against even a small obstacle".[4] This attitude runs contrary to Islamic teaching. The Quran says God will not change the fate of a people unless the people change it themselves.

On the whole Malays do not think rationally. They are more often led by sentiment.[5] In the past Malays did not exhibit discipline or punctuality. Indeed the absence of such words in the vocabulary of the Malays indicated the absence of the concept, hence the phenomena. Tha saying "janji Melayu" (Malay promise) is common to illustrate the unpunctuality of the Malays.[6] Industriousness (rajin) was present in the vocabulary. Malays show no spirit of perseverance in the midst of adversity. A Malay saying "Hangat-hangat tahi ayam" (Warm as a fowl's dropping) is invoked as a proof. The warmth of a fowl's dropping is short-lived.

"Malays desire wealth but their effort to acquire it is insufficient". They are not frugal and like to waste in unnecessary expenditure such as feasts, celebrations, and furniture far beyond their means.[7] Many Malays do not think of their future. They do not save for the future. Malays until now have shown less interest in science and technology than in the humanities as an academic vocation. They should modernize their traditional occupations. Some Malays consider the white man to be superior. The acquisitive instinct is not commonly recognized in Malay society.[8] The Malays lack also originality in thought,[9] imagination, and the spirit of enquiry. They lack a realistic attitude, and are not capable of effort (kurang usaha). They do not find the life of this world sufficiently important; they do not value time, and are not serious. They have no courage to take risks,[10] and it is the poverty of their soul (kemiskinan jiwa), not of money, that causes them to be backward.[11] As a nation they are not frank and forthright. They conceal their feeling in order not to hurt others.[12] These are then the traits suggested by the authors which have moulded the traditional Malay character. By implication the fourteen authors have become modernized and progressive. This Malay character, which is predominantly negative, is the target of transformation. The economic system is liberal capitalism and the philosophy of individualism. Emphasis is laid on the capacity of individual Malays to acquire wealth, social status, and professional progress, in emulation of the Japanese, Americans, Germans, Jews and Chinese. "The success of these people in the world of agriculture, trade and industry, proves that 'the method for oneself' in handling economic affairs is more superior than the 'collective' method, and our most inferior economic position in our country points to this."[13]

The Chinese alluded to are not from mainland China. The Germans are obviously from West Germany. Heads of states, business leaders, philosophers, die-hard capitalists from the Western capitalist world are revered in the pages of this book. So are some Western social scientists who uphold the capitalist system. Their views are quoted. The embodiment of tact and wisdom (kebijaksanaan) are some Malaysian Chinese millionaires, Ford, Rockefeller, Rothschild, and Krupp.[14] The modern hero is a business executive drawing over $2,000 (Malaysian), neatly dressed, with a tie on, carrying a James Bond bag, driving a Jaguar car, working in an air-conditioned room. The supreme hero is of course John Paul Getty, the American billionaire.[15]

This book which is a chaotic amalgamation of sound common knowledge of no depth, and absolutely ridiculous inferences, is perhaps the most naive, the most simple, and the least well-defined philosophy of capitalism, while claiming to represent the modern and indigenous philosophy of the Malays. The influence of colonial capitalism is strong. It avoided the issue of the indolence of the Malays. Its attitude towards this problem is ambivalent but definitely inclined to the view that the Malays are lazy. Unlike Rizal, it mentioned the British accusation that the Malays are lazy without either confirming or denying it.[16] It suggested that the Malay attitude in accepting fate is more powerful than his attitude towards effort and industry.[17] It suggested that the Malays lack effort and initiative. It mentioned that Malay farmers and fishermen are thought of as lazy and lacking initiative without denying or confirming this.[18] It suggested that the backwardness of the Malays is not due to the exploitation of others but to their own lack of effort.[19] In education, Malays are not considered lazy but lacking in effort.[20] The Secretary-General of UMNO, Datuk Senu bin Abdul Rahman, in his introduction to the book noted that the negative image of the Malays portrayed by foreign observers from the sixteenth century onwards is still current among the non-Malays of today. This image portrayed the Malays as lazy, unwilling to work like others, satisfied with the existing situation, and indifferent to affairs. This image had caused dissatisfaction against the government for taking special measures to promote the Malays. What is Datuk Senu's reaction? This is what he said: "On the other hand, these views need not be considered as a problem, but the time has come for the Malays to analyze again their background and their traits from the previous age."[21] He further said that if these negative traits were true, they should be abandoned and discarded. "It is no use for us to deny them or show our anger at such views and accusations. On the contrary let such opinions drive us to seek those qualities that shall allow us to compete with others."[22]

No wonder the book proceeds to characterize the Malays in negative terms unexcelled in the history of colonialism. While many British colonial writers stressed the laziness of the Malays they did not strip the Malays of so many other qualities which the *Revolusi Mental* did. No colonial British book had ever recorded so many negative qualities relating to the Malays or considered them to be the dominant influence in the formation of the Malay character. In another part of the book, there is a reference to the fact that not all Malay traits are bad. But the author says: "Nevertheless, the bad opinion on the Malays made by those writers should be a challenge to us to increase our good qualities to enable us to move forward so that we shall attain a similar position as the nations which have progressed."[23] The negative traits mentioned in the book governed the vast majority of Malays. There is a small group to which these traits, enumerated in the book, do not apply.[24] Hence the *Revolusi Mental* is a confirmation of the ideology of colonial capitalism as far as the Malays are concerned. It draws an image of the Malays which is even more negative in scope than that of colonial capitalism. It is this negative image which governed Malay life. It was in order to change this that *Revolusi Mental* was written. Many of the suggestions for progress in the *Revolusi Mental* are sound; they are common knowledge already among intellectuals and require no intellectual exertion. Ironically speaking, the traits of the Malay nature depicted by the authors, such as being easily satisfied, being inefficient, lacking in initiative, imagination, and effort, are manifested in the book. We shall discuss this later. In order to criticise the ideology of the *Revolusi Mental,* we have to show what it lacks, the weakness of its methodology, and the class affiliation of the authors. The *Revolusi Mental* is the political ideology *par excellence* of a conservative ruling group confronted with certain political problems.

In discussing the problem of false consciousness and ideology Mannheim suggested the following: "In the development of a new point of view, one party plays the pioneering role, while other parties, in order to cope with the advantage of their adversary in the competitive struggle, must of necessity themselves make use of this point of view."[25] The new point of view was developed by colonial capitalism. It was colonial capitalism which weighed the value of a community according to the degree of its serviceability to the group interest. In colonial capitalism, the European community was the most valued, next came the immigrant population, and lastly the indigenous people. About 70 years ago the well-known British colonial administrator Clifford proclaimed that the Malays had become "unprofitable and unsatisfactory members of the community" because the Malays did not supply the labour necessary to develop the resources of the country.[26] The *Revolusi Mental* has succumbed to this idea. While it mentioned the contribution of the Chinese immigrants to the increased wealth of the country, it did not mention the Malay contribution.[27] It analyses the past by means of categories of colonial capitalist thought. In the colonial capitalist ideology only those who directly contributed money were considered to be agents of development, or those who were directly involved in the colonial capitalist economy. The Malay contribution to development was played down. It was the Malays who administered the country. It was the Malays who supplied the police force. The Malays were the main food producers of the country, particularly during the colonial period. Even in the capitalist concept of development where the bulk of the profit goes into the pockets of the few, such services are considered to be an integral part of the process. Malay service to law and order was substantial. But the ideology of colonial capitalism only emphasized the direct involvement in the capitalist enterprise. The significance of law and order for development is beyond doubt. A handful of British administrators could not have accomplished this without the support of the Malay rulers and administrators of the country. Innumerable Malay contributions to the running of a well ordered government were simply ignored. The Malays had contributed substantially to create the setting wherein capitalist development was made possible. There is hence no need for the *Revolusi Mental* to accept the caste system of colonial capitalism which caused the Malays to be placed in the lowest position.

A slightly discordant note was sounded in two parts of the book.

The British were accused of crippling the spirit of the Malays by various means, one of which was calling the Malays lazy while they brought immigrants from China and India to exploit the rich resources of the country for the benefit of the colonial power and the immigrants. The Malays became the poor in their own country. [28] "Foreigners were encouraged to come to Malaya to work in rubber estates and tin mines. With the mass entry of immigrants from China and India into Malaya, small business under the Europeans were monopolized by these immigrants and when the Malays later wanted to enter this area, they were not given any opportunity by those who had come to control it. Because of the above causes the stage of progress attained by the Malays was not as before."[29] These discordant notes do not affect the overall tenor of the *Revolusi Mental*. They were probably written by two of the fourteen authors. This is a rare instance in the book when an extraneous sociological condition is invoked to explain backwardness. It conflicts with the spirit of self-reproach and self-degradation which characterizes the *Revolusi Mental*. The *Revolusi Mental* is a distorted ideology of a Malay ruling party sharing the false consciousness of colonial capitalism. The false consciousness distorts the reality. The Malay ruling party inherited the rule from the British without a struggle for independence such as that which took place in Indonesia, India and the Philippines. As such there was also no ideological struggle. There was no intellectual break with British ideological thinking at the deeper layer of thought. The leadership of this party were recruited from the top hierarchy of the civil service trained by the British, and middle class Malay school teachers and civil servants. The few professionals associated with it did not set the pattern.

Their emphasis on the individual as the dominant agent for change without sufficient consideration of the system reflected their powerful position. For about fifteen years through the government which it controlled, the party had initiated several projects to uplift the conditions of the rural Malays. Many of these projects were not entirely successful and criticism was voiced against them. To absolve themselves of responsibility the party put the blame on the Malays themselves. This attitude was expressed by many of their leaders before the 1969 general election. The book described the effort made by the government in various fields but it warned that individual efforts must ultimately be relied upon more than government measures. [30] It also complained of government failure to implement plans owing to the lip service of certain government officials. [31] It deplored the attitude of rural Malays in expecting the government and party leaders to solve their problems for them. It stressed that government ability to assist had its limit, and quoted the Quranic saying that God helps those who help themselves. The lack of the acquisitive drive to amass wealth and to achieve professional status, the weakness of individualism as opposed to collectivism, and the reliance on government and leaders, have made the Malays backward.[32] This is then the background of individualism and capitalism which constitute the spirit of the *Revolusi Mental.*

Apart from the above, many of the party leaders and dignitaries are involved in big business or business dominated by Chinese business men. The Secretary General himself occupied an important position in a shipping company. Many of the party dignitaries sit on the Board of Directors of important companies. Though not directly as owners and managers they are involved in the capitalist system; hence their enthusiasm for capitalism. The message that Malays through their individual efforts should become rich is an expression of their own life pattern. The fraternity between top UMNO leadership and big business interest is a well known fact. As we have noted in the introduction, an ideology contains an element of distortion. The unique factor about the UMNO ideology is the strong element of self-degradation. Historically speaking, the ideologies of ruling classes the world over contain a strong element of self-assertion, of pride of the group and its achievement. Not so with the UMNO ideology. The self-reproach and self-degradation reflect their own position in the economic set up inherited from colonial capitalism. They feel inferior because the criteria of measurement are derived from colonial capitalism. They are located on the outer fringes of big business, on the boards of directors. The wealth and power of big business must have impressed them. Hence their eulogy for capitalism, for Krupp, Rothschild, Rockefeller, John Paul Getty, and some Malaysian Chinese millionaires. Hence their lamentation that there are no such people amongst the Malays.

The type of distortion in the *Revolusi Mental* on the Malay character can be explained by the intellectual poverty of the authors. An intellectually more developed group could have built up a more sophisticated ideology of capitalism minus the element of degradation. The distortion is the result of fallacious reasoning. The thirty or more negative traits which are alleged to have predominantly moulded the Malay character are conclusions derived from false premises. They are neither based on research nor on sensible observations. It is true that with probably one or two exceptions, the authors themselves are not connected with big business. But it is the nature of ideologists that they need not be directly connected with all the major elements of the system which they are upholding. Hegel was a great ideologist of the Prussian state without himself being a state official of that state or politician openly preaching the message of the state. He was a university professor.

Certain major categories of thought dominate an epoch. One of these categories is the negative image of the Malays. Whether it is uttered by an UMNO leader or a British administrator does not make much difference as far as the supremacy of the idea is concerned. It belonged to a particular epoch. Malaysia is now undergoing a transition from colonial capitalism to a more national form of capitalism. In a period of transition it is often the case that the ruling ideas of the former epoch assert themselves with greater vigour. It was almost near the end of Spanish rule in the Philippines that the ruling idea of the Spanish colonial epoch, the indolence of the Filipinos, asserted itself with greater vigour, as evidenced by European and Spanish writing on the Filipinos in the second half of the 19th century. Hence the more thorough-going degradation of the Malays by the *Revolusi Mental* is not an indication of the emergence of a new image of the Malays. The existing ruling class in Malaysia forms an unbroken link with the colonial past. They operated with colonial categories of thought despite their anti-colonial pronouncements. Their concept of property, income-tax, business institution and the state, are still dominated by colonial categories. For instance, the government would never agree to tax relief for the maintenance of parents. It would not agree to the limit on income and profit while it is hospitable to the idea of restraining wages.

The problem arising from the *Revolusi Mental* is why did a ruling Malay party construct a capitalist ideology involving a more thorough degradation of the Malays than that expressed during the colonial period? Why should a ruling party be interested in degrading its own community? What is the vested interest which it camouflages in the process of degradation? There are three major explanations for this exercise. One is the sincere belief among some members of the ruling party that the Malays are in a bad situation, the causes of which have been attributed to the Malay character. The second is the desire to avoid the responsibility for the government failure to uplift the Malay community, relative to the progress achieved by others. The third is the need for a justification for definite plans to improve the general economic condition of the

Malays which in the first place contributed to the advancement of some Malays in power and Chinese business. By stressing the predicament of the Malays, funds are made available for projects which are ultimately tied up with the interest of some Malays in power. Undoubtedly all these things could have been accomplished without the element of degradation intruding, but this is due to an accident of circumstances. The formulators of the ideology are still under the spell of the colonial image of the Malays. There is a lack of people of high intellectual calibre capable of formulating a more sophisticated ideology, people who are aware of the sociology of knowledge, who are not only critical of current views and opinion but also the categories of thought underlying those views and opinions. The intellectual shortcoming of the UMNO ideologists will be examined in the next chapter and their image of the Malays critically assessed. We shall now turn to another view, in many respects similar to the *Revolusi Mental* but in at least one respect more extreme, that is the degradation of the Malays.

Mahathir bin Mohamad, a Malay physician and politician from Kedah published his reflections on the Malay problem in 1970 at the time when he was outside the party. He is now back with the party, occupying a position on its central executive committee. Mahathir added the hereditary dimension to the Malay problem. In his view, the Malays are by heredity inferior to the Chinese. Mahathir invoked the environment to explain the genesis and continuous transmission of what he considered to be hereditary racial traits. He first described the superiority of the Chinese. "The history of China is littered with disasters, both natural and man-made. Four thousand years ago a great flood was recorded, and subsequently floods alternated with famine, while waves of invaders, predatory emperors and warlords ravaged the country. For the Chinese people, life was one continuous struggle for survival. In the process the weak in mind and body lost out to the strong and the resourceful. For generation after generation, through four thousand years or more, this weeding out of the unfit went on, aided and abetted by the consequent limitation of survival to the fit only. But, as if this was not enough to produce a hardy race, Chinese custom decreed that marriage should not be within the same clan. This resulted in more cross-breeding than in-breeding, in direct contrast to the Malay partiality towards in-breeding. The result of this Chinese custom was to reproduce the best strains and characteristics which facilitated survival and accentuated the influence of environment on the Chinese." [33]

As to the Malays, their geographical environment contributed to the development of weak "racial" characteristics. Malays settled on the plains and river banks where cultivation was easy. "There was plenty of land for everyone and the hills were never necessary for cultivation or permanent settlement. The lush tropical plains with their plentiful sources of food were able to support the relatively small number of inhabitants of early Malaya. No great exertion or ingenuity was required to obtain food. There was plenty for everyone throughout the year. Hunger and starvation, a common feature in countries like China, were unknown in Malaya. Under these conditions everyone survived. Even the weakest and the least diligent were able to live in comparative comfort, to marry and procreate. The observation that only the fittest would survive did not apply, for the abundance of food supported the existence of even the weakest." [34] The crop cultivated had also its influence on the Malay character. "Rice cultivation, in which the majority of the Malays were occupied, is a seasonal occupation. Actual work takes up only two months, but the yield is sufficient for the whole year. This was especially so in the days when the population was small and land was plentiful. There was a lot of free time. Even after the gathering of other food-stuffs, there was still a lot of leisure time left. The hot, humid climate of the land was not conducive to either vigorous work or even to mental activity. Thus, except for a few, people were content to spend their unlimited leisure in merely resting or in extensive conversation with neighbours and friends." [35]

The clash between the hereditarily and environmentally weak Malays and strong Chinese had an adverse effect on the Malays. "The Malays whose own hereditary and environmental influence had been so debilitating, could do nothing but retreat before the onslaught of the Chinese immigrants. Whatever the Malays could do, the Chinese could do better and more cheaply. Before long the industrious and determined immigrants had displaced the Malays in petty trading and all branches of skilled work. As their wealth increased, so did their circle of contacts. Calling on their previous experience with officialdom in their own homeland, the Chinese immigrants were soon establishing the type of relationship between officials and traders which existed in China." [36] Chinese experience in graft and bribery at home served them in good stead in Malaya. "The organized open gratification of the ruling class soon firmly entrenched the Chinese in the towns and helped them establish complete control of the economy. The towns changed in character.

The small Malay shops gave way to rows of Chinese shops. As the Chinese increased in number and their business activities expanded, land prices in the town rocketed. Tempted by the high prices offered for their land, the Malays sold their holdings and began moving further and further into the outskirts of the towns. This pattern was already set when the British started their rule. The British at once recognized Chinese enterprise, and realized that a rich Chinese population would be good for British trade. The Chinese not only provided the infrastructure for the proper functioning of the big British import-export houses, but the wealth that they so readily acquired also made them good customers of the British. Chinese immigration was encouraged, and soon the towns began to assume the characteristics of the Malayan towns of today." [37]

The Chinese destroyed the self-reliance of the Malays in craftsmanship, skilled work and business. The Malays were completely excluded from these fields as a result of British encouragement regarding immigration. The town Malays were encouraged to hold on to administration. [38] The Independence of Malaya in 1957 did not change much the general situation of the Malays, although there had been an increase in the number of Malays in the profession and commerce. "But despite all this progress, the economic dilemma of the Malays still exists. It is there because for every step forward that the Malays make in the economic field other races make ten. It is there because other policies of the independent Government of Malaysia offset the policy towards helping the Malays. It is there because the concept of business has changed and changed again, even as the Malays begin to understand the orthodox methods which had originally defeated them." [39] The situation of the post-independence period was inherited from the past. This situation which grew out of the past favoured the Chinese immigrant. "The Chinese knew the local language and had all the contacts as well as the set-up necessary to enable the European traders to milk the Malay sultanates dry. In no time at all, perfect *rapport* was established between the Chinese traders and the conquering merchants of the West. As this partnership grew and as the Chinese partners proved their usefulness over and over again, Chinese migration to Malaysia was encouraged and speeded up. Now there came a bonus for the British who were the successors of the Portuguese and the Dutch in Malaya. The Chinese who grew rich under British protection themselves became good customers of the British. The market for British goods in Malaya enlarged and became very profitable. With the Chinese traders came the skilled workers and finally the unskilled coolies. To the British rulers of the country the influx of Chinese of all grades and classes meant a more sophisticated and organized society which facilitated their business as much as their administration. But for the Malays the influx meant a displacement. First it was in trade and commerce, then in skilled work and finally even in unskilled labour. There was also displacement in location, for the Malays had to move out of the towns, where, unless they were employed by the Government, there was no reason for them to stay. Indeed, the increased value of land in the towns and the various rates and taxes forced them to sell off their holdings and buy cheaper rural land." [40]

The displacement of the Malays by the immigrant population effected by colonial rule was partly due to the courtesy and self-effacing psychology of the Malays. "The Chinese and Indians coming from countries with vast populations are less concerned about good behaviour and manners. In their lives, nobility which is always associated with breeding, was totally absent. Age and riches are the only things they defer to. The Chinese and Indians have never understood the Malay habit of giving way. They saw nothing in it which bespoke good breeding. They do not admire it and they have never felt the need to copy it. But they certainly found it to their advantage. They found that they do not have to conform, that they can get away with anything. They found to their advantage that they can do things which the Malay cannot. They found in fact that in the land of the Malays they are privileged." [41] This courtesy and self-effacing habit of the Malays imposes a constant restraint upon them. "There is always an internal struggle, a conflict, and this conflict finds expression in a variety of ways. The first and most important result is a withdrawing into himself and his race. He is never frank except with those whose sympathy he can rely on absolutely. And he can rely absolutely only on his own people. His opinions as expressed to those not of his own kind are therefore different from those expressed to his own kind. Of course the difference only occurs when what he has to express to others is unpleasant or unpalatable. Where his true opinion will cause no unpleasantness or animosity, he does not hesitate to voice it to his own community as well as other communities. It is, therefore, fallacious to accept the Malay at face value. It is far better if his politeness and his abhorrence of unpleasantness is understood for what they really are. The conflict within him is potentially dangerous. It is perpetually seeking expression." [42]

Mahathir then suggested that running amok is an essential part of the Malay character. "*Amok* represents the external physical expression of the conflict within the Malay which his perpetual observance of the rules and regulations of his life causes in him. It is a spilling over, an overflowing of his inner bitterness. It is a rupture of the bonds which bind him. It is a final and complete escape from reason and training. The strain and the restraint on him is lifted. Responsibility disappears. Nothing matters. He is free. The link with the past is severed, the future holds nothing more. Only the present matters. To use a hackneyed expression, he sees red. In a trance he lashes out indiscriminately. His timid, self-effacing self is displaced. He is now a Mr. Hyde—cruel, callous and bent on destruction. But the transition from the self-effacing courteous Malay to the *amok* is always a slow process. It is so slow that it may never come about at all."[43] The relevance to the Malay problem is clear. "This brief examination of certain aspects of the Malay character is merely to illustrate that the Malay problem is more explosive than the evidence seems to indicate. It is meant to focus attention on the peculiarity of the Malays in suppressing their discontent. We can now understand why throughout history, the Malays appear to be contented to step further and further into the background. They gave up, apparently, politely, almost every vestige of power and authority in their own land."[44]

There is greater intellectual exertion exhibited in Mahathir's book than in the *Revolusi Mental*. Despite the use of the argument of heredity, Mahathir made use of numerous environmental and sociological arguments. Though there are historical inaccuracies here and there, the book, as a whole is a reasoned defence of the constitutional protection of the Malays.

We are interested here in his concept of the Malay character which is in many respects the same as that of the *Revolusi Mental*, for Mahathir followed the same trend of thinking. He found the Malays fatalistic. Malays lack the positive type of courage. "The firmness of will in agression, in withdrawal or in endurance directed by a true insight into a situation, as described by Plato, is not a part of the Malay make-up. Firmness in fact is not a Malay characteristic at all. The type of courage which requires firmness and adherence to a principle is therefore uncommon among Malays. Courage in most instances is equated with a willingness to face up to a hopeless situation. It is facing up to overwhelming odds which could certainly lead to defeat and destruction. To take on an adversary when it seems to be beyond one's capacity is courageous. To calculate and assess one's chances first is to exhibit cowardice. Time and again this inability or unwillingness to measure the odds against them has led to defeat and disaster for the Malays. The courageous or brave Malay is usually foolhardy, and because he is likely to do things without thinking of the consequences, the average Malay treats him with fear and respect. The ordinary man knows that it is not worthwhile to incur his displeasure and that it is safer to let him have his own way. The ordinary man therefore represents the other extreme when principle is easily set aside for the sake of safety."[45] Though there are exceptions to this, it is not the general rule. "It explains why Malays are adept in overcoming the enemy by stealth and cunning, and the infrequency of frontal assault in any situation."[46] The Malays have a peculiar way of decision making. "The need to control desires and to direct will-power is recognized, but wisdom is regarded mainly as the ability to circumvent a given situation. It is not restraint or direction which are highly regarded, but ability to avoid a clear cut decision and to be able to make corrections later on which are acclaimed. The Malay is never committed to anything. There is always a loophole somewhere for his escape. In trying to perfect an escape route for a given situation, decision making often becomes a tedious and time-consuming process. Indeed, where possible, a decision is avoided completely, thus preparing the ground for a reversal and later justification."[47]

Malays do not put a high value on time. "Disregard for time is seen in the careless way in which it is spent. Doing nothing, or sipping coffee, or talking is almost a Malay national habit. An invitation to a *khenduri* in a kampong is invariably for an indefinite time. One may arrive at any time, eat at any time and go off at any time. No one ever arrives on time for a meeting but once started there is no limit to the time it can last. A meeting would therefore start late and end even later, no matter how much the time of the meeting is adjusted to suit everyone."[48] The disregard for time has its consequences for Malay progress. Work and planning is never reliable. "A time-table is an essential part of the life of modern man. Indeed, the more technologically advanced the man, the more he is bound to time. The count-down symbolizes the absolute dependence of modern technology on time. Without mathematically perfect timing man would never have conquered space. A community which is not conscious of time must be regarded as a very backward society. What is more, it will remain a backward society. It can never achieve anything on its own and it can never be expected to advance and catch up with superior time-conscious civilizations. There is no doubt that the Malay failure to value time is one of the most important handicaps to their progress."[49]

On the theme of laziness Mahathir is not definitely clear but his view is perhaps more inclined to consider the Malays incapable of hard work. An extreme lassitude has descended on the Malays in the commercial and industrial sector. The potential in this sector is not developed. "Malays, except for those in Kelantan, may not be able to actually build a brick house on their own, but Malay architects are planning and directing the whole complex operation. Malay engineers can plan and direct the building of bridges of the most modern design. Malay agriculturists can conduct experiments and direct the cultivation of any and every crop. Malay doctors and lawyers compare well with those of any race. Malay administrators are much better than others. The potential is there but only in a limited field is it developed. Between the traditional Malay agriculturists and the educated *elite* there is a vast lacuna in which Malays are not to be found. Their potential in this area has not been developed. It is due partly to their apathy, and partly to the short-sightedness and apathy of their leaders. The fact is that even their responsible leaders suffer from the same lassitude that permeates their community."[50] On the capacity for hard work he said: "Malay leaders have been known to say that Malays are not suited for business or skilled work. They are agriculturists. Money does not mean the same thing to them as it does to the Chinese. They do not have the wish or the capacity for hard work. And above all they cannot change."[51] Mahathir did not deny the remark about the wish and capacity for hard work but he did deny that they could not be changed. His comparison between the Malays and the Chinese is a further clue to his concept of Malay capacity for hard work. "It is not the choice of the Malays that they should be rural and poor. It is the result of the clash of racial traits. They are easy-going and tolerant. The Chinese especially are hard-working and astute in business. When the two came in contact the result was inevitable. Before the onslaught of the predatory Chinese the Malays retreated to areas which were less attractive. The Government perceiving the result of this contest of racial characteristics hurriedly made Malay Reservation Laws which, while they do help the Malays, have also been instrumental in keeping the Malays rural."[52] He considered the Malays as inherently easy-going.

However a more perspicuous view is given in connection with

health amongst rural Malays. "Malaya abounded with various debilitating, endemic diseases like malaria and yaws. In addition, small epidemics of cholera and dysentery occurred at regular intervals. As often happens to a community subjected to continuous exposure to these diseases, the rural Malays developed a certain amount of resistance. They survived, but all their energy was depleted. Malaria, for example, affected practically all rural Malays. Rendered weak and dull by lack of blood and frequent bouts of fever, they were disinclined to work more than was necessary. The effort to plant and reap padi, which occupied two months of every year, taxed their strength. They had no more energy left to earn a better livelihood, or to teach themselves new skills."[53] On the whole his comments which occur in the book incline us to consider Mahathir's view on the Malay capacity for hard work as negative. His views on the Malays, like those of the *Revolusi Mental,* are dominated by colonial capitalism. Despite the deterioration of the Malays, brought about by British rule which he vividly described in his book, Mahathir cherished some good thoughts on the British. He said: "Before Independence the British ruled this country well. They may not have given the non-British inhabitants the best of everything,,but certainly they were expert administrators. They got jobs done efficiently. They built up an efficient civil service and a completely effective law-enforcing body. They brought law and order to the strife-torn tin-mining areas of Perak and Selangor, settled the minor wars of Malay rajas, and put down piracy. They built roads and railways and collected taxes which actually reached the treasury and were spent on public services. They were certainly a people well suited to administer."[54] There is in his mental world no complete break with colonial thinking. On the ability of the Malays to work hard his judgement is capitulative. Here is an instance. "The ordinary retail shops could easily employ Malay salesmen. They may not be as good as the Chinese, but they will certainly never be any good unless they have opportunities to learn. There will be dropouts, perhaps a considerable number at the beginning. But it is reasonable to expect a few at least to persist and succeed. In the bigger Chinese firms and banks where the business language is English there seems no valid reason why Malays could not be employed. Perhaps they do not work as hard as non-Malays. There seems to be some basis for this accusation, but again it cannot be as bad as it is made out. Government departments and a number of British firms have survived with Malay employees. It is unreasonable to put all the Malays into one category and label them as lazy. A more liberal and understanding attitude is needed."[55]

Similarly on the promotion of individual Malays to position of wealth, Mahathir showed the same attitude as the *Revolusi Mental.* He argued the benefits derived from the promotion of a few Malays to company directorship. His thinking on Malay reform must be seen within the context of capitalism. He did not question the capitalist system. His suggestion for reform is confined to the Malay attitudes and values which he considered basically negative, within the Malaysian constitutional context and the capitalist system. Adjustment of laws is implied in his thinking but this refers to part of the system rather than to an overall ideological change. He is even appreciative of feudalism. "In itself," he said, "the feudalist inclination of the Malays is not damaging. It makes for an orderly law-abiding society. People who could follow and observe an un-written code of behaviour are easily made to observe the written laws of a country. People who accept that a society must have people of varying degrees of authority and rights easily make a stable society and nation. A revolution in such a society is unusual unless led from above. A feudal society is therefore not necessarily a dormant or retrogressive society. It can be a dynamic society if there is dynamism at the top. But when the top fails, or is preoccupied with its own well-being, the masses become devoid of incentive for progress."[56] Here he stopped. Unlike Abdullah 120 years before him, he did not discuss the nature of feudal leadership in the Malay society. The weakness of both the *Revolusi Mental* and Mahathir's book is that they put the blame for the exploitation of the Malays on their character, British rule, and the impact of immigrant business but not to the same degree on the Malay ruling class which profited from colonialism. Thus when they say Malays are not frank, it also means they are not frank. In this respect, their silence on the contribution of the Malay ruling class to the deterioration of the conditions of the Malays, is an illustration of their hypocrisy. Unlike Abdullah bin Abdul Kadir Munshi, they themselves are not being frank. A critical discussion of both works follows in the next chapter. Both these works expressed the philosophy of the ruling elites in broad outline. While they attempted a detailed criticism of the Malays, they avoided a similar detailed treatment of the ruling elites. One or two brief references were made in passing but they never constituted a theme of a chapter or even a paragraph. It is a reflection of their position in the power structure, since they formed part of the status quo.

NOTES

1.   Senu Abdul Rahman, *Revolusi Mental*, p. 87. Penerbitan Utusan Melayu, Kuala Lumpur, 1971.
2.   *Ibid.*, p. 89. The translation is mine.
4.   *Ibid.*, p. 158. The translation is mine.
5.   Here the book expresses an absurd reasoning for an absurd conclusion. In the past Malays had no self-reliance because there was no word for it in the Malay language. The word for self-reliance, *berdikari* is new. So are "initiative" and "punctuality". This denotes the absence of the phenomena amongst Malays in the past. *Ibid.*, pp. 62, 159. The absurdity in the reasoning is to conclude that the absence of the words in the past denotes the absence of the phenomena. It is a glaring fact that initiative and self-reliance were shown by the Malays throughout history. Their sea-voyages, their agricultural activity, their wars, their piracy, their diplomacy, their trade, their social organization, surely these could not have been possible without self-reliance and initiative? Such an absurd reasoning can best be developed to draw the most absurd conclusion. Before the coming of Islam, Malays did not think at all, for there was no Malay word for "think". The present Malay word "pikir" is derived from Arabic!
6.   *Ibid.*, p.159. Number 10 is missing from the list. The paragraph heading is "Industriousness and Effort the Ladder to Wealth." Nowhere in this paragraph is stated that the Malays are industrious. But it is claimed that they are not disciplined or punctual.
7.   *Ibid.*, pp.161–162.
8.   *Ibid.*, p. 119.
9.   *Ibid.*, p. 75. In this part of the book seventeen negative traits are listed, based on Malay sayings, believed to have formed the traditional Malay character. Some of these are repeated elsewhere.
10. *Ibid.*, p. 76.
11. *Ibid.*, p. 351.
12. *Ibid.*, p. 442.
13. The translation is not completely literal owing to the syntactic defect of the passage. *Ibid.*, p. 122.
14. *Ibid.*, p. 99.
15. *Ibid.*, p. 172.
16. *Ibid.*, p. 41.
17. *Ibid.*, p. 71.
18. *Ibid.*, p. 115.
19. *Ibid.*, p. 214.
20. *Ibid.*, p. 316.
21. For the sake of accuracy the translation is kept as literal as possible without considerations of style, *ibid.*, p. 13.
22. *Ibid.*, p. 13.
23. *Ibid.*, p. 61.
24. *Ibid.*, p. 154.
25. Karl Mannheim, *Ideology and Utopia*, p. 67, *op.cit.*
26. Hugh Clifford, "Rival Systems and the Malayan Peoples", pp. 407–408. *North American Review*, vol. 177, 1903.
27. *Revolusi Mental*, p.103.
28. *Ibid.*, pp. 40–41.
29. *Ibid.*, p. 53. This part deals with the historical background.
30. *Ibid.*, pp. 99, 100, 105, 111.
31. *Ibid.*, p. 115.

32. *Ibid.*, pp. 118–120.
33. Mahathir bin Mohamad, *The Malay Dilemma*, p. 24. Asia Pacific Press, Singapore, 1970. Mahathir did not claim to make a scientific study. "At best it is an intelligent guess". The purpose is to awaken interest in the subject.
34. *Ibid.*, p. 21.
35. *Ibid.*, pp. 21–22.
36. *Ibid.*, p. 25.
37. *Ibid.*, p. 25.
38. *Ibid.*, p. 27.
39. *Ibid.*, p. 47.
40. *Ibid.*, pp. 35–36.
41. *Ibid.*, p.117.
42. *Ibid.*, p.117.
43. *Ibid.*, p.118
44. *Ibid.*, p.118.
45. *Ibid.*, pp. 160–161.
46. *Ibid.*, p.161.
47. *Ibid.*, p.161.
48. *Ibid.*, p. 163.
49. *Ibid.*, p. 163.
50. *Ibid.*, pp. 58–59.
51. *Ibid.*, p. 59.
52. *Ibid.*, p. 85.
53. *Ibid.*, p. 28.
54. *Ibid.*, p. 76.
55. *Ibid.*, p. 83.
56. *Ibid.*, pp. 170–171.

CHAPTER 11

The Distortion of Malay Character

The distortion of Malay character by the authors of the *Revolusi Mental*, and to some extent by Mahathir, is due to their lack of insight into the social sciences, their loose reasoning, and their unfamiliarity with Malay history. All are, however, sympathetic to the Malays. They resemble some American negroes who believe what white racialists say about them. In colonial times there were prominent indigenous personalities who believed in the moral and civilizing mission of the colonial powers. In ancient societies there were slaves who did not question the institution of slavery. As we have pointed out, once an ideology becomes supreme, it is accepted in some degree by the dominated party. Owing to the absence of a long and profound political struggle for independence in Malaysia and the continuity of the ruling class, there was no sharp break in the ideological consciousness of the Malay elites. Hence the resemblance between the *Revolusi Mental* and the colonial ideology. It is this persisting influence of colonial ideology coupled with scientific and intellectual shortcomings which characterized the *Revolusi Mental.* Our first criticism is its ignorance, or lack of awareness of previous thinking on the problem of Malay backwardness.

As we have seen, the subject of Malay backwardness had continuously attracted attention since Abdullah wrote his account of his trip to Kelantan in Singapore in 1838. Before the Second World War, a Malay, Dato Sedia Raja Abdullah, commented on the need to bring about a change of outlook amongst the Malays. He found the superstitious and magical practices amongst some Malay farmers inimical to progress.[1] The little booklet of the Council of Islam and Malay Custom, Kelantan, planned in 1918, discussed earlier, is another example of this. After the Second World War, Malay leaders like Dato Onn bin Ja'afar and Burhanuddin al-Helmy concerned themselves with Malay backwardness. Their views were scattered among their numerous speeches and newspaper reports.

After the Independence in 1957, this theme was frequently discussed. Ungku Abdul Aziz wrote on Malay poverty. I had myself made contributions to this subject since 1959. During that period, government planning and external institutional changes were believed to be sufficient. The idea of a mental revolution, a radical change in outlook was suggested by me in an article in a Malay daily published in 1959, dealing with the problem of change and the role of ideology.[2] Similarly in 1960, I noted three major problems facing the Malay community in Malaysia: to raise the standard of living of the people, to preserve the Malay language and culture, and "to accomplish a revolution in thought and attitude, abandoning that which obstructs progress, striving for that which is good."[3] In 1965, at a public lecture in Kota Bahru, Kelantan, organized by the Pan Malayan Islamic Party, I stressed the following: "The Muslim is required by his religion to perform good and just deeds and to eliminate evils. As given in the example of the Prophet Mohammed, the change that was first attempted was a change in thought and feeling. Only thereafter came the change in external action."[4] The concept of mental revolution with reference to the Malays was here suggested. A rejection of feudal values and ideas and retaining the valuable in Malay culture should "inspire a mental revolution (revolusi rohani) and our striving in the future, not a clinging to that which is stale and polluted."[5]

In 1965 I published a research paper on the influence of collective representations (types of beliefs conceptualized by French sociology) on the economic development of the Malays. I even made use of the term mental revolution.[6] In 1963 and 1970 two research papers were published in Paris touching on the problem of Malay development. The authors of the *Revolusi Mental* deliberately ignored these works, which were highly relevant to their themes, or were not aware of their existence. If the latter is the case it illustrates their intellectual and scientific consciousness. The first great error made by the *Revolusi Mental* was to view the Malay system of values as practised by the community in the form of a single, uniform and homogenous entity. The thirty or more negative traits which they attributed to the Malay character are more reflective of the Malay ruling class rather than the Malay community as a whole.[7] Indolence is more prevalent among the ruling class in traditional Malay society than among people. A certain number of indolent members exist in all societies. In the Malay society they are found in more significant numbers among the ruling class.

According to our definition the quality of indolence in all

individuals is to be distinguished from the decision to avoid certain works on account of their pecuniary outcome. A man who prefers to be a gardener and earn less rather than being a waiter need not be indolent so long as he works hard as a gardener. Hence the Malay preference for certain types of occupation cannot in itself be considered as proof of indolence; for instance rice farming as opposed to shopkeeping. The inclination of the *Revolusi Mental* to consider the Malays as indolent is unconsciously influenced by colonial capitalism. As we have shown, colonial capitalism considered industriousness from the point of view of the capitalist system of exploitation. The amazing thing is that both colonial capitalism and the *Revolusi Mental* never mentioned any indolent Chinese. In their view all Chinese were hardworking. While it is true that generally speaking the Chinese are industrious people, it would be absurd to think that there are no indolent Chinese. The image of an entirely industrious Chinese community as opposed to an entirely indolent Malay community is the creation of colonial capitalism. Amongst the Chinese there is a proportionately greater number of indolent members amongst the upper classes. Sons of millionaires, gamblers, playboys, mistresses, many of them are indolent. There are many indolent Chinese landlords who just wait for the end of the month to collect their rent. There are many indolent property owners, who buy plots of land and keep them, without doing anything to them, merely waiting for the prices to go up.

The error of the *Revolusi Mental* is to generalize from certain cases which the authors came across. There are Malays without initiative, Malays who are indolent, Malays who are not serious, and Malays who do not think of the future. All the negative characteristics listed by the *Revolusi Mental* exist in some Malays. But it is another thing to generalize. The temptation to generalize was based on folklore and proverbs. The fundamental premise in the reasoning is when a word is absent from the Malay language, the phenomenon is also absent. The second fundamental premise is when a number of sayings exist in the Malay literary record more than their opposite their central idea governs the Malay outlook. It requires only a little ingenuity to expose these fallacies. The *Revolusi Mental* utilizes a number of Malay sayings expressing negative characteristics which are then regarded as dominant elements in the Malay character. Thus the saying "Hangat-hangat tahi ayam" (the warmth of a fowl's dropping) is used to prove that the Malays lack enthusiasm and perseverance in an undertaking.

The warmth of a fowl's dropping is short-lived. The first elementary blunder of the *Revolusi Mental* is that it does not classify the sayings into types. These sayings can be classified, broadly speaking into three types, though at times the demarcation line is difficult to draw. We shall call them advocative, prohibitive and descriptive. The advocative saying is one which suggests something desirable or good, something to be accomplished. The prohibitive contains an element of rejection, disapproval, of avoidance. The descriptive merely portrays a situation, belonging to neither of the other two types. An instance of an advocative saying is "Tangan menetak bahu memikul", the hand chopping, the shoulders carrying, to portray diligence. The following indicates perseverance to complete a task: "Genggam bara api, biar jadi arang", grasping a burning wood, let it become charcoal. An instance of the prohibitive saying is this: "Jangan nantikan nasi disajikan dilutut", do not wait for the rice to be served at the knee (sitting cross-legged as in a Malay dinner). This prohibits expecting something without effort. A descriptive saying is the following: "Retak menanti pechah", the crack awaiting the break. It illustrates a tenuous friendship about to break.

Hence a saying in Malay by its mere existence cannot be used to establish a trait of character. It is society's response to a particular situation. An illustration of the system of values may be seen in the lists of the advocative and the prohibitive sayings. The saying "hangat-hangat tahi ayam" is prohibitive. When Malays say this, it is with the element of disapproval, a sneer. It is not advocative. The *Revolusi Mental* suggests that the Malays advocate it. Furthermore it suggests by implication, that the majority of Malays are influenced by this outlook. It suppresses Malay sayings which contradict the saying which they misinterpret. For instance they say Malays are fatalist. They quote the following: "Rezeki sechupak tidak boleh jadi segantang", a gain of one *chupak* cannot become one *gantang*.[8] This is supposed to indicate Malay fatalism. Strictly speaking a fatalist is one who does not believe that effort can influence a man's action. By this definition the Malays are not fatalists because they believe in free will. They believe human action can influence man's fate. There are several sayings, on record which are over a century old, stressing the value of human effort. The following are some: "Tanam lalang tidak akan tumboh padi", if we plant wild grass we shall not get a rice crop; "malu berdayong perahu hanyut", ashamed of rowing, the boat drifts; "segan bertanya, sesat jalan", too shy to enquire, the way is lost. All these indicate the Malay belief in man as a free agent. What is considered "takdir" by the Malays, is the unavoidable, the acceptance of that which man cannot stop from happening.

The *Revolusi Mental's* selection of sayings is biased and interpreted to suit its image of the Malays. In addition to this the reasoning is erroneous. It claims that the words initiative, self-reliance, punctuality, and discipline did not exist in the early Malay vocabulary. Its error lies in its conception of the nature of vocabulary. No vocabulary of a people entirely expresses the conscious thoughts and feelings of that people. An idea or a concept which is not formulated in a word, like initiative, can nevertheless exist and find expression in different forms. The Malays were definitely aware of the concept, since the Malay word "chergas" includes initiative. If it is true that the absence of a word means the absence of the phenomenon, then we shall reach the absurd conclusion that before the coming of Islam, no Malay ever thought because the word "think" in Malay is an Arabic introduction, "pikir"; there is now no original Malay word for "think". The *Revolusi Mental* further erred when it said that Malays did not know of discipline in the past because there was no word for discipline. The truth is there is a Malay word "patoh" to indicate discipline. Furthermore certain phenomena could not have happened in Malay history without discipline. The army organization of the Malay states in the past, the war, the raids, the administration, even the piracy could not have taken place without discipline. The kingdom of Malacca in the 15th century was a significant state. It is amazing that the *Revolusi Mental* ignored all these factors in its discussion of Malay discipline.

Another misconception concerns rationality. That Malays value rational action is obvious although rationality exists side by side with magic and superstition. This is a situation prevailing all over the world. Only in the modern highly industrialized society does the rational element predominate. However it is not true that in the past Malay society did not value rationality. Here are some sayings ignored by the *Revolusi Mental*. "Ikut hati mati, ikut rasa binasa", follow the heart you die, follow the feeling you are ruined. Maxwell commented on this as follows: "A maxim shewing the folly and immorality of taking one's wishes and feelings as the sole guide of one's actions, irrespective of law and social obligations."[9] "Turutkan gatal sampai ketulang"; to scratch an itch till the bone is reached, indicates giving way to passion to the bitter end, to indulge in unreasoned anger resulting in disaster.

If rationality meant justifying the ends by the means then the Malays did possess such a quality. Their handicraft, farming, fishing, trade and commerce during the 17th century, all indicated the presence of a rational outlook. If however the term rationality implied modern business practices, industrial ventures and commerce, this, it is true, was lacking. But one can hardly blame the Malay society of the past for lacking an institution created only in the 19th and 20th century in Southeast Asia by the colonial powers. It is like blaming the Malay society of the past for not knowing how to use electricity at a time when electricity had not yet been invented.

The same may be said of punctuality amongst the Malays in the past. Mechanical punctuality as measured by the clock did not exist owing to the nature of society and the absence of the clock. The productive processes of society were not mechanized, hence the need for the modern variant of punctuality did not exist. Take for instance shipping: owing to the fact that the movement of boats depended on the wind and human energy, the departure or arrival of a boat was not definable in terms of measurable units of time. The necessity for mechanized punctuality did not exist, therefore, in most areas of social life. There was no necessity for farmers and fishermen to work according to the clock. Despite all these factors, the Malays were not devoid of a sense of punctuality, which was connected with religion. The Malays of pre-colonial days as well as of subsequent periods until today, had always been punctual in saying their prayers, especially the dawn and sunset prayers. They observed the time scrupulously. The entire community in an area collectively broke its fast in the month of Ramadan to the minute. They strictly observed with utmost punctuality the call to prayer from the mosque. Hence it is misleading to claim that the concept of punctuality was absent from Malay society, but merely that it was not related to the clock. Modern science and technology, in so far as they affect the various sectors of modern Malay life, have widened the circumference of necessary punctuality and introduced the time measurement by means of the clock. The Malays like many other people have responded to this quite easily. They observe the clock when coming to work in the offices, when taking the train, when going to school. There are millions of Malays who observe the clock in their daily activities, and who have adopted punctuality for at least the past 50 years. [10]

On the other hand where strict observance of the clock is not required, Malays do not observe punctuality to the hour or half-

hour, as in a village feast. But this is also true of a highly industrialized modern society. The equivalent is an open house party
until late at night. Similarly cocktail parties ranging from 2 to
3 hours, with guests dropping in any time in between resemble
the Malay village feasts. In every society, there are areas of life
where punctuality according to time measurement is relaxed. The
frequenting of bars and clubs is another instance. In the Malay
village there were no bars or clubs, but this phenomenon was in
evidence at the village feasts. The *Revolusi Mental* and Mahathir
mistakenly accused the Malays of having no sense of time and
punctuality by selecting those instances in their life where punctuality
was not called for, while they ignored instances in Malay life where
punctuality and the sense of time were present. Their selection
of instances was highly biased, but what made them deliberately
distort the image of the Malays? Before we answer this let us
take the distortion of the image of the Malay rice farmer by
Mahathir. He suggested that the Malay rice farmer actually worked
two months in the year. Except for a few, people were content
to spend their leisure in resting or extensive conversation. This
is a distorted picture of the Malay rice farmer.

It was probable that in certain areas, such as Kedah and Perlis,
the rice farmers were under employed before the double cropping
period. This was due to the relative absence of secondary employment such as rubber tapping, road making, drainage and irrigation
works, fishing, and mat-making. But this is certainly not true of
the whole of Malaya. Research in the Kemubu area of Kelantan
involving 1,157 rice farms, indicated that the average working days
of a farmer was 123 days, excluding time spent on livestock keeping.[11] During the padi growing season where the farmer was
not employed on his field, he had to spend a great deal of time
feeding his animals in their stall. The research report suggested
that the farmer was employed 180 days in the year; 94 days were
spent in labour directly connected with rice-planting, a single crop
per year. Some of the farmers grew tobacco during the off season.
In 1967, 13,000 farmers in Kelantan had registered for tobacco
growing, out of the estimated 60,000 farm families. They also
grew food crops. Some cultivated rubber. The picture that the Malay
rice farmer worked for two months in the year is thus a crude
distortion. In the Kuala Selangor area the farmer worked on an
average of 131 days for padi cultivation alone.[12] In the double
cropping farms of Bachang in Malacca, the farmers were practically
fully employed. Out of 150 working days (6 months excluding

holiday) the farm operator was employed for 134 days, of which 42 days were spent for rice cultivation. The area is near the town of Malacca which offered employment for non-agricultural work. The farmers were employed temporarily as trishaw-riders, taxi-drivers, or participated in local trading or small scale business. They were also employed in cottage industries, making strings, mats, bags and wood cuttings. [13]

Mahathir, in assessing the average working days of the farmer have not compared the number with those who worked in the civil service and private firms. The high ranking workers in the civil service, the firms and industries, work on average 185 days in a year. Let us take government service and consider 8 hours as the working day, as the farmer's working day has been defined. Out of the 365 days in the year, 78 are Sundays and half Saturdays, about 30 days, are leave, 27 are holidays and medical leave. This leaves us with 230 working days. Since the government's actual working day is $6\frac{1}{2}$ hours, there is a further deduction of 43 days, plus a further 5 days of work in the fasting month Ramadan (until 1972). During this month, the offices only work 6 hours a day, from 8a.m. to 2p.m. Thus the total 8 hours working day amounts to 230 minus 48, which is 182 days in the year. Compare this to the rice farmer in Kelantan. The research report on Kelantan stated the following: "As for the farmer, he worked for the total equivalent of 123 days and of this more than half the work-time (68 work-days) was in off-farm employment. It is important to note that the farmer was under-employed for about 180 days in the year which is more than one-half of his work-time."[14] No-one speaks of the under employment of the civil service or its indolence. The difference between the lower ranks and the higher ranks is 7–14 days. As to indulgence in idle gossip, leisure and festivity, the civil service is not behind the farmers. Civil servants spend their leisure time, which is approximately 8 hours every working day and 16 hours during holidays, resting, chatting, watching TV, listening to the radio, visiting the cinema, the night-club, or gambling. In addition, a small group uses its leisure time for sport, reading, or cultivating a hobby. How is it that the urban dwellers of all communities, the office workers who are not victims of malaria, are not considered depleted of energy, as people who "were disinclined to work more than was necessary", by Mahathir?

Mahathir and the *Revolusi Mental* did not view the problem in its proper context. Malay rural dwellers work as hard as the urban dwellers; it is merely their income and opportunity which are more restricted. The negative traits of Malay character discussed by Mahathir are either an exaggeration or misplaced judgements. For instance, he suggested that the Malays are frank only towards those they can absolutely rely upon, and this happens to be their own people. This is nothing strange; in this, every community has this attitude. Who would express unpleasant and unpalatable remarks about other communities to members of that community, except those without moral restraints like the Nazis and white American racists? Most communities, both in Asia and the West, have a sense of politeness, or restraint. This is not peculiar to the Malays. Another exaggeration or misplaced judgement is Mahathir's evaluation of amok in the psychological make-up of the Malays. To begin with, the phenomenon described as amok is not confined to the Malays. Chinese and Indians have been known to kill members of their family in a state of mental pathology. Furthermore this phenomenon has substantially decreased amongst Malays owing to a change of historical conditions. A situation of extreme mental oppression exercised against a person, as for instance a Buginese slave cruelly treated in a Dutch household in 18th century Batavia, is no more common. In addition, Mahathir was wrong to consider certain phenomena pertaining to some individuals as indicating the character of a collectivity. The Japanese soldiers during the Second World War were very rarely captured. They preferred to commit suicide rather than surrender. But the Japanese nation did surrender, and did not commit suicide. The sense of honour which governed the conduct of individual Japanese soldiers impelling them to commit suicide rather than surrender, did not govern the conduct of the Japanese nation. Hence we cannot say that suicide in the face of defeat is a basic trait in the Japanese national character.

If we generalize about the character of a community on the basis of the action of a few individuals, then we are in for real confusion. Malays are prone to steal because some steal; Malays are lazy because some are; Malay women are disloyal to their husbands because some are; Malays are mad because some are; Malays are *ganja* smokers because some are. So we can indefinitely enumerate the negative traits of the Malay community based on the fact that some Malays at some times have exhibited these traits. Although mental disorders exist among particular communities, they cannot be automatically considered as part of the psychological make-up of the particular community. Amongst the Chinese in Singapore and Malaysia there is a mental disorder called "koro", a shrinking of the genital, predominantly amongst males. Just because it is primarily confined to the Chinese community, can we say that the loss of potency, the shrinking of the vital organ, is part of the basic psychological make-up of the Chinese? Such a conclusion would be a highly absurd and muddled one. Koro has nothing to do with Chinese character or the Chinese "dilemma". All it points out is that a small number of Chinese males are prone to it. Cultural and psychological factors may explain it although the cultural factors may not have a direct influence. But this has nothing to do with the collective character of a community.

What Mahathir and the *Revolusi Mental* attempted to do was strictly speaking, a national character study. There are serious problems connected with national character study which have baffled the best brains in social sciences, one of these is the definition of national character.

The difficulty of defining the national character is due to the fact that there are many classes in society with their sub-cultures, there are also the differentiations into age groups, into male and female, and into responses which arise from the national character in a given situation, or responses which arise from the situation only, without the dominant influence of the national character. It has been successfully shown by Ruth Benedict that Japanese society, for instance, was permeated through and through by the psychology of hierarchy. "In the family and in personal relations, age, generation, sex, and class dictate proper behaviour. In government, religion, the Army, and industry, areas are carefully separated into hierarchies where neither the higher nor the lower may without penalty overstep their prerogatives. As long as 'proper station' is maintained the Japanese carry on without protest. They feel safe. They are of course often not 'safe' in the sense that their best good is protected but they are 'safe' because they have accepted hierarchy as legitimate. It is as characteristic of their judgement on life as trust in equality and free enterprise is of the American way of life." [15] Here the author isolated a trait in the national character of Japan that dominated Japanese behaviour. She noted that it was Japan's mistake to try and apply it outside to the conquered territories. The conquered nations were expected to accept their lower station in the scheme of things. This was of course resented. I have myself witnessed this passion for hierarchy and organization in Java during the Japanese occupation (1942–1945). The concept of Asia for the Asians held by the Japanese, the "saudara tua", or elder brother, was basically a manifestation of hierarchy. Kawasaki noted that the Japanese operate best as a group. Decisions in a firm are usually in the nature of a consensus. [16] These are some instances which can be considered as constituent elements making up a national character. They dominate the psychology of the entire nation. They are transmitted through the socialization process; they are understood and taken for granted; their prevalence is not confined to a section of the community but generally to all. It is however, not always possible to delineate the national character of every nation or community.

The point we wish to stress is that it is possible in some instances to speak of national character but the problems are great. We shall not deny the possibility of the Malays having a national character but the constituent elements, with possibly one or two exceptions, are certainly not those cited by Mahathir and the *Revolusi Mental*. A great deal of expert research is required to establish trait by trait the national character of the Malays beyond what is obvious and of no profound consequence. For instance, Malays on the whole are soft-spoken, averse to shouting in conversation. A radical, heated and open dispute between individuals or groups is often avoided although not the dispute itself. There is a Malay manner for conducting and settling disputes, but even this is not a hundred per cent true. In the past, Malay rulers have fought against each other in direct and heated manner. Similarly religious disputes have been conducted in this way. Without denying the possibility of a Malay national character, we wish to point out here that the traits selected by Mahathir and the *Revolusi Mental* are by no means those of the national character. The history and current condition of the Malays contradicts the assertion that they were incapable of hard work, lacked discipline, and punctuality, while indulging in entertaining talks, etc. The authors mistook the actions of certain Malays for a general expression of the Malay community. Referring to the Japanese national character, Hasegawa suggested that it was less the property of a particular class than of the whole nation. A value, such as the sense of propriety in doing things, may originate in the upper class but if it extends to the entire nation it becomes part of the national character. [17] Values such as laziness, indiscipline, non-punctuality, are not upheld by Malay society. Neither is running amok a collectively accepted mode of reaction to difficult situations. It is merely evidence of a mental breakdown which affects some individual Malays. It cannot be considered part of the Malay national character. Suggesting a psycho-pathological disorder as part of the Malay collective tendency is a continuation of colonial thinking. As we had noted earlier it was the British colonial administrator Clifford who claimed that the psycho-pathological disorder called *latah* was inherent in the Malay psychology.[18] What Mahathir did was to use amok instead of *latah* as an element in the Malay community's psychological make-up; the suggestion has a colonial ring about it.

We earlier noted the impossibility of considering such disorders as part of the national character of any community. The reasons are as follows: it is not purposefully transmitted by the community; it does not govern collective responses towards national problems; it is not shared by the overwhelming majority, and it is not the approved or tacitly accepted mode of reaction. Only such values, attitudes, and modes of reaction conforming to the positive requirements of the above may be considered as the constituent elements of the national character.

If many Englishmen get drunk, and stagger on the street, making a lot of noise, this in itself does not represent part of the English national character. Only if it can be shown that the collective English reaction to national crises is somewhat conditioned by the peculiar phenomenon of drunkenness, that this phenomenon is a deep-seated national sentiment pervading English life, can we presume that particular form of drunkenness to be part of the English national character. Individual Englishmen can be drunkards whose life is entirely dominated by the bottle. But one can hardly conclude that this is a basic trait in the English character. Mahathir's unfamiliarity with social sciences made him suggest amok to be a basic part of the Malay psychology.

One last word about national character. It is not to be confused with religion, culture, rituals, institutions, practices or situations as such, although all or some may contribute to the formation of national character at a given point in a nation or community's history. Salvador de Madariaga stressed the predominance of the intellectual element in French collective life as compared to that of the English. The French state, in his opinion, marked an attempt to impose an intellectual order. "While in English collective life questions are solved at the very moment when they arise and by virtue of the very vital instinct which makes them arise, in France, the whole collective life is regulated beforehand and all cases are foreseen. This watch must naturally have a watchmaker. The State is in France the watchmaker in chief of the social mechanism. Thus it is that the tendency so typically French towards centralizing all public functions in the State appears as a natural consequence of French intellectualism. Let us remember in passing that it was an intellectual class which initiated and completed in France the centralization of authority."[19] No doubt French culture and history had contributed to the role of French intellectualism but it became part of the national character only after it had significantly influenced French life. The mere presence of an intellectual element in a community does not make that element supreme in the national life of that community. The more so a psychopathological disorder like amok.

There are numerous weaknesses in both the *Revolusi Mental* and Mahathir's book. I have published a detailed and separate criticism of the *Revolusi Mental* in Malay.[20] It would digress too much from the main theme of this book if all the erroneous statements from the two works were to be discussed. However Mahathir's idea on the racial inferiority of the Malays requires a comment. What he said about this was all vague. In other parts of his book he cited environmental influences. He believed in the racial inferiority of the Malays without actually specifying in detail where that inferiority lay. He did not say that the Malays were incapable of becoming good businessmen or professionals but he invoked a general racial explanation to account for the lag in capitalist development amongst the Malays. His use of the survival of the fittest hypothesis was inconsistent. While he applied it to explain the emergence of hardy individuals amongst the Chinese in the mainland, he did not apply it to the Malays. Amongst the Malays, there was also a serious struggle for existence. Malay fishing and rice-farming were not as easy as Mahathir suggested. The Malay village community had to struggle much harder against diseases in the pre-Independence days. Haynes, a member of the Malayan Civil Service, in his memorandum to the Rice Cultivation Committee of 1931, wrote the following: "I speak from considerable personal experience when I say that there are many deaths of small children amongst this population which occur from avoidable causes. Recently when I was walking over some padi fields where the population was clearly a healthy one I asked the only two Malay householders whom I saw how many children they had had and how many had died. One replied that he had had five children out of whom three had died; and the other replied that he had had eight children out of whom five had died. The fathers were both padi planters, and fine strong healthy men. These are merely samples of many cases which have come within my personal notice in places which are off the beaten track of doctors and health officers."[21]

Mahathir was also aware of the high mortality rate, particularly among infants. Why did not the survival of the fittest theory work amongst the Malays as it did amongst the Chinese? The explanation of cultural phenomena in terms of race and Darwin's evolutionary theory have long been discredited in the social sciences. It does not apply to China either. For thousands of years the Chinese peasants had to cope with difficulties. Yet it was only recently that advances were made in their social and economic progress.

It is true that the soil is conducive to cultivation, but this did not mean an easy life for the farmers. The farmers had to fight continuously against weeds, insects and pests. The great majority had also to fight indebtedness. As late as 1966, when the government had taken more interest in assisting the rice-farmers, crops were reported everywhere to have been attacked by rats and other pests. In one area about 25% of the crop was damaged by pests,[22] and in earlier periods the damage was even greater. 50 to 60% of the damage was caused by rats; there were also birds and floods.

In the 1931 it was found that indebtedness in different regions varied between 40 and 90% of the farming population. "Indebtedness takes two forms, namely, to Chetties and others for mortgages on land and to Chinese shop-keepers and others for advances either in cash or in kind to assist the cultivators during the period the crop is growing. Of the two, the latter is by far the most widespread and pernicious. It is commonly found that on this system cultivators obtain goods during the growing period of the crop and when repayment is made at the time of the harvest, the price they receive results in the producers being paid at a figure which is far below the true market value of the produce."[23] This situation prevailed for at least half a century; and since 1966 the situation has deteriorated. In an area where off farm employment opportunity is favourable as in Malacca, the estimated annual average income of the farmer was M$1,628, the family expenses were M$1,561, and the net saving was M$66. However the annual average borrowing was M$963. About 83% of the farmers in this area borrowed, and about 66% of the loan was for consumption purposes, namely for food and clothes. The bulk of the loan was in kind, from the provision shops. This loan alone constituted 68·5% of all loans, for the Malacca area.

The indirect rate of interest per annum charged by the provision shops in the form of higher prices on advances in kind was estimated to be 205%, while interest on cash from the pawn shop was 25%. Generally the farmer was able to pay about 70% of his debt at the end of the year. All these factors indicate that the life of a Malay rice farmer is not as easy and simple as suggested by Mahathir. Furthermore if they were easy going they would not become a profitable target for creditors. Here is another motivation for the Malay farmer to work hard, to pay his debt. "It should be observed that although provision shops provided more than 80 per cent of the total credit required by farmers, only a small percentage of such debts remained unpaid and was carried down to the following year. Most of the debts due to provision shops were repaid at the end of the year; for farmers fear that if such debts remain unpaid at the end of every month, shop-keepers would not allow them further credit."[24] The Rice Committee of 1956 listed the following conditions for the unduly small returns of the rice farmer: widespread and heavy indebtedness and the exorbitant interest charges paid by the producers; the lack of organized credit facilities; excessive marketing costs and margins, and malpractices by marketing functionaries and intermediaries; lack of recognized standards of quality; inadequate and defective storage facilities; lack of producers' organizations for financing, processing, storing and distributing, and poor communications in rural areas.[25] It is such factors which explain the slow progress of the Malays in emerging from a peasant society rather than the allegedly negative traits of their natural character or any hereditary qualities.

To summarize therefore, it would appear that both the *Revolusi Mental* and Mahathir painted a distorted picture of the Malay community. At best this picture reflects the life of the ruling elites, and was by no means a reflection of the Malay community. The foundation of their reasoning was loose and their knowledge of facts limited. Their interpretation is faulty and their thinking an extension of the colonial ideology. They have ignored many elements from Malay culture and history which stressed the values for progress. They have also confused the cultural and the historical. This we shall treat in the following chapter. The absence of the Malay trading class in Malaysia now is a consequence of historical factors, not a result of the Malay system of values.

The Second Malaysia Plan 1971–1975, aims at creating a Malay entrepreneurial class in 20 years' time, when 30 per cent of the country's business and industry should be owned and run by Malays.[26] The Plan is indirectly an admission of the failure of previous planning. After 14 years of independence, Malay participation in business and industry is negligible. The *Revolusi Mental* prepares the climate for an eventual failure of the *Second Malaysia Plan*. If it fails to achieve its targets, the attitude of the Malays is to blame. We are here not assessing the actual performance of the Malaysian government, we are only tracing the ideological motivational root of the *Revolusi Mental*. The degradation of the Malay character is an attempt by the ruling party to absolve itself from blame for real or expected failures to ensure the progress of the Malay community. Government publications and the pronouncements of various leaders have never made any reference to serious failures or shortcomings. This issue requires a separate study. Suffice it to say there is a growing anxiety amongst the Malay leaders in power that the situation of the Malays have not substantially improved. Publicly they do not admit that this is largely on account of corruption, nepotism, bad implementation of plans, and lack of institutional innovation. Their statements throughout the years that the people must respond indicate their anxiety that the people are not responding. Of course to assess this we have to know the issues, only then can we attribute responsibility either to the people or to the government. I have in this book merely attempted to prove the existence of this anxiety and its function as a motivational source to paint the Malay community in negative colours, so that the latter can be held responsible if the party in power fails to realize its declared objectives.

NOTES

1. Dato Sedia Raja Abdullah, "The Origin of Pawang and Berpuar Ceremony." *JMBRAS*, vol. V, pt. 2, November, 1927. In connection with magical and superstitious practices in farming, he said: "In conclusion, I cannot refrain from remarking it is idle to hope for the economic progress of the Malays so long as this and similar beliefs prevail among them. Where those beliefs are deep rooted, science cannot make much headway, for superstitions and scientific truths cannot exist side by side. It is difficult, if not impossible, to deal scientifically with pests if damage to crops is believed to be due to the ravages of evil spirits." P. 313.
2. Syed Hussein Alatas, "Erti Kemajuan Masharakat". *Utusan Melayu*, October 7, 1959, Kuala Lumpur. Here was stated: "Every great change in history, every revolution that occurred, has always been preceded by a great psychological change. There is no change in history which is not preceded by a change in man's conception towards life." The basic themes of the *Revolusi Mental* are found in this article, minus the treatment on Malay character. It deals with the concept of progress, the attitudes required, and the methods to achieve it. Though economic change is a major objective, economism should not be the dominant method of analysis.
3. Syed Hussein Alatas, "Sekitar Bahasa dan Kebudayaan Melayu." p. 82. *Dewan Bahasa*, IV, no. 2, February, 1960, Kuala Lumpur.
4. Syed Hussein Alatas, "Sejarah Melayu berisi Unsur2 yang tidak Sehat dari Segi Falsafah Perjuangan Islam." *Angkatan Baru*, October 1965, Kuala Lumpur. The lecture was printed in this monthly.

5. *Ibid.*
6. Syed Hussein Alatas, "Collective Representations and Economic Develop-ment". *Kajian Ekonomi Malaysia*, vol. II, no. 1, June. 1965, Kuala Lumpur. The following is suggested. "Collective representations in the realms of politics, medicine, technology, agriculture, fishing, reclamation of lands, building, trans-portation, etc. with their mystic participation, are, to my mind, one of the great influences bringing about the stagnation and underdevelopment of Southeast Asian societies. They possess the greatest of significance in the day to day life of the people. Before we can hope to achieve large scale and positive changes in the social and economic conditions of the Southeast Asian peoples, we must bring about a change of outlook, a mental revolution." Pp. 106–107. The way in which magical and superstitious beliefs influence development is discussed.
7. See Syed Hussein Alatas, "Feudalism in Malaysian Society: A Study in Historical Continuity", in *Civilizations*, vol. XVIII, no. 4, 1969.
8. Rezeki is from Arabic. It means sustenance, bounty, livelihood. The *Revolusi Mental* noted seven sayings to show that the Malays believe in fate. See *op. cit.,* p. 69. Maxwell, a great collector of Malay proverbs, did not see any fatalism in this. The saying, he said, described "one who is just able to support himself, whose daily earnings enable him to live but not to save." See W. E. Maxwell, "Malay Proverbs", p. 150. *JSBRAS*, no. 2, 1878.
9. W. E. Maxwell, "Malay Proverbs", p. 90. *JSBRAS*, no. 1, July, 1878.
10. I had earlier discussed the presence of punctuality as a value in some tradi-tional societies in refutation of Herskovits' generalization on the Sudan. See my contribution, "Modernization and National Consciousness", in Ooi Jin-Bee, Chiang Hai Ding (eds.), *Modern Singapore.* University of Singapore, Singapore, 1969.
11. S. Selvadurai, Ani bin Arope, Nik Hassani bin Mohammad, *Socio-Economic Study of Padi Farms in the Kemubu Area of Kelantan,* 1968, p. 91. Ministry of Agriculture and Co-operatives, Kuala Lumpur, 1969.
12. Udhis Narkswadi, S. Selvadurai, *Economic Survey of Padi Production in West Malaysia, Report no. 1, Selangor,* p. 143, table 37. Ministry of Agriculture and Co-operatives, Kuala Lumpur, 1967.
13. Udhis Narkswasdi, S. Selvadurai, *Economic Survey of Padi Production in West Malaysia, Report no. 2, Collective Padi Cultivation in Bachang Malacca,* pp. 144–146. Ministry of Agriculture and Co-operatives, Kuala Lumpur, 1967.
14. S. Selvadurai, Ani bin Arope, Nik Hassani bin Mohammad, *Socio-Economic Study of Padi Farms in the Kemubu Area of Kelantan,* 1968, p. 91, *op. cit.*
15. Ruth Benedict, *The Chrysanthemum and the Sword,* pp. 66–67. Routledge and Kegan Paul, London, 1967.
16. Ichiro Kawasaki, *Japan Unmasked,* p. 188. Charles E. Tuttle, Tokyo, 1970.
17. Nyozekan Hasegawa, *The Japanese Character* pp. 16–17. Tr. John Bester. Kodansha International, Tokyo, 1965.
18. Hugh Clifford, *Studies in Brown Humanity,* pp. 195–196, *op. cit.*
19. Salvador de Madariaga, *Englishmen, Frenchmen, Spaniards.* Oxford University Press, London, 1949, p. 37.
20. Syed Hussein Alatas, *Siapa Yangs Jalah.* Pustaka Nasional, Singapura. 1972.
21. *Report of the Rice Cultivation Committee,* vol. I, p. 53. Federated Malay States Government Press, Kuala Lumpur, 1931.
22. Udhis Narkswasdi, S. Selvadurai, *Economic Survey of Padi Production in West Malaysia, Report no. 3,* Malacca, p. 35. Ministry of Agriculture and Co-operatives, Kuala Lumpur, 1967.

23.   *Report of the Rice Cultivation Committee,* vol. I, p. 40, *op. cit.*
24.   Udhis Narkswasdi, S. Selvadurai, *Report no. 3, Malacca,* p. 147, *op. cit.*
       In Malacca the average rate of interest from provision shops was 267·5 per
       cent, see p. 157.
25.   *Final Report of the Rice Committee,* p. 16. Federation of Malaya, Government
       Press, Kuala Lumpur, 1956.
26.   For a critical analysis see Syed Hussein Alatas, *The Second Malaysia Plan
       1971–1975: A Critique,* Occasional Paper no. 15, Institute of Southeast
       Asian Studies, Singapore, 1972.

CHAPTER 12

The Disappearance of the Indigenous Trading Class

Historically speaking the Filipino, Javanese and Malay societies possessed a trading class. What happened to this trading class? It was destroyed by European colonialism. The process of destruction started at the beginning of the 16th century with the arrival of the Portuguese. With the Spanish conquest of the Philippines, Filipino trade became more and more restricted to petty inter-island trade. Pedro Chirino, a Jesuit priest sympathetic to the Filipinos, wrote about the flourishing Filipino trade around 1600, five years after the arrival of the Spaniards in 1565. He said the Filipinos were a most shrewd and skilful people in matters of trade.[1] Approximately half a century after the Spanish conquest, Morga had noticed some effects of the conquest on the Filipinos. We have earlier noted the forced labour and delivery of tributes, but a new factor restricting trade was introduced. The natives were not permitted to leave their towns on trading expeditions except with the permission of the Spanish authority.[2] Thus in the course of time more and more of the important trade fell into Spanish hands. We shall in this chapter devote more attention to the Malay and Javanese trading classes. Their trading activity was more extensive and wider in scope than the Filipinos. The Malay and Javanese traders in the 15th and 16th centuries were very influential. Their area of activity was between India and the Moluccas. Javanese sailors were believed to have reached Madagascar. That the Javanese had a sailing and trading community was an obvious fact. More than 50 years ago Schrieke asked why this class of Javanese had disappeared. His answer was only partially true, namely that the ruler of Mataram had prohibited the Javanese to trade in Java.[3]

The same applies to the Malays. With the conquest of Malacca by the Portuguese, and the subsequent growth of Dutch domination, the Malay trading class also disappeared. Thus when the British came to Malaya at the end of the 18th century, they did not find a Malay trading class of comparable status. This was after approximately three centuries of suppression by the Portuguese and the Dutch. In other words, the Malay and Javanese trading classes were eliminated in the course of those three centuries. The elimination of the trading class was not a uniform and simultaneous process. In Java, the elimination was very noticeable in the 17th century; in the Moluccas and Sumatra it occurred much later, and in Patani it was later still. Before we go any further, let us define what we mean by a trading class. By a trading class we mean the community of traders which imported and exported commodities on an independent basis, supplying its own capital, financing transactions, organizing shipping on a big scale, and using the most advanced vessels of the time to reach distant places. When the Europeans arrived in the 16th and 17th centuries, they were one amongst the many independent traders. European mastery in trade had not yet made itself felt. The Dutch control over the region became more effective in the 18th century. By the end of the 19th century, especially after the arrival of the steam boat, European control of the trade in this area became complete. By then the British had appeared on the political scene.

A conceptual clarification is required here regarding the terms "Malay" and "Javanese". By Malay we mean the ethnic group originating in Sumatra using as their mother tongue what is now considered to be Malay and Indonesian. Javanese indicates the ethnic group from the island of Java whose mother tongue was Javanese. This will exclude the inhabitants of West Java and Sunda area, whose mother tongue was Sundanese. Our historical sources referred to the great trading activity of these two groups, the Malays and Javanese. A third group was the Achinese. There were other ethnic groups involved, but mostly in local inter island trade. The Malays and the Javanese were involved in international trade, according to commodity, the nationality of the buyer and seller, as well as to the geographical location. Malay and Javanese traders were known to have been in Surat. In 1604 a Malay ambassador of Johore was in Holland. He returned from Holland to Johore with Matelief in 1606.[4] His trip was probably part of a preparation of the treaty of alliance between Johore and Holland against the Portuguese and the Spaniards.[5] He was probably the first Asian to have visited Western Europe. De Jonge suggested that an extensive trade had been conducted by the Malays since the middle of the 12th century.[6] This was indicated by the extent to which the Malay language had spread. We shall primarily be concerned here with the 17th and 18th centuries.

In a Dutch report available in 1603, the writer, probably a Mr. Stalpaert van der Wiele, discussing the different places and trading opportunities for the Dutch, mentioned Kedah as an excellent trading town. Johore and Patani were referred to as trading towns and the inhabitants of Johore traded a lot in Banda. The increasing trade of the Malays in Macassar was due to the Portuguese actions in Malacca which impeded trading there. The report noted that the Malays in Macassar carried on big business. They exported whole boatloads to China.[7] Around the middle of the 17th century observers were impressed by the growth of trade in Banten, Java. The people of Banten carried out a busy and lively trade, with the assistance of the English and the Danes, with Persia, Surat, Mocha, Corommandel, Bengal, Tonkin, Siam, China, Manila, and even Japan.[8] Jan van Gorcum, the Dutch governor of Ambon, cited in a letter to the Governor-General Carpentier in 1626, the view of the local ruler that the Malays and the Javanese had been trading in Macassar a century before the Dutch. This was in response to the Dutch attempt to ask the local ruler to prohibit them from trading.[9] In a similar letter of 1627, he noted the great profit made by the Malays and the traders of Macassar from the spice trade.[10] In a report on the situation in Macassar of 1637, the Dutch merchant, Hendrik Kerckringh, said the following: "The Malays there were held in good esteem. They were people of great means and their homes were built amongst the houses of the Macassarese in the village."[11] He then mentioned their trade in rice, clothes, porcelain and spices, and the seasonal voyages of their junks.

In a letter of 1638 to his superiors in Holland, the Dutch Governor-General in Java Antonio van Diemen cited how the big boats of the Malays and the Javanese from Banten and Mataram escaped their blockade in East Indonesia.[12] He also mentioned Kedah and Perak as places frequently visited. The Bugis, Malay and Javanese traders had exported a considerable amount of tin from these places. In 1649, the Governor-General Van der Lijn reported on the events in his area. He noted that the Dutch had obtained the agreement of the ruler of Acheh to prohibit Javanese, Chinese, Malay, and other traders, from trading in Perak and the entire West coast of Sumatra.[13] In numerous historical records of the 16th, 17th, and 18th centuries we find mention of Javanese and Malay traders as people who conducted business on an equal footing. One and a half century earlier Tom Pires mentioned the Malay and Javanese traders in places he had visited. He said that the people of Indragiri in Sumatra were accustomed to trade. During his time, Indragiri, Kampar and Jambi were the objects of much of the trading activity focused on Malacca. All these three places were under Malacca.[14] In almost the same period, 1518, Duarte Barbosa said that the city of Malacca was the richest sea port with the greatest number of wholesale merchants and abundance of shipping and trade in the whole world.[15] He mentioned among others, Malay and Javanese traders. Javanese trading activity according to Barbosa extended from the Moluccas to Bengal, Malabar, Pegu and Cambay. The junks from Java, which were different from the Portuguese junks, were built with thick timber.

In these junks they brought rice, beef, sheep, swine, deer, salt-meat, fowls, garlic, onions, weapons, spears, daggers and many other small articles. To the Indonesian islands they brought cotton goods of all kinds, quicksilver, wrought copper, bells and basins, porcelain, and Chinese coins. Barbosa mentioned the Malay traders, their language and social customs. De Barros, another Portuguese observer in the same period, noted how after the Malays were cast out by the Portuguese in 1511, they sought new settlements along the coast, taking the best ports for trade and navigation, not used by the local natives and made themselves masters.[16] Some Malay traders remained in Malacca but many of them moved out; others remained in Macassar. The Dutch reports on the activity of the Malays and the Javanese in East Indonesia a century later pointed to the fact that it was a gradual build-up from the preceding century. As Portuguese control around Malacca became more effective, the centre of activity shifted to East Indonesia. The retreat and the final elimination of the Malay and Javanese trading classes independently conducting international trade was correlative with European might in the locality. By the end of the 18th century, both in Malaya and Indonesia the indigenous trading class of independent international wholesale traders, who financed their own activity, organized their own shipping, on equal terms with other traders of the time, had disappeared. The reasons for this will be discussed later.

Schrieke commented as follows on the extent of Javanese trade: "The Javanese shipping trade took place within the Indonesian Archipelago including Farther India, and was there very heavy. The evidence for that is to be found in abundance in the Portuguese literature and the 17th century documents of the Dutch Company."[17] Of the Javanese port of Jaratan in 1600, the Dutch admiral van Heemskerck observed that it was the best and most efficient in the whole of Java. The language of the business contract was Malay.

The Javavese, Malays, Arabs, the Portuguese and Guijarah's were busy with the Banda trade.[18] Of Japara, Gresik and Surabaya, the "Account of Some Wars in the Indies", of 1622, noted the following: "From these places above mentioned, namely Grise, Jaratan, and Sedayu, great commerce is carried on at sea on all parts of the Indies, for they have a multitude of ships. In those places there can be a thousand and more boats of twenty, fifty, to two hundred ton, with which they steadily carry on their trade, and it must be taken into account that one never sees half the ships at home, for they sail with the monsoons. With the eastern monsoon they go to the Straits of Malacca, Sumatra, Palembang, Borneo, Patani, Siam, and a hundred other places too many to tell. With the western monsoon they go to Bali, Bantam, Bima, Solor, Timor, Alor, Salayar, Buton, Buru, Banggai, Mindanao, the Moluccas, Ambon, and Banda, which has now been taken from them. Also to the islands of Kai, Aru, Ceram, and other places too many to relate where they do business in bartering goods and make at least two or three hundred per cent profit before they return home." [19] Of Tuban the journal of the second Dutch voyage to the Indies (1601) said the following: "In this city dwell very many noblemen who do great trade in the buying and selling of silk, camlet, cotton cloth, and also pieces of cloth which they wear on their bodies, some of which are made there. They have ships that they call junks, which ships are laden with pepper and taken to Bali, and they exchange it for pieces of simple cotton cloth, for they are made there in quantity, and when they have exchanged their pepper there for that cloth, they carry the same to Banda, Ternate, the Philippines, and also to other surrounding islands more, and exchange the cloth in turn for mace, nutmeg, and cloves, and being laden therewith they sail home once more. The ordinary man occupies himself with fishing and tending his animals, for there is much livestock there." [20]

The effectiveness of Javanese and Malay trade could be judged by the fact that foreign traders were dependent on them for shipping. Another indication was the position of the Chinese traders in this pre-colonial time. They did not occupy a strong intermediary position in the trade structure of the period; they were just one of the traders. The position was then reversed. On Chinese trade Schrieke noted the following: "Partly as a result of the demands of the Gujarati served by Japanese shipping, the direct trade of the Chinese on the Moluccas mentioned by Barros, which judging from what can be deduced from the Chinese records of 1349, 1425–1432, and 1436 must have developed in the course of the 14th century and probably was continued until in the first half of the 15th century, was not able to maintain itself in the competition with the Javanese and Malay traders who were also carrying spices to Malacca and was already a thing of the past long before the coming of the Portuguese in 1511. At that time the Chinese went no further than Grise, which had them to thank for its rise around 1400."[21] The Malays and Javanese of that period had thus a strong trading class, and a strong control on shipping. In 1625, an English merchant, Sihordt observed: "The ones who sail these junks [from Macassar to the Moluccas] were most of them Malays from Patani, Johore, and other places who lived in Macassar by many thousands and controlled most of the shipping in all directions; few Macassarese travel by sea to distant places, but busy themselves with proas and small ships in the places lying around Celebes."[22] The shifting of the Malay traders to Macassar, as noted earlier was due to European encroachment. "At the coming of the Portuguese in the beginning of the 16th century, when Malays from Malacca and later Johore, and Javanese controlled the spice trade, Macassar did not yet play a role of any importance in the Indonesian Archipelago. As a result of the treatment they experienced in Malacca, some Malays had in the course of time emigrated to Macassar, which became a base for shipping on the Moluccas for them. The immigration of Malays increased after Achin in a number of expeditions had destroyed Johore and pretty much brought the peninsular of Malacca to submission. Finally, the Dutch Company's blockade of Malacca was also a factor."[23]

The Dutch Governor-General Hendrik Brouwer in 1634, noted the migration of Malay and Javanese traders to Macassar. The Malays came from Johore, Pahang and Lingga, while the Javanese came from Gresik, Giri, Jaratan, Sedayu and many other places.[24] Relations between the Dutch and the Sultan of Macassar were strained, owing to the liberal trade policy followed by the latter. The Dutch Governor-General Specx considered Macassar and Banten as the obstacles to the establishment of Dutch power and the development of its trade in the Malay Archipelago because they attracted all foreign and Muslim nations to their countries to trade. Macassar was described as a country allowing free and open trade, giving good treatment and demanding small tolls.[25] The idea of a liberal trade policy was thus not a new one. Raffles only repeated a policy which was practised centuries before him by some indigenous rulers. More than a century earlier before the

Portuguese conquest, Malacca similarly carried out a liberal trade policy. It took great pains to be efficient and conciliatory in trade demands. The following description illustrates this: "The goods were bought at the price agreed upon and then divided among the group of buyers in proportion to the share each had in the purchase. In Malacca, therefore, price formation was not entirely free, as it was in many other parts of Asia, but neither was the price dictated from above by the sultan. The Malaccan method meant that business was transacted quickly under conditions which were very favourable to the Malaccan merchants, while the vendors had no cause for dissatisfaction either. It was an established custom that the first ship to arrive was also first to be discharged. In this way the sellers disposed of their merchandise quickly and, since prices were generally well known in Malacca, they were not underpaid either. The whole system was aimed at reducing to a minimum the time required for doing business. The local merchants themselves played a part in this organization and had some hand in the imposition of the customs duties, for which there were fixed rules and fixed rates. Here too we see efforts being made to promote swift and efficient settlement. A committee of merchants was on guard against inflation. It could be said therefore that in Malacca the merchants did have some effect on the course of trade." [26]

Willem Lodewycksz, the author of the account of the first Dutch voyage to the East Indies under Cornelis de Houtman in 1595–1597, mentioned the Malays and the Indians (Klings) of Banten as traders who loaned money on interest for voyages and bottomry. The Gujarati Indians were commonly used as boat crews because they were poor, and were the ones who borrowed money for trade. [27] The role of the Javanese and the Malays in the trade of the period was clear. That Malay was the lingua franca, the official language of contracts and diplomatic correspondence showed the extent of Malay influence in trade and commerce. The position of Malay as a dominant language was however not conditioned by the State of Malacca in the 15th century. Two centuries and more after the disappearance of the Malay State of Malacca, Malay was still the dominant language of trade and diplomacy. The reasons were as follows: Malay predominance in shipping; the great influence of Malay traders; the great influence of Malay speaking coastal trading ports, and the migrating inclination of the Malays. Without a corresponding strength in the actual economic and political situation at that period, it would have been impossible for the Malay language to have attained such an influential status.

The elimination of the Malay and Javanese trading class was a gradual process started in the 17th century by the Dutch in Indonesia, the Portuguese in Malaya and to some extent by the local ruler in Java. By the end of the 18th century there were fewer and fewer centres of trade and the trading class dwindled. In the 18th century the Malay and Javanese trade which escaped the Dutch control was centred in Riau. It was to this place that Chinese and English traders came to exchange their goods. The Dutch Governor of Malacca, P. G. de Bruijn, appealed to the Governor-General in Batavia to allow him to develop Malacca as an exchange port, lest the Bugis might establish elsewhere an exchange port after the Dutch had driven them away from Riau in 1784.[28] Riau was perhaps the last significant trading centre and exchange port maintained by indigenous rulers and independent Malay traders. By this time the internationality of the trade had been transformed. Danish, Persian, Gujarati, Portuguese, Japanese, Arab, English, Dutch, Malay Javanese, Chinese and other traders who used to gather in the port of Banten in the 16th century as a group, were no longer there. The radius of direct indigenous trade was confined to the Archipelago. Javanese and Malay traders were no longer directly buying from India. They no more reached India. What were the events that shrunk the size of the class, that transformed their function, and eventually that eliminated them as a class?

For this we have to go back to the Dutch policy in the 17th century and onwards. Had the Portuguese been alone in this region, they would have stuck to Malacca, Timor and one or two other places. The Portuguese were not in a position to expand and impose their rule throughout the entire Malay Archipelago. It was the Dutch who did so.[29] Portuguese domination was confined to Malacca and the adjacent region. It was not in a position to subdue Johore, but merely to sack it. It was never able to control Riau or Sumatra. Without the Dutch the Malay and Javanese states would have continued to exist and the trading class would not have disappeared.[30]

The modus operandus was conspicuous in the 17th century Java, this time from the influential state of Mataram. But before this let us note the antecedents observed a century earlier by Tom Pires. It was a common feature that a conflict of interest occurred between the trading community at the coastal areas and the nobles and business men of the interior. Thus Pires noted that the Kingdom of Pasai in Sumatra had large towns with many inhabitants in the interior where important people of breeding lived. These sometimes disagreed with Pasai over pepper, silk and benzoin but the wishes of Pasai prevailed.[31] Similarly, Tom Pires observed between 1512 and 1515 the power of the Muslim coastal rulers "who are powerful in Java and have all the trade because they are lords of the junks and people".[32] The process of Muslim domination was described by Tom Pires. "At the time when there were heathens along the sea coast of Java, many merchants used to come, Parsees, Arabs, Gujaratees, Bengalees, Malays and other nationalities, there being many Moors among them. They began to trade in the country and to grow rich. They succeeded in way of making mosques, and mollahs came from outside, so that they came in such growing numbers that the sons of these said Moors were already Javanese and rich, for they had been in these parts for about seventy years. In some places the heathen Javanese lords themselves turned Mohammedan, and these mollahs and the merchant Moors took possession of these places."[33]

It was these coastal trading states which were subsequently ruined by the Dutch during the Mataran war in the 17th century. The turning point in Dutch colonial history occurred in 1676 with the entry of admiral Cornelis Speelman into the Javanese civil war on the side of Mataram against Taruna Jaya, the prince from Madura. Taruna Jaya and his allies had broken the power of Mataram. Bit by bit its territory fell into their hands. In the beginning the Dutch remained outwardly neutral. The capital Mataram itself was sacked. Finally in December 1679 Taruna Jaya surrendered to the Dutch. He was handed to the youthful King of Mataram, Amangkurat II, who personally stabbed Taruna Jaya to death. This whole event considerably extended the Dutch power in Java. The once powerful state of Mataram became dependent on the Dutch. Speelman extracted a great many concessions from the Mataram ruler in exchange for his assistance in saving his throne. Apart from an enormous bill which he presented, Speelman claimed the mortgage of all the ports in East Java and directed that their income should go to the Dutch East India Company. The residents of Mataram and the area under its jurisdiction were not to sell rice except to the Company or those approved by it. The Ruler of Mataram was also forbidden to import and sell Indian and Persian goods, and opium, from anyone except the Company. "By this regulation," said de Jonge, "the entire east-coast of Java was brought under the power of the Company's system of monopoly."[34] By the use of sheer brute force, the Dutch East India Company secured for itself an advantageous position. Independent Javanese merchants and financiers could not operate under such a setting. The Javanese trading class could not thrive.

Already much earlier, Amangkurat I, Ruler of Mataram, had restricted the trading activities of his subjects. He prohibited his Javanese subjects from sailing abroad, and controlled the major import and export business himself. As van Goens noted, he wanted others to come to him.[35] He controlled the sale of rice. But this monopoly was probably a reaction to the Dutch in Batavia. By centralizing such activities he made himself, but not the Javanese trading section, economically more powerful. This was one of the reasons why more and more Javanese traders left Mataram, a sizable area of Java, and spread throughout other areas. Subsequent Dutch monopoly and control over the area speeded up the process of elimination.

In addition to the above, there were the internal wars in Java such as the one which dragged three-quarters of Java into it, the Mataram war of the 17th century. This war had caused the ruin of towns and villages, starvation, destruction of food crops, forced migration of the population, heavy taxation, death, diseases, and the decline of trade. The Dagh Register of 1627 noted the following: "Owing to the internal wars and the great loss of life, the part of Java subject to the [ruler of] Mataram is much depopulated, many good trading towns situated on the coast are deserted, agriculture is neglected, and a very large proportion of the people is reduced to penury, so that Mataram's trade was insignificant this year. In the ten months since January only a scant twelve hundred tons of rice were received from there at Batavia, besides a few other necessaries."[36] The destruction and desolation continued throughout the 18th century. According to Schrieke "War on any appreciable scale was for the Javanese an economic catastrophe."[37] This was the internal event which contributed to the elimination of the Javanese trading class aside from the direct policies of the Javanese rulers and the Dutch East India Company. We shall now discuss the modus operandi. The best indications of this were the treaties engineered by the Dutch with the local rulers.

The first treaty made with a Malay state of the Peninsula which affected the Malay trading class was the one between Johore and the Dutch East India Company in April, 1685. It allowed the Dutch a monopoly of the trade in important commodities along the coast of Siak, with an unlimited number of boats, without payment of toll. This monopoly covered tin and gold. The treaty mentioned the role of the Johore subjects. They were free to trade along the river in provisions, salt, fish, rice and other Javanese items sold there.[38] In April 1689 the treaty was tightened further. Other European nations and Moors (Arab, Indian, Turkish and Persian Muslims) were not allowed to trade in Johore and Pahang. The Moors were accused of draining away the profit which rightly belonged to the people of Johore.[39] Later in the 18th century, after the Dutch had occupied Malacca, an agreement with Perak was repeated in March, 1753. Only the Dutch East India Company was able to buy the tin from Perak. The Sultan of Perak was to direct all boats leaving his kingdom to approach first the Dutch stations for inspection.[40] In November 1754 the treaty with Johore which included Pahang and Trengganu, stipulated Malacca as the only source for its import of wool and silk.[41] The Company was in a much stronger position to impose its will. In the first two treaties with a Malay state, Johore, in May and September, 1606, Malacca was to be returned to the Sultan of Johore. After the defeat of the Portuguese in 1641, the Dutch permanently occupied Malacca.

Johore was not then considered a vassal state. It conducted direct negotiations with the Dutch authority in Holland as evidenced by the embassy which arrived in Holland in 1604. The ambassador, Megat Mansur, died on the way but he was accompanied by Inche Kamar.[42] Inche Kamar was the first South-east Asian, if not the first Asian to have visited Western Europe. He returned to Johore in 1606, with Admiral Matalief. One hundred and fifty years later the situation had changed all over the Archipelago. Dutch monopoly extended with Dutch power. By the end of the 18th century, the downfall of Mataram, Malacca, Banten and other coastal states, as well as the various sultanates in Sumatra, had caused major structural changes in the Malay and Indonesian world which we shall discuss later. An essential cause of this major structural change was the Dutch hold over the trade of the Archipelago, as illustrated in a series of agreements. Basically it was the same with all the states in the Archipelago; the tone and content of the agreement depended on the size and strength of the other party. Thus in the contract with the Yang Dipertuan of Trusan on the West coast of Sumatra, which was revised and tightened in February, 1755, His Majesty was made aware of full obedience to the Company, of His duty to develop the cultivation of pepper, to sell all the products of His land to the Company, to ask permission from the commander at Padang if He wanted to send His boats further than Chingkuk Island.[43]

During the latter part of the 18th century, the Dutch treaties with the Malay states such as Selangor and Pahang, included a clause forbidding entry of Chinese junks to these states, apart from the customary monopoly rights. In the agreement with Johore of November, 1784, Johore, Pahang and Riau were made even more subservient to the Dutch. The Bugis had assumed power in Riau and fought against the Dutch. Riau was abandoned by the Bugis in October, 1784. The Dutch took it and imposed a treaty of capitulation on the Sultan of Johore and Riau, Sultan Mahmud. A curious part of the treaty was the financial compensation for the Dutch Commander for not plundering and burning Riau. The Sultan was to bear part of the war expenses.[44] The once powerful Mataram one and a half centuries previously had suffered the same destiny as Riau. It fell into Dutch hands. In December, 1749, the dying ruler of Mataram, exhausted by the civil war, unconditionally ceded his territory to the Dutch Company, five days before he died. To appease the contenders and to maintain its supremacy, the Dutch eventually divided Mataram into three sultanates. Everywhere it was the internal dissension between states or powerful individuals within the states which allowed the Dutch to execute its policy of divide and rule, the favourite policy of the Company, as van Deventer put it.[45]

In the treaty of February, 1755, with Sultan Hamangku Buwana of Jogjakarta, a state carved out of the old Mataram, a pledge was made by the Sultan to sell to the Company all moveable products at fixed prices. He also pledged to care for the proper delivery and cultivation of the prescribed crops.[46] The treaty which the Dutch at Malacca made with the adjacent principality of Rembau and Klang stipulated that all the tin from Linggi, Rembau and Klang should be sold to the Company at fixed prices. No boat, whoever owned it, was allowed to sail from the North to the South or the other way round passing Malacca, without coming for a permit to Malacca itself on its way. There was the customary prohibition to trade with other European nations. The treaty also stipulated that it was the duty of the inhabitants to be law abiding and avoid piracy, in return the Company would offer her "favourable and fatherly protection".[47] Included in the report of the Dutch Governor of Malacca Balthasar Bort to his successor, Jacob Jorisz Pits, in October, 1678, was the treaty imposed upon Nanning and the surrounding villages. This area was to pay an annual tithe from the rice fields as well as fruits, betel and pepper. There was a sales tax of 10 per cent of the price in the transaction between the inhabitants. If a Minangkabau inhabitant of Nanning died without an heir, the Company would take half the property and the Captain of Nanning the other half. If he had heirs, the Company would take one tenth, and the Captain half of the property.[48] This was a sure way of impoverishing the Minangkabau property owners while enriching their captain and the Dutch Company.

Even the fowls of Nanning were coveted by the Company. "If the inhabitants of Nanning wish to depart from their dwelling place and go elsewhere, they must show said collector a permit in writing from the Captain and stamped with the seal of the Company, together with a fowl as a present from each person for the profit of the Honourable Company aforesaid."[49] The inhabitants were not permitted to trade with any foreign nation directly or indirectly. They were bound to bring their goods down to the Malacca river only.[50] In the course of the 17th and 18th centuries, the Dutch had succeeded in bringing about hundreds of such restrictive agreements with the indigenous chiefs and rulers throughout the entire region from Malacca to Ternate. During this period the Dutch East India Company emerged as the most formidable single power. It fought and won the greatest number of wars by any single power. It encouraged conflict in some areas and peace in others. By the end of the 18th and the beginning of the 19th century, the rise of Dutch power in Indonesia had brought about a number of novel structural changes in the society of the region. For the first time in the history of the region, there was a power strong enough to dominate the entire Archipelago. This power was highly centralized and maintained a remarkable cohesiveness for more than two centuries until the outbreak of the Second World War.

The first major change was in the class structure of the area. An independent trading class operating at the highest level of business was eliminated. The elimination was not brought about by the downfall of one state such as Malacca or Mataram. The trading class and centres of trade could shift. The elimination was brought about by the grinding and steadily expanding Dutch power which eventually annihilated the numerous states of Indonesia and kept some intact as a tool of the Dutch administration. The Dutch monopoly of buying and selling important commodities made an independent, high level, internationally operating, indigenous trading class superfluous. Its function was taken over by the Dutch Company. Indigenous traders were pushed into restricted internal trade at a subsidiary level. Another great change accomplished by the Dutch which was inimical to the development of a strong indigenous trading class, was the conversion of indigenous rulers and chiefs into suppliers and supervisors for the Dutch Company. The rulers and the nobility were made agents of the Dutch Company. They supervised the cultivation of cash crops and mining and they supplied the Company with the products. Thus they became part of a consortium with vested interest in the Dutch Company. Some of them, as a number of 19th century reports indicated, became oppressive to their subjects. It was this institutionalization of the rulers and nobility as the business agents of the Dutch Company, together with the monopoly and restriction, which eliminated and prevented a re-emergence of an independent and powerful trading class.

The sociological mechanism preventing the emergence of this kind of trading class was illustrated by the Sultanate of Banten and its dependency Lampong at the end of the 18th century. Our account is based on the biography of Nakoda Muda, a Malay pepper trader, by his son, written in approximately 1788. Nakoda Muda and his family revolted and killed the Dutch soldiers who arrested them on an unfounded accusation that Nakoda Muda traded with the English. After being honoured by the Sultan, Nakoda Muda was humiliated by the Dutch. He and his family was tricked on board a Dutch naval vessel and thereafter arrested. They escaped and killed the Dutch soldiers and thereafter proceeded to the English settlement at Bengkulu to seek asylum which was granted to them. In this biography we get a glimpse of the role of the Sultan of Banten. The Malay traders in Lampong could buy the pepper for 7 *reals* a *bara*. They sold it to the Sultan of Banten for 12 *reals* and the Sultan sold it to the Dutch for 20 *reals*. Whatever the quantity of pepper brought to Banten, the Sultan would buy it all. The traders were not allowed to sell it directly to the Company. The sentence for such an offence was death.[51] The Company in turn found it convenient to deal with the Sultan. The decision regarding prices always came from above. The Sultan was the biggest intermediary trader in the state. By dealing directly with small traders who were under his control, he had no need of other big traders in the state. In other areas where there was no more a sultan or raja, the Dutch transferred the function to the Regent of a province.

As to the import of major commodities, this was also directly controlled by the Dutch. They were the sole major importers on the spot. Everybody had to buy from the Company. Hence in the import business there was no scope either for a powerful indigenous trading class to emerge. Whatever traders were left operated at the lowest level of supply and distribution. The scene in Banten had drastically changed from the situation which had prevailed in the 16th and part of the 17th century when Banten was a flourishing international centre of trade. No more were traders of different nationalities assembled in Banten. No more were there Javanese and Malay traders importing and exporting with distant countries, financing expeditions, organizing their own shipping and acting as independent traders, selling to customers and buying from sources of their choice. This was the Banten observed by Tom Pires at the beginning of the 16th century. At that time the role of the Sultans was different. Their revenue came from taxes; they did not monopolize business. They knew too well that if they did so the traders would migrate to other parts. It was in their interest to attract traders. This was the reason why most of the states in the area had not imposed the policy of monopoly and price control which the Dutch did. Furthermore none of the states was strong enough in the 15th century to dominate the entire region as the Dutch Company eventually did, for a monopoly policy could only work if a substantial part of the region fell under the domination of the monopoly authority.

Another significant factor which emerged from our historical study was an event which changed the course of history in the Archipelago. The growth and expansion of Dutch power in the 17th and 18th century arrested the development of a process already noticeable in the 15th century, namely the rise of commercial coastal states. In the 15th and 16th centuries, a number of Muslim coastal states which revolved around commerce came into being: Malacca, Banten and Demak, preceded by Pasai and Perak. Acheh in the 16th century was an influential state, extending its influence along the west coast of Sumatra and parts of the Malay Peninsula. With their own independent states to back them up, the Malays were provided with opportunities for demonstrating their ability which were subsequently curbed by the Portuguese and Dutch powers. The extent of their involvement is reflected in the following account: "Achinese ships sailed to India and even ventured as far as the Red Sea, while not only Gujarati merchant ships but also Turkish vessels from Egypt came to Achin. As a matter of fact we know that as early as 1346, Ibn Battuta, returning from Zaitun (Chuanchow), went to Sumatra in a junk manned by Malays, and he mentions Malays among the traders who frequented Calicut, on the Malabar Coast, at that time. He also found Malays along the coast of Bengal, where they had settled. In 1440 'Abd arRazzaq met with Malays even at Hormuz.

Much earlier, Idrisi, writing in 1154, had stated that Malay ships, or at least ships from the 'Zabag Islands', regularly fetched iron from the Sofala Coast of eastern Africa."[52] By the end of the 18th century the entire Indonesian world had been transformed with Acheh as the last bastion of resistance against Dutch power which dragged on until the power of Acheh was broken at the end of the 19th century.[53]

The loss of independence, just at the time when the commercial coastal states were emerging, eliminated numerous activities connected with these states and with them the classes and occupational groups associated with them. From the point of view of the development of this region it was thus a terrific set back. Let us cite an example. The loss of a state meant the loss of the army belonging to that state. This meant the loss of opportunities for the indigenous weapon industry. This subsequently led to the disappearance of the weapon craftsmen as a class. In the 15th century Java was exporting weapons. By the 19th century there was no trace left of this export industry. The only export industry which grew and developed was the cultivation of cash crops since this was demanded by the colonial power; hence the expansion of the peasantry and the shrinking of the other classes. Thus colonial rule had effected a restructuring of the indigenous economy long before the advent of modern capitalism in the nineteenth century. This restructuring of the economy was attended by the destruction of the trading class and a number of occupations. The process was gradual and affected each area differently. By the end of the 17th century the influence of once seafaring Javanese of Mataram was no longer felt in Java. In his letter of 1657, the Regent of Japara requested the Dutch Govenor-General Maetsuijker to assist the Ruler of Mataram by providing Dutch pilots for his commercial boats sailing along the coast of Java. He said that "the sea is large and the Javanese cannot sail it".[54] The Dagh-Register of 1677, twenty years later compared the inhabitants of Banten and the eastern Javanese of Mataram. The Javanese of Mataram "besides their great ignorance at sea, were now completely lacking in vessels of their own, even for necessary use."[55]

It was true that the migration of the seafaring Javanese to Macassar was the result of the policy of the Ruler of Mataram. Amangkurat I. But had the Dutch not intervened on Mataram's behalf in the civil war between the commercial coastal principalities and the interior agrarian Mataram, seeking to impose its rule by crippling the seaport towns, it would have been defeated as events subsequently showed. It would be the often recurring instance of one state formation succeeded by another, all indigenous without the attending destruction of classes and occupation groups.

Without the Dutch in Batavia, the Javanese seafaring elements would have entrenched themselves along the coast and succeeded in overthrowing the power of Mataram. What happened subsequently intensified the elimination of the Javanese trading class and its seafaring community. This time it was the Dutch Company which succeeded Mataram. "The dynasty of Mataram, rent by inner discord, was saved from certain downfall, but at the cost of important territorial concessions to the Company in 1677 and 1678. And from that moment on there was a change in the relation between the *susuhunan* and the governor general, who was now called the 'protector', 'father', presently 'grandfather' of the Javanese ruler whereas before he had been called 'brother' even by the coastal regents who had orders to place. At the same time Dutch money was declared legal currency and the Company was granted a monopoly for selling cloth and opium in the ports of Mataram, the latter partly in compliance with the strict order of the Company directors in 1676 to intensify the monopoly."[56]

Power falling into Dutch hands was different from power falling into the hands of an indigenous successor. An indigenous power was generally more liberal in trade. It did not destroy its own trading class throughout the whole area, and continued to use the products of its own industry. It built its own boats, and last but not least, was incapable of imposing a monopoly throughout the major part of Indonesia. It promoted the abilities of its own people even though a tyrant was on the throne. The control on trade imposed by some powerful indigenous ruler was different from that practised by the Dutch. In the 17th century, one of the most exacting rulers, at the height of his power, Sultan Iskandar Muda of Acheh demanded a quarter of the value of the pepper sold by his subjects after the price had been fixed. His tendency was to raise the selling price to foreigners. In 1615, the English obtained a monopoly to buy pepper in Acheh for two years. This agreement was not renewed owing to the opposition from his chiefs and merchants.[57] This was not possible under Dutch rule. Had the Dutch controlled Acheh instead of Iskander Muda, the chiefs and merchants would have been relegated in function and potential to become collectors of pepper on a commission basis, or the Sultan would have been the super middleman as was the case with the Sultan of Banten at the end of the 18th century.

The danger to trade by the rulers who participate directly in it was described by Ibn Khaldun in his book written in 1377. The ruler's participation harmed his subjects, as he was in a position to lower the price when he bought and increase the price when he sold. As it was unlikely for the ruler to tax himself, the state would then lose revenue; his other competitors would be taxed and rendered incapable of competing. Finally he would destroy the incentive to trade and the merchant class itself.[58] This was precisely what the Dutch East India Company did in Indonesia. The chiefs and rulers of independent bearing were gradually changed to those acting as the agents of the Dutch Company. An independent and indigenous trading class operating at the highest level of business was eliminated. A gap emerged in the class structure of indigenous society. Subsequently this gap conditioned the trend of colonial ideological thinking. Native society was considered as alien to business and commerce. Since business and commerce formed part of the colonial capitalist concept of industriousness, a society lacking in such a class was considered indolent. The destruction of the trading class was also accomplished in the Philippines by the Spaniards. The details of the process differed but the basic pattern was common, the strangulation of an independent and leading indigenous trading class. It was a basic element in the colonial system not to share power with the natives in matters of great social significance, such as economic power.

NOTES

1. Pedro Chirino, S. J., *The Philippines in 1600*, p. 240. Tr. Ramon Echevarria. Historical Conservation Society XV, Manila, 1969.
2. Antonio de Morga, *Sucesos de Las Islas Filipinas*, p. 247. Tr. J. S. Cummins, *op. cit.*
3. B. Schrieke, "Javanen als Zee-en Handelsvolk", p. 427. *TITLV*, deel LVIII, 1919.
4. P. Tiele, "De Europeers in den Maleischen Archipel", p. 61. Zevende Gedeelte. 1606–1610. *BTLVNI*, pp. 49–118, vol. VIII, 1884. See also Hendrik P. N. Muller, "The Malay Peninsula in the Past", p. 59. Abstracted and tr. from the Dutch, P. C. H. van Papendrecht. *JSBRAS*, pp. 57–84, no. 67, December, 1914.
5. The Dutch texts of two treaties are in J. K. L. de Jonge, *De Opkomst van Nederlandsch Gezag in Oost-Indie* (1595–1610). vol. 3, 1865, *op. cit.*
6. *Ibid.*, p. 115, (1595–1610), vol. 2, 1864.
7. J. K. J. de Jonge, *op. cit.*, vol. 3, pp. 149–163.
8. *Ibid.*, vol. 6, pp. LXXVII–LXXVIII, 1872.
9. P. A. Tiele, J. E. Heeres, *Bouwstoffen voor de Geschiedenis der Nederlanders in den Indischen Archipel*, p. 109, vol. 2. Martinus Nijhoff, 'S-Gravenhague, 1890.
10. *Ibid.*, p. 113.
11. *Ibid.*, p. 336.

12. *Ibid.*, p. 339.
13. P. A. Tiele, J. E. Heeres, *Bouwstoffen voor de Geschiedenis der Nederlanders in den Maleischen Archipel*, p. 469, vol. 3. Martinus Nijhoff, 'S-Gravenhage, 1895.
14. Tom Pires, *The Suma Oriental*, vol. I, p.153. Tr. A. Cortesao. Hakluyt Society, 2nd Series, no. 89, London, 1944.
15. Duarte Barbosa, *op. cit.*, p.175.
16. In appendix I, Duarte Barbosa, Ibid., p. 243. Extracts from Joao de Barros, "Decadas", Book ix, ch. 3.
17. B. Schrieke, "Javanese Trade and the Rise of Islam in the Archipelago", in B. Schrieke, *Indonesian Sociological Studies*, Part One, p. 19. W. van Hoeve, the Hague, 1955.
18. J. K. J. de Jonge, *op. cit.* (1595–1610), vol. 2, pp. 448–454, 1864.
19. Quoted and translated in B. Schrieke, *op. cit.* p. 20.
20. *Ibid.*, p. 20. Quoted and translated.
21. B. Schrieke, *Ibid.*, p. 25.
22. B. Schrieke, *Ibid.*, p. 66. Quoted and translated from *Daghregister 1625*, p. 125.
23. *Ibid.*, pp. 66–67
24. P. A. Tiele, J. E. Heeres, *op. cit.* vol. II, p. 260.
25. *Ibid.*, p. XLVIII.
26. M. A. P. Meilink-Poelofsz, *Asian Trade and European Influence in the Indonesian Archipelago between 1500 and about 1630*, p. 45. Martinus Nijhoff, the Hague, 1962.
27. Willem Lodewycksz, "D'Eerste Boeck", in G. P. Rouffaer, J. W. Ijzerman (eds.), *De Eerste Schipvaart der Nederlanders naar Oost-Indie onder Cornelis de Houtman 1595–1597*, vol. 1, p. 121. Martinus Nijhoff, S-Gravenhage, 1915.
28. "Trade in the Straits of Malacca in 1785. A Memorandum by P. G. de Bruijn, Governor of Malacca". Tr. Brian Harrison, *JMBRAS*, vol XXVI, pt. 1, July, 1953.
29. The reasons for the Dutch victory against the Portuguese were superior economic resources, manpower and sea-power. "The populations of the two countries were probably roughly equal (1,500,000 to 1,250,000 each); but whereas Portugal had to supply cannon-fodder in the service of Spain before 1640 and against her thenceforward, the Dutch could and did make extensive use of neighbouring German and Scandinavian manpower in their armies and fleets. The disparity in sea-power was even more striking, and was cogently expressed by the great Portuguese Jesuit, Antonio Vieira, in 1649. He estimated that the Dutch possessed over 14,000 vessels which could be used as warships, whereas Portugal did not possess thirteen ships in the same category. The Dutch, he claimed, had a quarter of a million sailors available to man their shipping, whereas Portugal could not muster 4,000. Vieira was evidently exaggerating, but he was not exaggerating very much. A census taken at Lisbon of seamen available for manning the fleet in 1620 listed only 6,260 men for the whole country. At a meeting of the Viceroy's advisory Council at Goa in November 1643 it was stated that there were not sufficient qualified pilots at Lisbon to navigate any ships to India, since all those with adequate qualifications (fewer than ten individuals) were then in the three Indiamen detained by the Dutch blockade at Goa." C. R. Boxer, *The Portuguese Seaborne Empire*, p. 114. Hutchison, London, 1969.
30. A reminder is here necessary. By trading class we mean independent big time traders, financiers, exporters and importers, distributors, not peddlers,

vendors, and village shopkeepers, operating at the fringe of the distribution network.

31. Tom Pires, *The Suma Oriental of Tom Pires*, vol. 1, p. 143, *op. cit.*
32. *Ibid.*, p. 182.
33. *Ibid.*, p. 182.
34. J. K. J. de Jonge, *op. cit.* vol. 7, p. XXXV, 1873. Translation mine.
35. Ryckloff V. van Goens, "Corte Beschrijvinge van 't Eijland Java's", p. 366, *BTLVNI*, vol. 4, 1856.
36. Quoted and translated in B. Schrieke, *Indonesian Sociological Studies*, Part II, p. 149. W. van Hoeve, the Hague, 1957.
37. *Ibid.*, p. 143.
38. E. Netscher, *De Nederlanders in Djohor en Siak*, Bijlagen p. V. Bruining en Wijt, Batavia, 1870.
39. *Ibid.*, Bijlagen p. IX.
40. F. W. Stapel, *Corpus Diplomaticum Neerlando-Indicum*, pp. 1–2, vol. 6. Martinus Nijhoff, 'S-Gravenhage, 1955.
41. *Ibid.*, p. 23.
42. E. Netscher, *op. cit.*, pp. 8–9.
43. F. W. Stapel, *op. cit*, pp. 30–31.
44. *Ibid.*, pp. 549–551.
45. M. L. van Deventer, *Geschiedehis de Nederlanders op Java*, vol. 2, p.188. Tjeenk Willink, Haarlem, 1887.
46. F. W. Stapel, *op. cit.*, pp. 41–45. The prices for different commodities were fixed by the treaty.
47. *Ibid.*, p.187.
48. C. O. Blagden, "Report of Governor Balthasar Bort on Malacca 1678", *JMBRAS*, vol. V, p. 56, August, 1927.
49. *Ibid.*, p. 58.
50. *Ibid.*, p. 59.
51. G. W. J. Drewes, "De Biografie van Een Minangkabause Peperhandelaar in de Lampongs," p. 105, Malay text. *VKITLV*. Vol. 36, Martinus Nijhoff, 's-Gravenhage, 1961. This contains a Dutch translation and the Malay text.
52. B. Schrieke, *Indonesian Sociological Studies*, Part II, pp. 244–245. W. van Hoeve, the Hague, 1957.
53. For an instructive account, see Anthony Reed, *The Contest for North Sumatra*. Oxford University Press/University of Malaya Press, Kuala Lumpur, 1969.
54. *Dagh-Register 1637*, p. 198. Quoted in B. Schrieke, *Indonesian Sociological Studies*, Part I, p. 78, *op. cit.*
55. *Dagh-Register 1677*, p. 436. Quoted *Ibid.*, p. 79.
56. B. Schrieke, *ibid.*, p. 78.
57. P. A. Tiele, "De Europeers in den Maleischen Archipel," *BTLVNI*, vol. xxxvi, p. 243, 1887.
58. Ibn Khaldun,*The Muqaddimah*, pp. 93–95, vol. 2, *op. cit.*

Conclusion

In the twelve preceding chapters we have discussed the image of the Malays, the Filipinos and the Javanese as it evolved from the 16th to the 20th century. The most striking feature of that image is the alleged indolence of the native. We have tried to show that indolence has not been the characteristic of the community. We have also attempted to explain how the idea emerged and its function in the colonial ideology. However there remains one thing to be said. An image or a prejudice need not be entirely devoid of truth. The European colonial image of a lazy, incapable, treacherous and scheming native partly did reflect a section of native society. The natives with whom the European came into close contact in the 19th century, were mainly from the ruling class. By this time the ruling class, or the principal class of native society had undergone a transformation. They were unable to wage war against each other on a sufficient scale which demanded much ingenuity, courage and leadership. They were not in control of major ports of trade which required their interest and vigilance in international commerce. They no longer possessed the independence of their country which required talents of diplomacy and statesmanship. They exerted no influence on the economic activity of their subjects which would have demanded a serious interest in economic growth. Thus the area of interest and the scope for action of the native principal classes had shrunk to such an extent that all that was left was their interest in land and receiving benefits from the colonial rulers.

The number of independent, forceful native rulers and chiefs had been totally decimated by the end of the 19th century. By the middle of the 18th century most of them had disappeared from the scene. Occasional rebellions took place here and there, like the one of Pangeran Diponegoro in Java from 1825 to 1830. The chiefs and rulers who rebelled against the colonial government were all defeated. None of the rebellions were successful. This meant that the ensuing generation of native leaders in areas where colonial control was effective became a passive or docile type. In other areas like trade and the administrative service, the passive and docile type was given the opportunity to develop. Big business and important offices were held by the European ruling class. The process of displacing the natives from the top positions in the political, economic and administrative hierarchies was completed throughout the Archipelago by the 19th century except in places where the colonial government wanted them to be, like the regents in Java, serving as subordinates to the Dutch rulers. All the top positions in the political, economic and administrative hierarchies were reserved for the members of the colonial ruling elite. The result was the blocking of upward mobility amongst the native aspirants. Thus colonial rule had blocked the social mobility of native society. It had restrained the growth of motivation amongst the natives to aspire for a better position in life. This phenomenon was in turn used by the colonial elite as an argument in support of the contention that the natives lacked drive and ambition. They attributed to the natives traits which they had created themselves. After the colonial power destroyed the leading native trading class, the natives were accused of having no interest in trade. What was the effect of colonial rule generated decades or centuries earlier was interpreted as the nature of native society by the colonial observers of the 19th and 20th centuries. This reasoning follows what we shall call the principle of misplaced responsibility.

The principle of misplaced responsibility is based on the following: a situation is created by colonial rule. This situation affected a change in native society, and native society is then blamed for the resultant situation. The best instance was the spread of opium amongst the natives. Opium was consumed before the coming of Western colonial powers. The consumption was confined to native rulers and chiefs and well to do people in the coastal towns. After the Dutch conquest of Malacca in 1641, the Dutch had easier access to the supply from Bengal. Ninety years after this, Baud noted that the consumption of opium in Batavia had become a general public vice (eene algemeene volksondeugd).[1] The Dutch East India Company gradually obtained the monopoly in the opium trade. By 1808 the local authorities were used by the Governor-General Daendels to sell the opium supplied to them by the government. Thus opium was distributed throughout the length and breadth of Java by the government. This was done to prevent smugglers and unauthorised dealers from reaping the profit which the government felt should go to it, and also to ensure that the average

Javanese got his supply. Daendels in his letter to the Dutch Minister of Colonies explained that opium had become a permanent need to the Javanese however harmful the drug was.[2] It was an incontestable fact that the European powers greatly influenced the promotion of the drug, with their bigger boats and more efficient organization. They themselves did not cultivate the habit but they pronounced it as evil while they promoted it. The responsibility for the spread of the habit was misplaced to the consumer who became a victim of colonial manipulation.

A Dutch scholar who did not condemn opium smoking and who even sounded apologetic about the practice admitted that it was the East India Company which increased its import into Java.[3] In 1914 the public revenue of the Netherlands Indies was 281·4 million guilders of which 34·9 millions, or 12·4% were from the sale of opium by the government.[4] The revenue fluctuated but as a single item it was substantial since the 17th century. It was the British, however, who promoted the spread of opium throughout Asia more than any other power known in history. It went to war with China finally to succeed in compelling it to allow the sale of Indian opium by British merchants. In 1729 the export of opium from India to China was 200 chests, each chest containing about 140 pounds of opium. In 1773 the East India Company made their first transaction in opium with China with heavily armed ships. Until the year 1800 opium was considered as medicine in China and its importation did not attract much attention. Thereafter the Chinese Government prohibited its import, realising the moral and financial consequences of its spread as a drug used for pleasure. In 1860, however, it did away with the prohibition as the problem had grown in magnitude owing to the intensive smuggling done by the British with the collaboration of Chinese smugglers. By 1875, the export of opium from British India to China was as many as 85,454 chests worth $10,000,000, of which 8,443 chests were sent to Malacca. During the same year the consumption of opium for medicinal purposes in Great Britain was 165 chests.[5]

Opium was greatly promoted by the British also in the Straits Settlements and the rest of Malaya. So was it in Sarawak and Brunei. Between 1918 and 1921 the entire area of British Malaya which embraced the three Straits Settlements (one of which was Singapore) and the 9 Malay Sultanates, had an opium revenue ranging from 25% to 60% of the total revenue. In 1918 the opium revenue of the Straits Settlements was 60% of the entire revenue and was practically equal to the expenditure. In 1918 the opium revenue of the State of Johore was 46% of the total revenue and covered 72% of the total expenditure.[6] In the Philippines, prior to its annexation by the United States in 1898, a substantial amount of revenue was obtained by farming out the right to sell opium. The United States abolished this and in its place allowed the importation of opium with high customs duty.[7] The difference between the government's policy is revealed by the comparative import figures. While the Philippines as a whole in 1899 imported approximately 120,000 pounds of opium, the Straits Settlements imported from Bengal 10 years earlier more than 1,924,000 pounds (13,749 chests of 140 pounds).[8] In the Straits Settlements the great majority of consumers were Chinese, who assumed the habit after arrival in the Straits. There is an enormous amount of evidence, statistical and otherwise to show that the colonial governments in the Philippines (before the American period), in Indonesia and in Malaysia, greatly promoted the opium trade, throughout the greater part of their history until the outbreak of the Second World War.

Judgements on the principle of misplaced responsibility are involved here. The blame for the increased addiction to the drug was put upon the Asian inhabitants. Although the anti-opium opposition in the West emerged from the time of the Opium War in China (1839–1842) and even earlier, its influence was minimal compared to those in favour of the opium trade. The arguments which they marshalled were as follows: every nation requires a drug; the Oriental opium, the Occidental alcohol. The moderate use of opium is not harmful. The abuse is bad but so is the abuse of alcohol; if you abolish opium, the Oriental will take a worse drug, namely alcohol. Thus, as recently as 1939, a Dutch scholar defended the trade while also paying homage to its suspension. He claimed that the question whether a moderate opium smoker causes more injury to his health than a tobacco smoker, or an alcohol drinker, has not been definitely solved. If he smokes good opium in moderation there is no fear of injury to health for many years. However his ambivalent and hesitant attitude is expressed in the following: "The bad working conditions in the countries in which opium smoking is customary is one of the causes of opium smoking among the workers and the reason for buying bad quality opium which again has an unfavourable influence on the mortality figure. Then comes the fact that opium smoking gives rise to the great danger of addiction. An immoderate drinker *does* sometimes return to the good path but a habitual opium smoker practically never. Everything is therefore to be said for the total suppression in the long run, of the smoking of prepared opium in the world. This is however easier said than done. It appears that man cannot do without a stimulant. If the opium smoker is deprived of his pipe, he will try to satisfy his craving by illicit traffic or by means of another form of luxury. If he chooses hashish or alcohol for instance, the consequences are much worse, so that a substitution of opium by hashish or alcohol is probably the last thing to be desired. Alongside this, it must be taken into account, that the deficiencies in the medical provision of the peoples in those countries where opium smoking is still customary, is a cause why prepared opium is used as a medicine, a fact which also forms an obstacle to a rigorous abolition of the habit."[9]

The above expresses the general trend of thought from the 18th century onwards of those indulging in the opium trade. The native society was blamed for using opium as a medicine, but not the Western society for the same practice. The big-time promoter of the drug, the colonial government was not blamed. Medical opinion on the injurious effect of even moderate addiction was ignored and the fact that the increasing use of opium takes away the appetite was ignored. The fact that both the rich and the poor opium consumers are known to have become emaciated was not considered, while the colonial system of farming out opium, or selling it to merchants led to the intensive promotion activity by this group was not regarded as a decisive factor in its increase. The case of Burma illustrates this point. In the Indo-Chinese districts of British Burma, the action of a government department in promoting the sale of opium had become a public scandal. Prior to the introduction of British rule into Arakan, the punishment for using opium was death. In 1817, a report was issued which stated: "The people were hard-working, sober, and simple-minded. Unfortunately one of the earliest measures in our administration was the introduction of the Abkari rules by the Bengal Board of Revenue. Mr. Hind, who had passed the greater part of his long life amongst the people of Aracan, described the progress of demoralisation. Organised efforts were made by Bengal agents to introduce the use of the drug and to create a taste for it amongst the rising generation. The general plan was to open a shop, with a few cakes of opium, and to invite the young men in and distribute it gratuitously. Then, when the taste was established, the opium was sold at a low rate. Finally, as it spread throughout the neighbourhood, the price was raised and large profits ensued."[10] In this area an observer saw "a fine, healthy generation of strong men succeeded by a rising generation of haggard opium-smokers and eaters, who indulged to such an extent that their mental and physical powers were alike wasted". [11]

From the overwhelming pile of committee reports, newspaper articles, books and private correspondence it is indubitably clear that the colonial power promoted the opium habit on a scale hitherto unknown. Even the defenders of the trade did not contest this. They argued for its perpetuity but they did not deny that they had promoted the trade on a big scale. Not only was the sale of opium promoted, but even the circumstances surrounding such a sale were at times defended against any change. In 1924, the committee appointed by the British Malayan government to enquire into matters relating to the use of opium in British Malaya was opposed to the policy of registering addicts, on the ground that it could affect the free influx of Chinese labour into Malaya. It said: "Any check on a free flow of labour from China would have disastrous effects on the economic position of British Malaya, and these territories would be faced with a steadily dwindling revenue and a steadily increasing expenditure, owing to costly preventive services and establishments required to make the system effective." [12] On this, Willoughby, Professor of Political Science at the John Hopkins University, who had once been the legal adviser to the Chinese government, commented: "It is not always that one finds the economic and financial element in the opium problem so frankly announced." [13] A fully-fledged colonial ideologist was even more frank twenty years earlier. He said: "As far as I am aware, no one has ever tried to make people believe that gambling and opium-selling are licensed in many Far Eastern countries because it is hoped by that means to eradicate those vices; the reason why they are licensed is because the sale of the monopolies produces a good revenue. But although eradication is impossible, a certain degree of control may be effected by granting to some one person or firm the opium and gambling monopoly." [14] This author, with complete disregard for history blamed the Chinese people. Three hundred years of contact with China had taught that no legislation or repression could turn the Chinese away from opium and gambling. [15]

He and others like him have been guilty of making judgements on the basis of misplaced responsibility. Such judgements have not been confined solely to opium comsumption but also extended to cover many other phenomena in South-east Asian history.

Paradoxically, Sinibaldo de Mas, the Spanish colonial writer mentioned before, who was once the Spanish plenipotentiary in

China, complained in 1858 that the Filipinos did not take to opium. He said: "At present opium is little cultivated elsewhere, because it can be grown so very cheaply in India. In the Philippines, the cultivation of it has been prohibited from a fear, as I have before stated, that the natives might take to smoking it, and thus become even more indolent than they already are. For my part, I consider this to be an entirely mistaken policy, for the indolence of the Philippine natives proceeds from their having absolutely no wants whatever, so that if a taste for opium was allowed to spring up amongst them, they naturally would be forced to work, in order to gratify the acquired desire."[16] Thus the natives were blamed not only for what they did but also for what they did not do. In the earlier period of European expansion, the colonial power was unfavourably inclined towards the competing native trading classes. They then destroyed this trading class as the example of the Dutch showed. Thereafter native society was looked down upon for not manifesting commercial values. The succeeding generations of colonial ideologists were often not aware of, or deliberately distorted past history. They condemned certain conditions of native society without taking into account that those conditions were generated by colonialism. While they blamed native society for harbouring these conditions, they credited the colonial government for condemning, often only in theory, these conditions which it had itself generated in earlier periods. Colonialism was not only the imposition of foreign rule for the purpose of extracting economic benefits. It was also an imposition of culture, values, ethics, attitudes and modes of reasoning. The native society was expected to accept these judgements based on misplaced responsibility. The radius of this judgement was wide and the subjects were diverse. Let us take other instances, apart from opium.

First, let us start with slavery by which we mean the condition wherein one human being is in bondage to another for the purpose of supplying labour. Slavery in South East Asia has a different connotation from that in the West. Generally speaking, a slave in South East Asia was a domestic help or a farm assistant integrated into the family organization. The cruel treatment of slaves found in the West Indies and the United States before, had never characterized the South East Asian institution of slavery. Before the coming of the foreigners, both Oriental and European, the main sources of recruitment for slaves had been war and incurred debts. After the coming of the Europeans with their towns and trading posts, the slaves developed into a commercial commodity, an article of export. Organized slave raids increased as the main source of recruitment, accompanied by an increase in inhumane treatment. In his letter of June 22, 1821 to the Duchess of Somerset, Raffles wrote about slavery on the island of Nias. The population was about 230,000, the island about 1,500 sq. miles. The country was highly cultivated, the soil rich, and the people industrious and intelligent.[17] According to Raffles, the slave export from Nias exceeded 1,500 annually. He was informed by the rajas that the commercial export of slaves originated from the foreigners. Many of those rajas took the opportunity to become exporters themselves. Some, as Raffles noted, refused to take part in the slave trade and even refused to allow the transit of slaves from the interior through their own district. In another letter of 1819, Raffles deplored the East India Company's employment of 200 to 300 negro slaves in Sumatra. In Indonesia, the Dutch had been active in commercial slavery since the 17th century. An import duty was introduced at Batavia in 1720. A figure available showed 4,000 slaves per year during the time of Van der Parra. The slaves were mostly employed as domestic servants or hired out for profit by the owners. In 1689, one Dutch lady had 59 slaves in her household. In the household of Van Riemsdijke in 1775 there were about 200 slaves. In 1782, the slaves owned by a deceased were assessed at 33,000 Dutch florins. During the British interregnum in 1816, about 12,000 slaves were counted in Batavia and the surrounding area. The highest figure owned by one person was 165. In the 18th century, and perhaps earlier, the slave population of Batavia far outstripped the free population in number.[18]

Compared to the condition in traditional native societies, two novel sociological factors were found in the colonial territory. The first was that in traditional native society there is no instance of a town where the slaves represented the majority of the population. The second, was that only important rulers and chiefs had a large number of slaves in their possession, not ordinary citizens. In Batavia, the Dutch middle class had a great number of slaves. With the introduction of large scale commercial slavery by the Europeans in the 17th century, came the introduction of laws relating to the treatment and exploitation of slaves, most of whom were obtained through raids. In the words of Raffles on the slavery when the British took over, "These slaves were the property of the Europeans and Chinese alone: the native chiefs never require the services of slaves, or engage in the traffic of slavery."[19] The census taken by the British in 1812–13 is indeed revealing. The second largest single section of the city population of Batavia were slaves. Out of a total population of 47,083, 1,928 were Europeans and 14,239 were slaves. In the environ of Batavia there were 5,244 slaves out of a population of 218,777. The census for the whole of Java and Madura pointed out that the slaves were concentrated in and around the city of Batavia.[20] According to Raffles, there were more than 30,000 slaves throughout Java. A later estimate indicated the Surabaya and Semarang divisions as other points of concentration. It is clear that the degree of slavery was proportionate to the degree of European control of the area.

Many European observers of native society in the 19th and 20th centuries, as suggested earlier, were often not aware of the changes wrought by their compatriots in the earlier centuries. It was these changes which had upset traditional social institutions and generated what appeared as undesirable to the observers of the succeeding centuries. Slavery as they found it in the 19th century was then attributed to the intrinsically savage nature of traditional society. There were no doubt some exceptions like Raffles. The same could be said of native enterprise. The observers of the 19th century and later, by means of the printing press, portrayed native society as decadent and declining, not realizing that what they observed were the effects of earlier European plunder and monopolistic trade policy. As Braddell observed, not one of the flourishing native trading ports in the Indian Archipelago of the 16th, 17th, and 18th centuries was extant in the 19th century. Indiscriminate ruin had fallen on them all.[21] It was the predatory and lawless action of the early European powers which drove many native rulers to piracy and resistance. Braddell has summarized the situation in the following words: "The early Dutch and English appear to have vied with each other in enforcing, under the pretence of treaties, a more strict monopoly of commodities at the ports where their influence was all powerful. On obtaining a territorial position, they forced, under a similar pretext, the production and exclusive sale to themselves, of the produce of the country. This system had the effect of raising the opposition, and at last the deadly enmity, of all classes of the natives. The chiefs saw their ports deserted, their revenues destroyed and their authority relaxed by the overweening arrogance and tyranny of their European visitors, while the people were reduced to a state little better than slavery. The natural resource for the chiefs was piracy. They only followed the example set by the Europeans themselves, in taking possession of whatever they were strong enough to retain. Afterwards, when the Europeans had ruined all the native trading ports in the Archipelago, and had drawn all the available trade to settlements formed by themselves, they became obnoxious to the attacks of those they had driven to such courses. They then gave the name of piracy to the exact course which they had seen no impropriety in following themselves." [22]

So it is with the alleged disinterest of the Malays and the other peoples such as the Filipinos and the Javanese. They were reacting to a situation generated by colonial rule. They were forced to work and denied the complete fruits of their labour. Both the early European and the native rulers subjugated by the Europeans were engaged in accumulating wealth for themselves leaving no room for others to accumulate wealth beyond that necessary for subsistence and comfortable living for the higher classes. For the majority of people there was neither rational motive nor sufficient opportunity to acquire wealth beyond that required for subsistence. In Indonesia, the system of monopoly and forced delivery, the culture system, and subsequently the capitalist organization of crop cultivation and related industries controlled by European investors backed by the government in power, with its numerous rules and regulations in favour of the colonial government, made it impossible for the Indonesians themselves to acquire wealth and prestige comparable to the Dutch and European commercial and industrial men of success. What was actually lacking in the peoples of Indonesia, Malaysia and the Philippines was not so much the will to work as the will to acquire greater and greater wealth in the Western capitalist sense. There was a lack of the aggressive and acquisitive spirit of modern capitalism. This was mistakenly interpreted as indolence by many observers. It is a fact that the peoples of the area during the colonial period had not shown much interest in the kind of capitalistic economic activity introduced by the colonial powers. The question is why should they have been? Why should the Filipinos have been interested in ventures which would enrich the Spaniards? Why should the Javanese have toiled in the Dutch plantation? Why should the Malays have hastened to the mines and the estates when their life in their villages offered greater satisfaction?

It was only when they were judged by the criteria of colonial capitalism that they were found wanting. The ideology of colonial capitalism evaluated people according to their utility in their production system and the profit level. If a community did not engage in activities directly connected with the colonial capitalist venture, that community was spoken of in negative terms.

One final example of the ideology of colonial capitalism was furnished by an author around the turn of the century. It was an unashamed, crude, vulgar, and malicious expression of the ideology accompanied by all the major distortions. We are mentioning this case because the author was not an illiterate layman, a sailor on a quick visit, a small town journalist, or a narrow minded administrator, he was supposed to be a scholar. He was commissioned by the University of Chicago to study the administration of tropical dependencies, in 1901. During his visit to Southeast Asia he wrote a series of articles for magazines in London and New York which he subsequently published as a book. It is here that the nature of ideological distortion manifests itself in an extreme form. Scholarship in this book becomes a joke; all reason disappears. What emerges from the book is hostility and resentment against particular groups. Opinions are suggested which can only be described as totally absurd.

This colonial ideologist said the following of the Malays: "As far as my own observation extends, I should say that the Malay of the Peninsula is the most steadfast loafer on the face of the earth. His characteristics in this respect have been recognized by every-one who has come in contact with him. He will work neither for himself, for the Government, nor for private employers. He builds himself a house of bamboo and attaps, plants enough rice to fill out the menu which stream and forest afford him, and for nine tenths of his waking hours, year in and year out, he sits on a wooden bench in the shade and watches the Chinaman and the Tamil build roads and railways, work the mines, cultivate the soil, raise cattle, and pay the taxes."[23] How could such an author allow his imagination to run wild as to suggest such an absurdity? If the Malays spent nine-tenths of their waking hours sitting on their wooden benches, year in and year out, they would all have died.

Such opinions on the Malays are too mischievous and malicious as to require any serious refutation here. But the interesting thing is the ideological root. The author of the book relied on the opinion of a Resident-General in the annual report of 1901. The report said: "The Government, with a system of taxation which barely touches the Malay, raises a large revenue and incurs a large expenditure in developing the resources of the country by means of roads, railways, irrigation works, and so forth. But the labor force engaged in their execution is supplied almost entirely by foreign coolies under the superintendence of foreign engineers and superintendents. The Malay, with his rooted disinclination to steady work of any kind, will neither give his work to the Government undertakings, nor to mines or plantations."[24]

As is apparent the Malays were judged to be opposed to steady work because they avoided colonial capitalist ventures. Here also on the question of taxation, is revealed the inability of the colonial ideologist to evaluate in contextual terms. The majority of the Malays were subsistence farmers and fishermen; their earnings were very modest. If they did not pay much tax, they did not benefit either from the roads and railways. It is a fact that the predominantly Malay east coast was greatly neglected by the colonial government. Why should the Malays have been expected to pay taxes to a government which neglected them and one which served the interests of colonial capitalism? The towns which were given the most attention during the colonial period were in the tin-mining and rubber growing areas.

I have sufficiently exposed the roots of the image of the lazy native to demonstrate that it was an important element in the ideology of colonial capitalism. It was a major justification for territorial conquest, since the degraded image of the native was basic to colonial ideology. Imperialists of different times and nationalities have shared many common ideas. Thus the American social philosopher Benjamin Kidd, an imperialist, compared the inhabitants of the tropics to a child, in the same manner as some Dutch imperialists considered the Javanese.[25] Similarly he claimed there could never be a good native government.[26] Like the Spanish friars who blamed the Filipinos for the moral deterioration of the Spaniards, Kidd blamed the natives for pulling the white man down. This served as the ideological justification for bad colonial government. Kidd went to the extent of saying we had no right to expect a good European colonial government. He gave the followings reasons: "In climatic conditions which are a burden to him; in the midst of races in a different and lower stage of development; divorced from the influences which have produced him, from the moral and political environment from which he sprang, the white man does not in the end, in such circumstances, tend so much to raise the level of the races amongst whom he has made his unnatural home, as he tends himself to sink slowly to the level around him."[27] The colonial ideologists frequently stressed the inability of native governments to exploit the natural wealth of the country. Hence native ability was questioned, and the image of the backward native grew up. The peoples of Southeast Asia such as the Malays, the Javanese and the Filipinos did not belong to a pre-literate, simple society. They had to be judged incapable, with retroactive application, of developing their resources. Since they were judged incapable they forfeited the right of independence. Kidd put it in the following: "It will probably be made clear, and that at no distant date, that the last thing our civilization is likely to permanently tolerate is the wasting of the resources of the richest regions of the earth through the lack of the elementary qualities of social efficiency in the races possessing them. The right of those races to remain in possession will be recognized; but it will be no part of the future conditions of such recognition that they shall be allowed to prevent the utilization of the immense natural resources which they have in charge." [28]

The other historical alternative was not considered, namely that the indigenous society might develop its own resources, assimilating modern Western science and technology. Countries like Burma, Indo-China, Malaya, Java, Sumatra and the Philippines were historically *not simple and non-literate*. They had developed social organizations, technology and statecraft, as described earlier. It is true that they contained simple non-literate communities as well but this did not detract from the fact that these countries had been managed by developed societies at the time when the Europeans arrived around the beginning of the 16th century. The colonial ideologists projected the view that the scientific and technological gap between Western society and native society which lasted until the outbreak of the Second World War could be traced back several hundred years, but in reality the gap was hardly there during the 16th and 17th centuries. As noted earlier it was colonial bondage which blocked the flow of assimilation from the Western world. Had there been a free intercourse between independent Acheh and the Western world from the 16th century onwards, Acheh and similarly other Indonesian states would have reached an advanced state of development by now. Instead, the Dutch destroyed Acheh by a prolonged war. Until now, Acheh has not recovered its former status. If the Dutch had not overthrown the Javanese states, by now there would also have been some Javanese states. Like Japan, Russia, Turkey, and Thailand, by the 19th century these states would have recognized the benefits of modern science and technology from the West, as they did recognise similar benefits from other societies in the past.

The portrayal of the native was part of a total ideological

campaign, which was carried out without any deliberate instruction. It was a collective reaction of a group moved by a common outlook and consciousness of interest. The degradation of the native brought in its train a similar phenomenon with reference to native activities. Let us take the economics of native life.

Economic studies of the colonies had mostly focused on those items which brought profit to Western capitalists. This is still the case today, for instance in Malaysia and Indonesia. I am not aware of any study on the trade of a town, but there are hundreds of studies on the trade of Amsterdam or Hamburg. The reason for this phenomenon may be traced to the fact that economics which were not related to the profit pursuit of colonial capitalism were not paid any attention. Inter-regional studies within Southeast Asia were neglected. The economics of native society was not studied. What was studied were exports to and imports from the West, the production of commodities required by the West, capital inflow from the West, and profit transfer to the West. The general definition of economics relies heavily on the concept of the satisfaction of wants and the means therof; the colonial capitalist attitude towards economics was the satisfaction of profit by the colonial interest groups and the means thereof.

Historically speaking, an ideology of an epoch rarely expresses itself bluntly, consciously revealing its entire nature. But it is also not entirely concealed; here and there it reveals itself, as for example in the work of a Dutch professor of economics who defined economic history entirely in terms of Western capitalism. "Economic history," he said, "presupposes economic change. Villages, towns and nations that year in and year out and century after century satisfy their wants in the same manner, have no economic history".[29] By this definition, China, Japan and India before the 19th century had no economic history. Gonggrijp was referring to traditional Indonesian society. Villages, he said, existed also in Central and Western Europe but the Indonesian village life missed the individualism present in the European village of earlier centuries.[30] European individualism is here considered as a significant criterion of what constitutes economic history. Here is a cultural imperialism in the realm of scientific conceptualization. Consequently an economic process which does not conform to such a concept of significance is abandoned by the ethnocentric colonial scholarship.

As I have noted in the Introduction, the colonial ideology influences scholarship in the selection of themes as well as in analysis and conclusion. Similarly, as regards the image of the natives the negative traits were intensively treated while the positive were neglected; hence a distorted and unbalanced picture emerged. Consequently what was important in the history of the natives was also neglected. There has been, for instance, no study on the effects of the destruction of the native states on the natives themselves, where as there have been some references to the effects on the colonial power. One reason for this is the negative image of the native which does not awaken the desire to study its contemporary affairs. This explains the fact that generally during the colonial period only the anthropologist and the colonial adviser studied native affairs not scholars from other disciplines like economists, political scientists and sociologists. Some Indonesian exceptions can be mentioned such as Schrieke, Boeke, Wertheim, and Douwes Dekker. In Malaysia, scholarly interest in the natives was generated by some British administrators like Clifford, Swettenham, Maxwell and Windstedt, but their interest merely served to strengthen the image of the indolent, unpredictable, fun-loving, superstitious and imitative native. They compiled dictionaries, published Malay literary materials, wrote histories of the Malays, very much in the fashion of amateurs without the application of science in their works. Their works as a whole was the pillar of the colonial ideology with reference to native society.

In this book we are not attempting to evaluate colonialism as a historical phenomenon or the contribution of colonial scholarship to knowledge. Our attention has been focused on the colonial image of the native and its function in the colonial ideology. We have also noted the negative influence of ideology on scholarship. In the Introduction we have classified the influence of Ideology into negative and positive. The negative influence of ideology is distortive, one sided, generative of inconsistencies and superficiality. Some time a point of view is offered, which appears objective and dispassionate, but lurking beneath it is the sympathy with colonialism. To my mind, a truly objective scholar will pronounce his sympathy and then argue for it in the most reasonable manner. Camouflaging an attitude by a posture of objectivity and impersonality serves to retard scholarship more than to advance it. Let us take the following instance: "Whether imperialism was good or an unmitigated evil is beside the point. Such judgements belong to the individual conscience. Here we treat imperialism as a fact requiring explanation rather than censure or apology."[31] Hence an attempt to evaluate colonialism whether it has been beneficial or not to the colonized society, cannot be considered scientific. It is a matter of conscience, but imperialism as a "fact" is not a matter of conscience, it is a scientific treatment.

To consider the evaluation of colonialism as non-scientific entails a similar judgement on the evaluation of the various aspects of colonialism, in our case the colonial ideology and its negative image of the native. Are we not allowed to say that the colonial image of the native did not promote inter-ethnic harmony, that it was a blend of prejudice, that it was an unprovoked insult, that it was a distortion of reality, in short, that it was something which it should not have been?[32] Agreeing to the two authors means to allow the colonial image to prevail and influence scholarship. Any effort to reject the image is considered outside the purview of scholarship. To expose the distortion, the untruth, and the prejudice behind the image, is another way of saying that the image is bad, even if we do not use the word "bad". The treatment of imperialism and colonialism as a "fact" without involving any value judgement is a delusion. Either we are unconsciously influenced by values or allow values to intrude into our scholarship. Let us take the phenomenon of imperialism and colonialism as a "fact". What do we mean by this?

Modern Western imperialism marked the expansion of Western rule and dominance over the greater part of the non-Western world. It had profound effects both on the West as well as the non-Western world. This is a "fact". But this is a "fact" only in the general and abstract sense. The moment we go into the concrete our discourse on the "fact" entails a value orientation. We may not use terms such as "good" and "bad" in our discourse but the moment we say that colonialism has generated peace and stability, has introduced modern sanitation, has developed the natural resources, we are proclaiming it to have been good. On the other hand, we may select the negative influence of colonialism and by so doing we are proclaiming it to have been bad. It is not the intention of this book to evaluate the total effect of colonialism and imperialism. As Moon had warned us, "In the end, some of the benefits and evils of imperialism would still be imponderable, and the final judgement would be subjective rather than scientific, for no scientific balance can be devised to weigh ships against schools, raw materials against wars, profits against patriotism, civilization against cannibalism."[33] The difficulty is no doubt there, to assess the myriad of events which constituted the phenomenon of imperialism; events which changed in nature and effect in different times. For instance, the British fought malaria in Malaya. But they did this after increasing it on a large scale, with their haste to plant rubber, their massing of physically weak immigrant labour in infested area, and their neglect of medical welfare for the populace. To evaluate this aspect of colonialism we would have to ask the question what would have happened to the population of Malaya if a Western colonial capitalist government had not been there, but since it did exist what could it have done to prevent malaria? All aspects of the problem have to be looked into. It is here that Moon and others who believe in the impossibility of an objective explanation are wrong. To proclaim that the social and historical sciences are not in a position to offer objective evaluations is to proclaim the impotence of human reason. If we cannot evaluate colonialism we cannot evaluate anything in history. We cannot proclaim such and such a ruler is a tyrant. We cannot proclaim such and such a government is weak. We cannot proclaim such and such a system is retrogressive. We cannot proclaim the benefits of Western civilization. The difficulty in evaluating colonialism is practical, not theoretical.

However, while Moon admonished us to hesitate in proclaiming colonialism as evil, he was quick in pronouncing its virtues. He said: "When capital waves its magic wand over jungle and wilderness, railways, mines, oil-wells, cities, plantations, wharves, factories, power-plants, telegraphs, and warehouses appear. Of the profits, the native population may at first receive a niggardly share. On the other hand, with material progress are linked the vices, diseases and problems of modern industrialism. Backward countries such as India go through the Industrial Revolution, with its low wages, child labour, excessive working hours, overcrowded slums; colonies suffer from high mortality rates due to labour conditions unsuited to native physique. The medal has its two faces. Perhaps it is not unduly optimistic to hope that the evils of uncontrolled exploitation and the problems of economic transformation are passing phases which will in time be corrected, as they have been, at least partly, in progressive countries, while the benefits of industrial progress will be more enduring. Let those who will lament the invasion of the Orient by hustling business and noisy machine, or the passing away of tribalism in Africa."[34] Here his value orientation came in. Unlike Hobson he was not averse to imperialism. There is also the familiar invention of arguments. Shocking and inhuman conditions were camouflaged by the phrase "labour conditions unsuited to native physique". There is an element of misplaced responsibility here. Native physique was blamed for the high mortality rate. What exactly of this physique which caused the high mortality was not suggested. Here we find another trait of colonial studies, their fondness for generality when it comes to matters outside their interest or which may cause embarrassment. Human relations are discussed in the language of commodities. On the image of the native we have noted that it was constructed on the basis of generalities without any operational foundation. The alleged indolence of the Malays was not operationally defined, as we have previously pointed out. However, on rare occasions, the operational background of the alleged image appeared. In this connection, we have to examine in detail the use of abstract phrases as illustrated in Moon's book and the possibility of an objective evaluation of colonialism. The reminiscences of a British planter in Malaya offer just this.

Let us deal with the notions of indolence, indentured labour and physique as a cause of low productivity. On the Malays our planter said: "The Malay labourers on the plantation were very much in the minority, for no other reason than their intense dislike of work, and more particularly that type of work which entailed constant hard manual labour combined with a rigid daily routine. Such drudgery was like poison to their temperamental natures, so that we could only employ them on work that could be done on a contract basis, as the felling of trees and on haulage and cartage; at both of which they excelled, since the Malay has few rivals in the art of jungle felling and in the handling of bullocks and buffaloes."[35] Here he openly admitted that the Malays disliked drudgery, a perfectly ordinary and human attitude. He himself and other planters were not subjected to a rigid daily routine. It was alright for them to dislike drudgery, but not for the Malays. Felling jungles was apparently not considered work which disqualified the subject from being classified as "indolent". The colonial capitalist criteria of industriousness are here fully revealed. Only labour which directly promoted profit could disqualify the subject from being labelled as "indolent". A more revealing document was the official annual report. On Malay labour is said: "This labour is of very little importance. No large estates depend to any great extent on Malays and the total number engaged at any one time on estates in the Federated Malay States is roughly 3,500 persons. The reason why more Malays are not employed as labourers is that they are unwilling to work regularly. They merely use the estate as a convenience to supplement whatever livelihood can be made out of their kampongs and cannot be relied on to remain on the estates when their services are most urgently required. They are, as a rule, not desirous of earning any more money than is sufficient to support them and to provide them with needs of the moment. As is the case with the locally engaged Javanese small numbers of Malays supplement regular labour forces of Indians or Chinese on many estates but the Malays work even less regularly than locally engaged Javanese."[36]

Here important labour meant estate labour. Apart from the figure, and the addition of one phrase, the same paragraph was repeated in successive annual reports. In 1934, however an exception was made for Kedah and Kelantan, two of the Malay States, the rest of the paragraph being the same. In 1935 and 1936 this paragraph was repeated. However in 1937 a different tone was noted. The report said: "During the year Inspecting Officers of this Department were instructed to make careful enquiries as to the extent and conditions of employment of local Malays. Though the total employed is not great some facts were brought to light to show that the kampong Malay like the rest of the world is changing in unexpected ways. In Kelantan, as one would expect, some estates are run entirely by Malays. One successful system adopted there is for each family to take on one or more task and for some member of the family to turn out and tap it. It is only under some such arrangement that it is possible to employ Malays successfully. It was then found that on a European-owned estate in Malacca exactly the same system had been worked up. The Malays had learned the necessity of regular attendances and proved themselves good workmen and were being paid standard rates."[37] The dislike for regular work was not mentioned any more. The Malays had turned "good"; they had come to the estates. A novel element emerged, employment by family and payment by standard rates. Earlier there was official discrimination against the Malays. The Honorary Secretary of the Malay Settlement, Kuala Lumpur, described the situation in 1908. "At present the Malay candidate for Goverment employment is, on the whole, rather worse off than the Tamil or the Chinaman. He has, of course, a reputation for laziness, which, whether justified or not, always stands in his way. Moreover, the rates of salary offered to him are in some cases actually less than those offered to other Asiatics in the Federated Malay States. It was only quite recently that the Malay police were allowed the higher rate of salary which the Sikh police had enjoyed for years. The official schedule of wages for Chinese coolies is still higher than that for Malays. A Malay assistant teacher gets a lower salary than a

Tamil peon. Jaffna Tamil clerks are allowed leave to return to their homes on half-pay, while a Malay clerk who wishes to visit his parents on leave is granted no pay at all. To get half-pay leave he must go abroad."[38]

In 1938 mention was made of the better response of the Malays towards estate work as partially determined by bicycles. "The bicycle too seems to play an important part in making it easy to cover the distance between the kampong and the estate or mine."[39]

If all the historical and sociological factors surrounding the attitude of Malays towards estate labour were considered then the general and abstract imputation of indolence would appear as a vulgar distortion. Some of these factors have been mentioned already, such as discriminatory wages, trying condition, distance from the home, an estate life cut off from the community. These are ordinary human reasons for avoiding particular occupations. One need not rely on abstract notions such as being "naturally indolent" and "dislike for regular work", or the culture and national character, to explain Malay evasion of estate labour. It is the characteristic of colonial ideology that it relied on nebulous notions for arguments supporting some of its rationalization. Its thought construction was not inclined to the concrete in all its complexity except in matters of economic and administrative interest.

In colonial works the subject of labour, on the whole, was treated as a commodity, an abstract and statistical process. To them, labour meant the phenomenon of people working to earn wages. The actual historical condition of labour was glossed over. It is to this actual historical condition that man reacts. When a topic such as indentured labour was discussed in many colonial works, it was the dollars and cents, the formal terms and conditions of labour, the laws covering it, its relationship to production, to immigration, and to the general circumstances affecting the labour force. Rarely did a scholar's account contain a description of the actual condition of indentured labour. Indentured labour in Malaya up to at least the late twenties was in practice a form of slavery. This was confirmed by some planters. In an earlier part of this book we have discussed the abuses of labour in the mines and estates. A description of indentured labour in an estate in Kedah, presumably in the late twenties pointed to the inhuman treatment of indentured labour. The supervisor, a Eurasian carried a gun, while the Chinese foreman carried a whip. Whenever a coolie stopped working the foreman would shout at him to continue; if this order was not obeyed quickly he got a blow on the legs with the whip. If he showed any signs of turning on the foreman in retaliation for such punishment, he found himself shouted at by the supervisor and threatened by his colleague.[40] The author who had recently arrived from England was shocked to see such a treatment. These indentured labourers from China were bound for three years and were paid ten cents a day at a time when the rate was between thirty-five cents and fifty cents. They had to pay off a debt of approximately 10 pounds for their passage. After work they were herded back to their quarters and guarded by two Sikh watchmen with rifles, to prevent revolt or escape. Our newly arrived planter thought they were slaves to all intents and purposes.[41]

There were also the endless fights over women. The Indian labour force in the estate was predominantly male. Owing to an extreme shortage of women, leading an isolated community life in the estates, a number of women had several men. There was also homosexuality.[42] The European planters also had relation with the estate women. A Bengali Indian ran amok killing two persons arising from jealousy. In the mornings the manager and two other British employees inspected the quarters to see that all got up in time. If a labourer was found still asleep, he would be seized by the ankles and with a quick jerk pulled straight off the platform so that he fell two feet on to the ground with a resounding bump. Then there was the continuous illness of some and frequent deaths, at the estates. Such a condition was fairly widespread, particularly due to bad sanitation. The estate labour force comprised of Indian labour and indentured Chinese labour. The bulk was Indian. As to Moon's statement "labor conditions unsuited to native physique" what was historically implied amounted to a callous disregard for human life. There was nothing instrinsically wrong with native physique. It was the exposure to malaria which killed thousands of labourers. In 1908, twenty-one estates had an average death rate of over 200 per thousand.[43]

Malaria was the number one killer. In four States of British Malaya, the Federated Malay States, with a total population of 1·16 million in 1929 there were 85,000 cases of malaria registered in hospitals and 4,300 deaths in 1928 and 1929. During this period there were approximately 72 medical officers in this area, 45 hospitals, 30 town dispensaries and 24 travelling dispensaries. The area was 27,500 sq. miles. The death rate from malaria on the hospital cases alone was 50·6 per thousand patients or 5%. The doctor population ratio was 1:16,000. Malaria cases and deaths for the entire population of the area would easily be 3 times the hospitalized figures. The second biggest killer was pulmonary tuberculosis. There were 4,600 cases with 2,100 deaths. Thus the fatality rate was 45·6%.[44] Eight years later in 1937, with an increased population, malaria was reduced. There were 35,000 cases in government and estate hospitals with 800 deaths. The fatality rate was reduced to 2%. In 1937 there were 1,994 cases of pulmonary tuberculosis. 791 died resulting in a fatality rate of 39·8%.[45] There had been a slight improvement owing to the general improvement of world medical science but the disparity was impressive between England and her dependency. For the whole of British Malaya in 1939 the doctor population ratio was 1·4:10,000 while in the United States it was 10:10,000. The second largest illness in British Malaya was venereal disease.[46] In 1929 there were 6,000 cases hospitalized in the Federated Malay States. In 1937 there were in Singapore alone 22,800 new patients out of a population of 1·25 million and 185,000 old patients. In the Straits Settlements the rate of syphilis in 1937 was 49·4 per 10,000 population while the rate for England and Wales in 1936 was 1·7 per 10,000, that of Holland 1·06, and Sweden 0·67. Thus the rate for the Straits Settlements was approximately 30 times that of England and Wales, 47 times that of Holland, and 75 times that of Sweden.[47] In 1944, the authors of a book on epidemiology promoted the following conclusion on the health situation in Malaya: "Public health, hospital and medical facilities under the British regime, although they were efficiently organised and maintained, were inadequate for the health and medical requirements of the Malay States."[48]

The main diseases of Malaya: malaria, venereal disease, dysentery, pulmonary tuberculosis, beri-beri, diarrhoea, and pneumonia, except the first two, had each a fatality rate ranging from between 10 to 50%. The highest was tuberculosis. In incidence the highest by far was malaria. Out of 70,000 hospitalized cases in 1928 in the federated Malay States, 48,500 were suffering from malaria. The total deaths from all cases were 6,800. The general fatality rate was thus 9·7%. The growth of many of these diseases such as malaria, tuberculosis, venereal disease, dysentery, were the results of colonial capitalism. The hasty development of settlements, the crowding of people, bad sanitation and sewage, prostitution, injurious habits such as opium smoking and drinking amongst those of modest means, had resulted from the opening of the mines and estates with its attendant urbanization. We shall confine our discussion to the biggest disease, malaria, based on the findings of a colonial doctor with a pronounced colonial ideological affiliation.

The main factors responsible for the outbreak of malaria were the opening up of lands and road building. "Roads and other public works, by producing breeding-places for mosquitoes, are important agents in spreading malaria and filaria. Roads in flat country, especially when parallel to the coast, are injurious in two ways: during their construction borrow pits are formed, and these remain afterwards as mosquito breeding-places; when completed, roads may interfere with drainage of land on the inland side of the road."[49] The location of the labourer's quarters near ravines in estates or hill land contributed to the rise in malaria amongst the workers. A twenty-eight mile railway line completed in 1914 caused an outbreak of malaria. Whenever there was an outbreak in a certain district it re-infected districts which had previously been cleared of malaria. The immigrant estate labourer was a particularly vulnerable victim. He lived in areas which often harboured malaria mosquitoes. The newly arrived immigrant labour were suddenly exposed to the disease. Some of them came from famine stricken districts in India (1906). The high incidence of malaria had nothing to do with their physique. It was more their economic circumstances. The poor died from the illness not the well-to-do. The bodily resistance of the poor and the facilities for cure were both inferior to those of the well-to-do. In 1909, of 29 Europeans living on ten hilly land estates in Selangor, 25 had malaria at some time or other. In this period Watson could say that no European had died from malaria.[50] At this time thousands of labourers, farmers, and poor town dwellers were dying from malaria. However if we were to reverse the position, had the Europeans become estate labourers, and had come from poor classes at home, they would have died by the thousands. Later in the subsequent decades there was much improvement. The Oriental physique was the same. Only the circumstances had changed. This change was due to the fact that malaria hit the capitalist purse. "The whole success and, in fact, the very existence of tropical agriculture depends on a healthy and contented labour force."[51] Estates could not function efficiently; the cost of treatment was high. The labour force was cut down below the optimum production level. Many labourers deserted the estates.

It is such instances, and facts, which had often been neglected in colonial studies of the colonies. The problem was first generated by the colonial power then a solution was attempted, and then they claimed the credit for it. Malaria is an example of this. As

Watson, the Chief Medical Officer of the Estate Hospital's Association in the Federated Malay States put it, "If the history of other tropical enterprises was to be taken as a guide, the opening up of the land, especially when done with imported labour, was likely to produce virulent outbreaks of malaria, and to be costly in lives, both of Europeans and Asiatics. My hospital returns showed how severely the existing estates were suffering already, and I determined to study the matter in more detail."[52]

No attempt has been made to study the introduction of colonial capitalism into Malaya, in the forms of mining and plantation agriculture, in terms of the cost to human lives. The thousands who died under the rubber trees and along the mining pools, along the roads and railways, deserve our memory and attention. They should not be cynically brushed aside as digits in the balance sheet of colonial development. There is, however, nothing in the social sciences which prevents a social scientist from calling a spade a spade, from identifying exploitation for what it really is, from depicting misery, cruelty, and oppression in the course of time. The problem here is the accurate portrayal of reality, not the permissibility of the attempt. A poor estate labourer suffering from a dysentery which dragged him to his grave experienced the misery of the disease and that misery was a fact. The social sciences do not ban facts. Similarly the miserable condition of estate life around the beginning of the 20th century in Malaya was a fact, the only difference being that it was more complex and more difficult to portray than a simple case of dysentery. To hedge theoretical objections around studies of such facts is to defend the colonial attitude of camouflaging those facts. Hence the idea of a value free social science, if applied to the former colonies, is an ideological device to prevent the exposure of colonialism: A reappraisal of the colonial scholarship on the region would entail a focusing of attention on hitherto neglected areas and perspective. If it was possible for Dutch scholars to write on some Indonesian tyrants, and they rightly did so in cases which warranted it, why should it not be possible for Indonesian scholars to write about Dutch tyrants provided they were really so, according to a responsible and operational definition of tyranny?

The social system during the colonial period was fairly reflected in the ideology. The image of the natives and their place in the scheme of things was a reflection of an actual state of affairs. The image of the lazy Malays reflected a discriminating system. Malays had a lower salary scale. The habit of grading nations in terms of high and low, with the European nations at the top was parallel to a similar grading in society with the Europeans at the top. The status system alluded to earlier, was a system based on racial discrimination and apartheid. This apartheid and discrimination were not as absolute as in contemporary South Africa. Violation of apartheid did not entail imprisonment but nevertheless apartheid did exist in the social and psychological sense. This was expressed in administrative measures. For instance, the hospital system of the Straits Settlement included a special European ward and a special European operating theatre.[53] The ward was spacious and never overcrowded. The medical statistics gave separate European and non-European figures. In 1906, the only patient entitled to free treatment at the General Hospital in Singapore was a poor European.[54] The colonial ideology with its emphasis on European superiority and their right to rule imposed the status system on the dominated territory. The European colonial community had the best of everything. In the administration and in business they held the highest posts. In agriculture they owned the biggest estates. In their social life they kept to the best clubs, hotels and restaurants, and they lived in the best residential area. They created in the colonies a social world which enjoyed all the benefits of health, wealth, status, residence, power, prestige, and influence. In Indonesia Europeans also went to separate courts.

The privileged position of the Europeans and the superior economic circumstances which they created for themselves after gaining power in the colonies had caused a much lower mortality rate amongst them than amongst the natives and foreign immigrants. The hospital death rate showed that Europeans had a much lower casualty rate. In 1887, the death for Europeans in all hospitals in the Straits Settlements (Singapore, Dindings, Malacca, Penang, Province Wellesley) was approximately half of the others (4·15%–8·42%).[55] The estimated population of the Straits Settlements in 1907 were 611,796 of which 5,436 were Europeans, 8,114 Eurasian, 323,182 Chinese, 216,459 Malay, 59,651 Indian and 6,954 other nationalities.[56] In 1907 the general death rate of the Europeans was 15·45 per 1,000 population. The Malay, the Indian and the Chinese were 31·12, 43·49, and 44·02 respectively.[57] As to the birth rate there was hardly any big difference but the European excelled the Malay, Chinese and Indian. Thus while the European had a slightly higher birth rate, the non-European had a considerably higher infant mortality rate. In 1907, the mortality rate for the Chinese was 274·99 per 1,000 infants, the Indian 256·78, the Malay

218·93, while the European infant mortality rate was 37·04. In absolute numbers there were 5,883 Malays born in 1907 and 1,365 died while 162 Europeans were born and only 6 died.[58]

In 1927 the same general trend prevailed. The estimated total population of the Straits Settlements in 1927 was 1,059,968. The European population was 11,305, the Chinese 615,149, the Malay 270,552, the Indian 141,777, and other nationalities 10,800. The death rate per 1,000 of the European population was 8·67 while the Malay was 36·68, the Chinese 33·34 and the Indian 32·40. Thus the death rate for non-Europeans was more than four times that of Europeans.[59] The birth rate of Europeans showed a great difference with the Malay rate which was 43·03. The European rate was 19·37, the Chinese 35·27, and the Indian 22·08. Statistically, the European rate is the most accurate owing to size, location, and administrative habits of the population. Next comes the Chinese and Indian while the Malay rate is the least accurate. There were certainly many more births and deaths amongst the Malays who were more spread out in the rural area. We have confined our statistics to the Straits Settlements because it had the earliest and the most developed statistical organization during that period. It was furthermore the region most developed by colonialism, since it was directly under British rule. There was no Malay sultanate there. The infant mortality rate was even more disparate. The European rate was 18·27 per thousand and while the Malay, Chinese and Indian were 269·03, 188·45 and 208·24 respectively. Thus the infant mortality rate of the three major communities was on the average 13 times higher than the European community.[60] For the same period the infant mortality rate of England and Wales was 70 per 1,000.[61]

In 1937, the estimated population of the Straits Settlements was 1,245,739, of which 14,397 were Europeans, 770,645 Chinese, 294,565 Malays, 142,703 Indians, 12,402 Eurasians and 11,657 other nationalities.[62] The Malay infant mortality rate was still very high. In Malacca it was 215·12 per thousand. In the preceding thirty years there was no doubt a general improvement, but there still remained a considerable gap between the European and other communities. There was improvement in some areas and deterioration in others. A conspicuous instance was venereal disease. In 1887, there were 3,213 patients suffering from venereal disease admitted to hospitals.[63] This was 0·5 per cent of the population in 1907. It could very well have been 0·8 per cent of the 1887 population which was not given in the annual report. By 1937, half a century later the percentage of population with venereal disease must have been more than 20%. The total population of the Straits Settlements between 1933 and 1937 was between 1·04 million and 1·25 million. During this period the health institutions received 110,000 new patients suffering from venereal diseases. The number of re-attendances was about 1·04 million. If one patient returned 15 times to the clinic or hospital there would have been 69,000 additional cases. Thus the treated cases would have been about 179,000. The statistics excluded cases of troops and other services. There was also a considerable percentage of cases treated outside government clinics. It was estimated that 13·2% of cases were treated by private practitioners, not to mention those treated by traditional methods. Thus the government statistics represented only those cases treated by modern medical methods. On this basis alone, 14·3% of the population suffered from venereal diseases. This group, those confined to government treatment, constituted, as suggested, only 86·8% of cases treated by modern medical practices. Including those treated by traditional medical practices, the percentage must have been more than 20 on a very conservative estimate.[64]

The Straits Settlements had become a seething cauldron of venereal diseases. In 1907, the annual report acknowledged the number of brothels and prostitutes in the Straits Settlements. There were in total 3,867 prostitutes and 541 brothels. There were 28 European prostitutes, all operating in Singapore.[65] The brothels themselves were introduced into Malaya during the colonial regime. By 1937 the number must have increased considerably. The spread of venereal diseases was even more alarming in relation to the adult population of the Straits Settlements. The 1931 census reported a population of 1,114,015 persons in the Straits Settlements of which 671,080 were males.[66] The population in the age group between 20 and 54 was 638,000.[67] Between 1933 and 1937 there were 110,000 new cases of venereal diseases and an estimated 69,000 re-attending for treatment in government clinics. At least 179,000 had been patients of venereal disease out of an adult population of 638,000, that is 26·3 per cent of the adult population between the age groups of 20 and 54. Bearing in mind the cases treated by private practitioners and traditional physicians it could easily have gone beyond the 30 per cent mark. The percentage was even higher if we relate it to the male population in this group, which was two-thirds of the total. The victims of venereal diseases were predominantly male.

There is no way to know how much the government spent to

cope with this disease. The total medical expenditure for 1937 (things connected with medicine and health) was 3·5 million Straits Dollars. The entire government expenditure was 42·04 million dollars. Thus the medical expenditure for the entire range of diseases and preventive measures was 8·3% of the entire government expenditure. Expenditure for the police was 2·9 million dollars while that of the military was 4 million. Thus for the armed forces the expenditure was 6·9 millions of which 3·36 millions were spent in the Straits Settlements. The total receipts of the Straits Settlements in 1937 were 226·65 million (216·04 plus the opening balance). The sum of 218·26 million was further spent in investments, loan, deposits, etc., leaving a balance of 8·39 millions.[68] Part of this balance, let us say 42%, if allocated to the medical services would have increased the medical expenditure by 100 per cent. The revenue from liquor alone was 3·92 million, while from opium it was 9·65 million.[69] If only the entire revenue from opium had been spent on the medical services, it would have gone a very long way to alleviate the health problems of the Straits Settlements, particularly the prevention of malaria and the treatment of venereal diseases, not to mention other diseases.

The prevalence of mortal diseases among the native population, and also the high death rate among foreign Orientals, became facts from which the colonial ideologist deduced his conclusion that the natives were weak. In almost all fields except in birthrate the natives appeared to be weak. Economically, politically, technologically, militarily, and educationally, judged from the modern capitalist standards, the native population lagged behind. This was obvious from the 18th century onwards. To this was also attributed the moral, intellectual, cultural and social backwardness. The entire native society was characterized in negative terms, including his motivation to work. The colonial ideology characterizing the natives in negative terms was partly conditioned by the objective circumstances surrounding the native population. They were indeed weak from the 18th century onwards. This weakness was extended by the colonial ideology to cover morality and civilization. The tendency to degrade the native was further reinforced by the sense of ethnic superiority which was predominant in Europe at the time. The sense of ethnic superiority was so overwhelming that it even influenced the founders of Communism and other revolutionaries who were supposed to be against exploitation and to preach the brotherhood of man.

The tendency to treat Asian civilization lightly was noticeable amongst Marx and Engels. Their condescending attitude, their carelessness about facts, their misinterpretation of Asian institutions, and their ethnic pride, were clearly revealed in their writings. Marx called Chinese isolation barbarous, ignoring the fact that in such isolation China had built a grand civilization.[70] In the apprehension of great changes Orientals used to hoard.[71] His view of the Indian peasant and village life excelled that of the British Colonial administrator in its distortion and insulting tone. The destruction of the village community, which he considered to be semi-civilized, was hailed by him as the "only *social* revolution ever heard of in Asia". Here is what Marx said of the Indian village: "Now, sickening as it must be to human feeling to witness those myriads of industrious patriarchal and inoffensive social organizations disorganized and dissolved into their units, thrown into a sea of woes, and their individual members losing at the same time their ancient form of civilization and their hereditary means of subsistence, we must not forget that these idyllic village communities, inoffensive though they may appear, had always been the solid foundation of Oriental despotism, that they restrained the human mind within the smallest possible compass, making it the unresisting tool of superstition, enslaving it beneath traditional rules, depriving it of all grandeur and historical energies. We must not forget the barbarian egotism which, concentrating on some miserable patch of land, had quietly witnessed the ruin of empires, the perpetration of unspeakable cruelties, the massacre of the population of large towns, with no other consideration bestowed upon them than on natural events, itself the helpless prey of any aggressor who deigned to notice it at all. We must not forget that this undignified, stagnatory, and vegetative life, that this passive sort of existence evoked on the other part, in contradistinction, wild, aimless, unbounded forces of destruction, and rendered murder itself a religious rite in Hindustan. We must not forget that these little communities were contaminated by distinctions of caste and by slavery, that they subjugated man to external circumstances instead of elevating man to be the sovereign of circumstances, that they transformed a self-developing social state into never changing natural destiny, and thus brought about a brutalizing worship of nature, exhibiting its degradation in the fact that man, the sovereign of nature, fell down on his knees in adoration of Hanuman, the monkey, and Sabbala, the cow."[72]

Karl Marx, a man who had never set foot on Asian soil, who had never seen an Indian village, never met and spoken to a single

Indian or Asian in his life, had the courage to pronounce such pontifical judgements, degrading the Indian village, the Indian peasant, and the Hindu religion. The role of England in India as a colonial power was extolled. "England," he said, "it is true, in causing a social revolution in Hindustan, was actuated only by the vilest interests, and was stupid in her manner of enforcing them. But that is not the question. The question is, can mankind fulfil its destiny without a fundamental revolution in the social state of Asia? If not, whatever may have been the crimes of England she was the unconscious tool of history in bringing about that revolution."[73] It was the method that he condemned not the presence of England in India. Engels spoke of Oriental ignorance, impatience, prejudice, and the vicissitudes of fortune and favour inherent in Eastern courts.[74] How Oriental ignorance, impatience and prejudice differed from similar Occidental phenomena was not explained but the Oriental version was much worse. Though he attacked the British during the Anglo-Chinese war, he described the war from the point of view of the Chinese as "a popular war for the maintenance of Chinese nationality, with all its overbearing prejudice, stupidity, learned ignorance and pedantic barbarism if you like, but yet a popular war."[75] Thus the Chinese nationality was characterized by overbearing prejudice, stupidity, learned ignorance and pedantic barbarism, traits which Engels did not claim to have been present in Western European nations. While in their description of their own society Marx and Engels used the notion of class, in the case of other societies they often used the notion of ethnicity. Thus Engels considered what he called the Moors in Algeria as a race of a very low moral character.[76]

Engels, the avowed preacher of international brotherhood, evinced a sense of ethnic superiority. He talked about Celtic credulity with reference to Irish politics.[77] In a letter to Bernstein, a fellow German, he spoke of German theoretical superiority over the French and Italians.[78] He was in favour of colonialism, but a socialist one. In a letter to Karl Kautsky in 1882, he wrote the following: "In my opinion the colonies proper, i.e. the countries occupied by a European population—Canada, the Cape, Australia—will all become independent; on the other hand, the countries inhabited by a native population, which are simply subjugated—India, Algeria, the Dutch, Portuguese and Spanish possessions—must be taken over for the time being by the proletariat and led as rapidly as possible towards independence. How this process will develop is difficult to say."[79] In this respect the views of Engels were of the same kind as those of the civilizing mission with the only difference that the mission was to be socialistic. It was this view of colonialism which had dominated socialist circles for decades. His friend Bernstein openly preached German colonialism, by means of strange and unreal arguments. Bernstein said: "But if it is not reprehensible to enjoy the produce of tropical plantations, it cannot be so to cultivate such plantations ourselves. Not the whether but the how is here the decisive point. It is neither necessary that the occupation of tropical lands by Europeans should injure the natives in their enjoyment of life, nor has it hitherto usually been the case. Moreover, only a conditional right of savages to the land occupied by them can be recognized. The higher civilization ultimately can claim a higher right."[80]

Bernstein echoed the views of the masters that it was the method not the principle of colonialism which was wrong. Bernstein was an influential Marxist socialist thinker in Germany. His logic was strange. If the Germans enjoyed tropical bananas, it was all right to seize the country cultivating them. However if the Japanese enjoyed Dutch potatoes it was not all right for the Japanese to seize Holland. In the Stuttgart Congress of the Second International in 1907, Bernstein invoked the authority of Marx and Lassalle for his pro-colonialist view. A certain amount of tutelage of the civilized over the uncivilized was regarded as a necessity.[81] There was a lively debate between those who were for and against colonialism in principle. Kautsky was one of the prominent socialists opposed to colonialism. But the Socialist Second International adopted the reformist view of colonialism, condemning only its capitalist form. For two decades it became the majority socialist view of colonialism. Its anti-colonialism was confined to its current capitalist version, which it condemned. Only in 1928 did the Socialist International adopt at its Brussels Congress a new policy calling explicitly for self-government and independence.[82]

The great majority of the socialists of the time, including Marx and Engels, were not free of their Eurocentric outlook. Apart from their condemnation of capitalist injustice, they shared a common basic outlook on the history, culture, religion, and society of the non-Western world. Their bias, ignorance and prejudices were basically the same. Engels called Islam a fake religion without any explanation.[83] Although they considered religion as essentially untrue, they did not describe Christianity as a fake religion. Expressions to describe abominable phenomena were often culled from Oriental history such as when Engels referred to Russia as a country "surrounded more or less effectively by an intellectual Chinese wall erected by despotism".[84]

The impression was given that there was an Oriental variety of ignorance, stupidity, intolerance, and despotism. This variety was considered worse than the Occidental one. Similarly when Marx spoke of Oriental peoples his tone was derisive and contemptuous. This was what he said of the Turks, one of the most accomplished Oriental peoples: "Their way of promoting trade, when they were yet in their original nomadic state, consisted in robbing caravans; and now that they are a little more civilized it consists in all sorts of arbitrary and oppressive exactions. Remove all the Turks out of Europe, and trade will have no reason to suffer. And as to progress in general civilization, who are they that carry out that progress in all parts of European Turkey? Not the Turks, for they are few and far between, and can hardly be said to be settled anywhere except in Constantinople and two or three small country districts. It is the Greek and Slavonic middle class in all the towns and trading posts who are the real support of whatever civilization is effectually imported into the country."[85]

A colonial ideologist could not have done better in degrading another nation. He suggested that the Turkish power should be eliminated. Marx further twisted the Koran by saying that it treated all foreigners as foes. Had he read the Koran it would have been clear to him that the Koran made a distinction between friendly unbelievers and hostile unbelievers. The Muslims were to be the friend of those friendly to them. He drew a caricature of the Islamic faith as a fanatical, intolerant and backward religion.[86] The despotism in Russia, "whose arbitrariness and caprice we cannot imagine in the West", Engels called "Oriental despotism".[87] Engels divided the nations of Europe into "great historic peoples", such as the Italians, the Poles, the Germans, the Hungarians, the French, the Spaniards, the English and the Scandinavian, and the inconsequent nationalities such as the Serbians, Croats, Ruthenes, Slovaks, Czechs and others. The right to form independent nation states was recognized by him only for the "great historic peoples".[88]

The condescending and at times contemptuous attitude towards Asian affairs was a phenomenon generally found amongst European thinkers of different persuasions, the monarchist, the revolutionary, the atheist, the religious, the conservative, the radical, the racialist and the non-racialist. They were children of their time and culture. A great Russian revolutionary, a humanist, like V. G. Belinsky (1811–1848) when it came to Asian affairs lost his sense of rationality. There was the familiar theme of using Asian society as a whipping post. He said: "National pride is a lofty and noble sentiment, an earnest of true excellence; but national conceit and susceptibility is a purely Chinese sentiment."[89] Like the Spanish priests who blamed the Filipinos for the decline in morals of the Spaniards, Belinsky blamed the Tartars for what he considered to be the negative traits of Russian life. "Seclusion of women, slavery in notions and sentiments, the knout, the habit of burying money in the ground and going about in tatters for fear of showing one's self a rich man, corruption in the affairs of justice, Asiatism in ways of life, mental sloth, ignorance, despising of self—in a word, everthing that Peter the Great had been eradicating, everything in Russia that was directly opposed to Europeanism—all this was not our native characteristics, but *ingrafted* upon us by the Tartars."[90]

Another great Russian revolutionary thinker and humanist, very advanced in thought and sentiments of social justice, Alexander Herzen (1812–1870), revealed the same shortcoming when it came to judging Asians. The Chinese had sunk in slumber. The people of India "has outlived its prime and is wasting away in senile impotence".[91] These he contrasted with the Russian people who had not attained complete growth, but were in a period of change. To show the strength of Eurocentrism, the sense of ethnic and cultural superiority, it is best to refer to the group from whom one could least expect it, the socialist and radical revolutionary thinkers of Europe.

Up to the Second World War it seemed to be the dominant trend in Europe to view the Asian and non-European world as an inferior world not only technologically and scientifically but also morally, culturally and religiously. The great Asian civilizations such as Hinduism, Buddhism and Islam, judged by contemporary European standards did not show any inferiority except in technology and science which eventually caused a less developed system of production and economic organization. The superiority of the West in this field gave rise to the claim that it was also superior in all fields, and this also applied retroactively to history. It was this sense of superiority and righteousness which had caused the distortion of history by colonial writers, the hegemony of the principle of misplaced responsibility in the writing of history, the placing of events out of context, and the construction of the distorted image of the native. Attempts from within European society itself to correct this image, to introduce a measure of objectivity in the study of native life and customs, were made from time to time but with little success. After the Second World War, a Dutch author summarized the position. He said: "Being Western in education and thought, we easily criticize or condemn institutions and customs intimately connected with the mentality of the Easterner. What seems absurd or reprehensible to us, through the centuries has often proved not only acceptable but the only workable solution. The fact that the East is different from the West should not automatically mean condemnation of the institutions of the East. For centuries this prejudice and lack of knowledge had created a very bad impression of the native population. The Portuguese had warned the Dutch that the natives could not be trusted. This bad impression had remained during the whole period of the East India Company although there were some noticeable exceptions."[92]

Between the First and Second World Wars there was a genuine interest among an influential section of the colonial administrators to improve the condition of the native population, both in Indonesia and Malaysia. But this policy of improvement was within the colonial hierarchical structure. As we have earlier stated, it is not our intention to evaluate the merits of colonialism which could be considered only after the First World War. There are four areas to which questions of merit apply. They are the area of education, the area of health, the area of earning a livelihood, and the area of status and power. We judge a colonial measure meritorious if it improved conditions in these four fields. Had the native population benefited in these fields? Before the First World War definitely not. After the First World War there were improvements here and there such as when a school or a hospital was built but this action, this return gesture, had to be judged within the entire context of profits and advantages obtained by the colonial power from the colonized country, and the historical and social cost for the country concerned. This social cost took the form of the destruction of the trading classes, the loss of freedom to interact with various nationalities and countries, the loss of an indigenous ruling class, the loss of an indigenous class and status mobility which would have taken place in the modern era had it not been restricted by colonialism. Studies of colonial rule by colonial writers had focused attention on colonialism as an agent of social change but there is also another side to it. Colonialism had impeded social change. It had retained and consolidated feudal elements from traditional society while it transformed the feudal order to suit its purpose.

The image of the native constructed by colonialism has been

an impediment to a profound and genuine understanding of native life. This image, as we have shown earlier, is still influential today. Hence the relevance of a deeper enquiry into the origin and function of the colonial image of the native. Our exposition of the ideological roots of this image should in no way be regarded as an attempt to establish the opposite image, an image of perfection. There are many defects in native society now and in the past, and one such defect is the absence of an effective and functioning intellectual community.[93] Before the arrival of the Europeans in the 16th century, there was no functioning intellectual community in the Philippines, Indonesia and Malaysia. Some records of intellectual activity in Pasai and Malacca were available but they did not indicate the presence of a socially functioning community of intellectuals as in ancient Greece and 15th-century Italy. This is only to indicate that not all shortcomings of native society are to be attributed to colonialism, granted the fact that the presence of such a thing as an intellectual community is a desirable one from the point of view of development. Neither is it the intention here to establish a general and homogenous image of the native in South-east Asia. We are not attempting a complete and detailed personality and culture study of the native, a national character study. There is a vast difference between the Javanese and the Malays but these differences are on a different plane. They do not refer to characteristics selected by colonial ideology, such as indolence, treacherousness, lack of originality, and so on. It is however the colonial ideology that attempted to construct a homogenous and negative image of the native. The tracing of this image to its ideological roots and the circumstances surrounding them is the task of the present work.

NOTES

1.   J. C. Baud, "Proeve van Eene Geschiedenis van den Handel en het Verbruik van Opium in Nederlandsch Indie", p. 91, *BTLVNI*, vol. 1, 1851.
2.   *Ibid.*, p. 145.
3.   J. F. van Bemmelen, "Opium", p. 158, in D. G. Stibbe (ed.), *Encyclopaedie van Nederlandsch-Indie*, III, Martinus Nijhoff, E. J. Brill, Leiden, 1919.
4.   W. W. Willoughby, *Opium as an International Problem*, p. 112. Johns Hopkins Press, Baltimore, 1925.
5.   Theodore Christlieb, *The Indo-British Opium Trade and the Effect*, p. 22. Tr. David B. Croom. James Nisbet, London, 1881.
6.   Ellen N. la Motte, *The Ethics of Opium*, pp. 53, 62, *op. cit.*
7.   W. W. Willoughby, *op. cit.*, p. 18.

8.   For the Philippine figures see *Use of Opium and Traffic Therein*, p. 160. Senate Document no. 265, 59th Congress, 1st Session, Government Printing Office, Washington, 1906. For the Straits Settlement figures see M. van Geuns, *De Opium Cultuur in Nederlandsch-Indie, eene Nieuwe Bron van Inkomsten*, p. 54. J. H. de Bussy, Amsterdam, 1903.

9.   Tj. J. Addens, *The Distribution of Opium Cultivation and the Trade in Opium*, pp. 85–86. Enschede en Zonen, Haarlem, 1939.

10. From *Report, East Indian Finance*, 1871, no. 5097, quoted in J. F. B. Tinling, *The Poppy-Plague and England's Crime*, p. 7. Elliot Stock, London, 1876.

11. *Ibid.*, p. 7.

12. Quoted in W. W. Willoughby, *op. cit.*, pp. 85–86, from *Proceedings of the Committee appointed by His Excellency the Governor and High Commissioner to enquire into Matters relating to the Use of Opium in British Malaya, p. A54*. Government Printing Office, Singapore, 1924.

13. W. W. Willoughby, *op. cit.*, p. 86.

14. Alleyne Ireland, *The Far Eastern Tropics*, p. 47. Archibald Constable, London, 1905.

15. *Ibid.*, p. 47.

16. H. H. Sultzberger (ed.), *All about Opium*, pp. 104–105. London, 1884 (no publisher indicated). It contained amongst others, extracts from *England, China, and India*, by Sinibaldo de Mas, Paris, 1858.

17. T. S. Raffles, *Memoir*, vol. 2, p. 173.

18. F. de Haan, *Oud Batavia*, pp. 450–453, A. G. Nix, Bandoeng, 1935.

19. T. S. Raffles, *The History of Java*, vol. 1, p. 76, Oxford Univ. Press, London, 1965.

20. *Ibid.*, p. 63. On slavery see also D. G. Stibbe (ed.), *Encyclopedie van Nederlandsch-Indie*, art. "Slavernij", vol. 3. Nijhoff, Brill, The Hague, Leiden, 1919.

21. T. Braddell, "The Europeans in the Indian Archipelago in the 16th and 17th centuries", p. 329. *JIAEA*, New Series, vol. 11, no. 4, 1857, Singapore.

22. *Ibid.*, p. 328–329.

23. Alleyne Ireland, *The Far Eastern Tropics*, pp. 115–116, *op. cit.*

24. *Ibid.*, p. 116. Historically, the remarks were not accurate. Malays did work for the government in the Malay States, as well as the Straits Settlements.

25. Benjamin Kidd, *The Control of the Tropics*, p. 52. Macmillan, New York, 1898.

26. *Ibid.*, p. 51.

27. *Ibid.*, p. 50.

28. *Ibid.*, pp. 96–97.

29. G. Gonggrijp, *Schets eener Economische Geschiedenis van Nederlandsch Indie*, p. 3. Erven F. Bohn, Haarlem, 1928. The translation is mine.

30. *Ibid.*, pp. 5–6.

31. G. H. Nadel, P. Curtis (eds.), *Imperialism and Colonialism*, p. 25. Macmillan, New York, 1964.

32. The most concise definition of prejudice is "thinking ill of others without sufficient warrant". See Garden W. Allport, *The Nature of Prejudice*, p. 6. Addison-Wesley, Massachusetts, 1966.

33. Parker T. Moon, Imperialism and World Politics, p. 526. Macmillan, New York, 1937.

34. *Ibid.*, p. 537.

35. Leopold Ainsworth, *The Confessions of a Planter in Malaya*, pp. 53–54. Witherby, London, 1933.

36. C. D. Ahearne, *Annual Report of the Labour Department for the Year 1931*, pp. 19–20. Federated Malay States, Kuala Lumpur, 1932.

37. C. Wilson, *Annual Report of the Labour Department, Malaya, for the Year 1937*, p. 72. Federated Malay States Government Press, Kuala Lumpur, 1938.

38. B. O. Stoney, "The Malays of British Malaya", in Arnold Wright (ed.), *Twentieth Century Impressions of British Malaya*, p. 228, *op. cit.*

39. C. Wilson, *Annual Report of the Labour Department, Malaya, for the Year 1938*, p. 76. Federated Malay States Government Press, Kuala Lumpur, 1939.

40. Leopold Ainsworth, *op. cit.*, pp. 46–47. The date of this incident was not given but the book was published in 1933.

41. *Ibid.*, p. 47.

42. *Ibid.*, p. 71.

43. M. Watson, *The Prevention of Malaria in the Federated Malay States*, p. 102. John Murray, London, 1921.

44. The basic figures are derived from *Handbook of British Malaya 1930*, p. 189. Malayan Information Agency, London (undated).

45. J. T. Simmons, T. F. Whayne, G. W. Anderson, H. M. Horacle, *Global Epidemiology*, vol. I, pp. 168, 171. Heinemann, London, 1944.

46. *Ibid.*, p. 164.

47. *Ibid.*, p. 169.

48. *Ibid.*, p. 173.

49. M. Watson, *op. cit.*, p. 39.

50. *Ibid.*, p. 94.

51. *Ibid.*, p. 48.

52. *Ibid.*, p. 42.

53. *ADRSS 1907*, p. 455. Government Printing Office, Singapore, 1908.

54. Arnold Wright, *op. cit.*, p. 247.

55. *SSAR 1887*, p. 163. Government Printing Office, Singapore 1888. Unfortunately the total population figure and ethnic breakdowns were not given.

56. *ADRSS 1907*, p. 394, *op. cit.*

57. *Ibid.*, p. 398.

58. *Ibid.*, pp. 396, 400.

59. *ADRSS 1927*, pp. 619, 623.

60. *Ibid.*, p. 625.

61. *Ibid.*, p. 733.

62. *ADRSS 1937*, p. 1002, Vol. II (1939).

63. *SSAR 1887*, p. 136, *op. cit.*

64. For the figures see *ibid.*, pp. 1033–34.

65. *ADRSS 1907*, p. 41, *op. cit.*

66. C. A. Vlieland, *A Report of the 1931 Census and on certain Problems of Vital Statistics*, p. 128. Table 10. Malayan Information Agency, London, 1932.

67. *Ibid.* Compiled from Table III, pp. 232–233, and rounded to the nearest thousand.

68. For the above figures see *ADRSS 1937*, vol. II, pp. 104, 82, 87, 145, 31, 30, 32, *op. cit.*

69. *Ibid.*, vol. I, p. 243.

70. Karl Marx, Frederick Engels, *On Colonialism*, p.19. Progress Publishers, Moscow, 1968.

71. *Ibid.*, p. 23.

72. *Ibid.*, pp. 40–41. From the *New York Daily Tribune*, June 25, 1853.

73. *Ibid.*, p.41

74. *Ibid.*, p.122.

75. *Ibid.*, p. 124. From *New York Daily Tribune*, June 5, 1857.

76. *Ibid.*, p. 156.
77. *Ibid.*, p. 264.
78. *Ibid.*, p. 340. "In all questions of international politics the sentimental party newspapers of the French and Italians are to be used with utmost mistrust, and we Germans are dutybound to preserve our theoretical superiority through criticism in this sphere as well."
79. *Ibid.*, p.341.
80. Eduard Bernstein, *Evolutionary Socialism*, pp. 178–179. Tr. E. C. Harvey. Schocken Books, New York, 1963.
81. H. C. d'Encasse, S. R. Schram (eds.), *Marxism and Asia*, p. 130. Allen Lane /The Penguin Press, London, 1969.
82. Julius Braunthal, *History of the International 1864–1914*, p. 319. Tr. H. Collins, K. Mitchell. Thomas Nelson, London, 1966.
83. Karl Marx and Frederick Engels, *Selected Correspondence*, p. 96. Foreign Languages Publishing House, Moscow (undated after 1953) Religion according to Marx and Engels is an illusion. It was born out of human distress. The happiness it creates is illusory. It is the opium of the people. Karl Marx and Frederick Engels, *Religion*. Progress Publishers, Moscow, 1966.
84. *Ibid.*, p. 561. Letter to Plekhanov, February 1895.
85. Karl Marx and Frederick Engels, *The Russian Menace to Europe*, pp. 137–138. Edited and selected by P. W. Blackstock, B. F. Hoselitz. Free Press, Glencoe, Illinois, 1952. The title was chosen by the editors. This work is a selection of articles, speeches, and news dispatches. The quotation is from *New York Tribune*, April 19, 1853.
86. *Ibid.*, pp. 142–143. *New York Tribune,* April 15, 1854.
87. *Ibid.*, p. 215. Article in the Volkstaat, Leipzig, April 21, 1875.
88. *Ibid.*, pp. 99–100. Articles in *Commonwealth*, March 24, 31, April 5, 1866.
89. V. G. Belinsky, *Selected Philosophical Works*, p. 125. Foreign Languages Publishing House, Moscow, 1956.
90. *Ibid.*, p. 127.
91. Alexander Herzen, *Selected Philosophical Work*, p. 481. Tr. L. Navrozov. Foreign Languages Publishing House, Moscow, 1956.
92. D. W. van Welderen Rengers, *The Failure of a Liberal Colonial Policy*, p. 41. Martinus Nijhoff, the Hague, 1947.
93. I have discussed this problem in another book on the intellectuals in developing societies. The shortcomings of Asian societies are discussed there. A separation is made between those arising from colonialism and those from indigenous history. See Syed Hussein Alatas, *Intellectuals in Developing Societies*, Frank Cass, London, 1977.

Bibliography

Abdul Rahman, Senu. *Revolusi Mental.* Penerbitan Utusan Melayu, Kuala Lumpur, 1971.

Abdullah, Dato Sedia Raja. 'The Origin of Pawang and Berpuar Ceremony', in *JMBRAS*, vol. V, part 2, Nov. 1927.

Addens, Tj. J. *The Distribution of Opium Cultivation and the Trade in Opium.* Enschede en Zonen, Haarlem, 1939.

ADRSS 1907, Government Printing Office, Singapore, 1908.

ADRSS 1927, Government Printing Office, Singapore, 1928.

ADRSS 1937, vol. 1, 2. Government Printing Office, Singapore, 1939.

Agoncillo, Teodoro A. *Malolos.* University of the Philippines, Quezon City, 1960.

Agoncillo, Teodoro A. 'Rizal and the Philippine Revolution', in Leopoldo Y. Yabes, (ed), *Jose Rizal on His Centenary.* University of the Philippines, Quezon City, 1963.

Agustin, Gaspar de San. 'Letter on the Filipinos', in E. H. Blair, J. A. Robertson, (eds.). *The Philippine Islands 1493–1898.* Vol. XL, 1690–1691. A. H. Clark, Cleveland, Ohio, 1903–1909.

Ahearne, C. D. *Annual Report of the Labour Department for the Year 1931.* Federated Malay States, Kuala Lumpur, 1932.

Ainsworth, *The Confession of a Planter in Malaya.* Witherby, London, 1933.

Alatas, Syed Hussein. *The Sociology of Corruption.* Donald Moore, Singapore, 1968.

Alatas, Syed Hussein. *Thomas Stamford Raffles (1781–1826): Schemer or Reformer?* Angus and Robertson, Singapore / Sydney, 1971.

Alatas, Syed Hussein. 'Erti Kemajuan Masharakat', in *Utusan Melayu,* 7 Oct. 1959, Kuala Lumpur.

Alatas, Syed Hussein. 'Sekitar Bahasa dan Kebudayaan Melayu', in *Dewan Bahasa,* IV, no. 2, Feb. 1960, Kuala Lumpur.

Alatas, Syed Hussein. 'Sejarah Melayu berisi Unsur-Unsur yang tidak Sehat dari Segi Falsafah Perjuangan Islam', in *Angkatan Baru,* October, 1965, Kuala Lumpur.

Alatas, Syed Hussein. 'Collective Representations and Economic Development', in *Kajian Ekonomi Malaysia,* vol. II, no. 1, 1965, Kuala Lumpur.

Alatas, Syed Hussein. 'Modernization and National Consciousness', in Ooi Jin Bee, Chiang Hai Ding, (eds.), *Modern Singapore.* University of Singapore, Singapore, 1969.

Alatas, Syed Hussein. *The Second Malaysia Plan 1971–1975: A Critique.* Occasional Paper no. 15. Institute of Southeast Asian Studies, Singapore, 1972.

Alatas, Syed Hussein. *Siapa yang Salah.* Pustaka Nasional, Singapore, 1972. (In Malay.)

Alatas, Syed Hussein. 'Eliminate Social Greed', in *PHP* (Peace, Happiness, Prosperity), September, 1972, Tokyo.

Alatas, Syed Hussein. 'The Grading of Occupational Prestige Amongst the Malays in Malaysia,' in *JMBRAS*, vol. XLI, pt. 1, 1968.

Alatas, Syed Hussein. 'The Weber Thesis and Southeast Asia', in *Archives de Sociologie des Religions*, no. 15, 1963, Paris.

Alatas, Syed Hussein. 'Religion and Modernization in Southeast Asia', in *Archives Européennes de Sociologie*, XI, 1970.

Alatas, Syed Hussein. 'Some Comments on Islam and Social Change in Malaysia', in *International Yearbook for the Sociology of Religion*, vol. 5, 1969, Cologne.

Atalas, Syed Hussein. 'Theoretical Aspects of Southeast Asian History', in *Asian Studies*, vol. 2, no. 2, 1964, Manila.

Alatas, Syed Hussein. *Modernization and Social Change*. Angus and Robertson, Sydney, 1972.

D'Albequerque, Alfonso. *The Commentaries of the Great Alfonso D'Albequerque*, vol. III. W. de Gray Birch, (tr., ed.). Hakluyt Society, London, 1880.

Ali, Abdullah Yusuf. *The Holy Quran*, vols. 1–2. Khalil Al-Rawaf, New York, 1946.

Allport, Gordon W. *The Nature of Prejudice*. Addison-Wesley, Massachusetts, 1966.

Allen, G. C., Donnithorne, A. G. *Western Enterprise in Indonesia and Malaya*. Allen and Unwin, London, 1957.

Andreski, Stanislav. *The Uses of Comparative Sociology*. University of California Press, Berkeley and Los Angeles, 1964.

Andreski, Stanislav. *Parisitism and Subversion*. Weldenfeld and Nicolson, London, 1966.

Angelino, A. D. A. de Kat. *Colonial Policy*. 2 vols., tr. G. J. Renier, Martinus Nijhoff, the Hague, 1931.

Anson, A. E. H. *About Others and Myself*. John Murray, London, 1920.

Alzona, E. *Selected Essays and Letters of Jose Rizal*. Rangel and Sons, Manila, 1964.

Arsalan, Shakib. *Our Decline and Its Causes*, tr. M. A. Shakoor. Muhammad Ashraf, Lahore, 1952.

Arsalan, Shakib. *Mengapa Kaum Muslimin Mundur dan Mengapa Kaum Selain Mereka Madju*, tr. into Indonesian by H. Moenawar Chalil. Bulan Bintang, Djakarta, 1967.

(Author Unknown), 'Een Voorbeeld van Javaansche Luiheed', in *TNI*, part 3, 1869.

Author Unknown (an Englishman). *Remarks on the Philippine Islands and on their Capital Manila, 1890–1822*. W. Thacker, St. Andrew's Library, Calcutta, 1828. Reproduced in E. H. Blair, J. H. Robertson, (trs. eds.). *The Philippine Islands 1493–1898*, vol. LI, 1801–1840. A. H. Clark, Cleveland, Ohio, 1903–1909.

Balestier, J. 'View of the States of Agriculture in the British Possessions in the Straits of Malacca', in *JIAEA*, vol. II, no. III, March, 1848.

Ballard, G. A. *Rulers of the Indian Ocean*. Duckworth, London, 1927.

Barbossa, Duarte. *The Book of Duarte Barbossaa*, tr., ed., M. L. Dames. Hakluyt Society, vol. 2, 2nd Series, no. 49, London, 1921.

Bastin, J. *The Native Policy of Sir Stamford Raffles in Java and Sumatra*. Oxford University Press, London, 1957.

Battuta, Ibn. *Travels in Asia and Africa 1325–1354*, tr. H. A. R. Gibb. George Routledge, London, 1929.

Baud, J. C. 'Proeve van eene Geschiedenis van den Handel en het Verbruick van Opium in Nederlandsch Indie', in *BTLVNI*, vol. 1, 1851.

Baumgarten, F. L. 'Agriculture', in *JIAEA*, vol. 3, 1849.

Belinsky, V. G. *Selected Philosophical Works.* Foreign Languages Publishing House, Moscow, 1956.

Bemmelen, J. F. van. 'Opium', in D. G. Stibbe, (ed.), *Encyclopaedie van Nederlandsch-Indie*, vol. III. Martinus Nijhoff, E. J. Brill, 1919.

Benedetto, L. F. *The Travels of Marco Polo*, tr. Aldo Ricci. Routledge-Kegan Paul, London, 1950.

Benedict, Ruth. *The Chrysanthemum and the Sword.* Routledge and Kegan Paul, London, 1967.

Bernstein, Eduard. *Evolutionary Socialism*, tr. E. C. Harvey. Schocken Books, New York, 1963.

Bird, Isabella L. *The Golden Chersonese.* Oxford University Press, Kuala Lumpur, 1967. (Reprinted from 1833.)

Blagden, C. O. 'Report of Governor Balthasar Bort on Malacca 1678', in *JMBRAS*, vol. V, August, 1927.

Blair, E. H., Robertson, J. A. (eds), *The Philippine Islands 1493–1898.* Vols. XL, LI. I, XXVIII. A. H. Clark, Cleveland, Ohio, 1903–1909.

Bleackley, J. T. *A Tour in Southern Asia.* John Lane, London, 1928.

Blythe, W. L. 'Historical Sketches of Chinese Labour in Malaya', in *JMBRAS*, vol. XX, part 1, June, 1947.

Boeke, J. H. 'Dualistic Economics', in *Indonesian Economics.* W. van Hoeve, the Hague, 1961.

Boeke, J. H. *The Evolution of the Netherland Indies Economy.* Netherlands and Netherlands Indies Council/Institute of Pacific Relations, New York, 1946.

Boeke, J. H. *The Interests of the Voiceless Far East.* Universitaire Pers Leiden, Leiden, 1948.

Bosch, J. van den. 'Memorie van den Commissaris-General J. van den Bosch', in *BTLVNI*, vol. 7, no. 11, 1864 (Amsterdam).

Bowrey, Thomas. *A Geographical Account of Countries round the Bay of Bengal.* Ed. R. C. Temple. Hakluyt Society, Cambridge, 1905.

Bowring, Sir John. *A Visit to the Philippine Islands.* Smith, Elder, London, 1859.

Boxer, C. R. *The Portuguese Seaborne Empire.* Hutchison, London, 1969.

Braddell, T. 'Gambling and Opium Smoking in the Straits of Malacca', pp. 66–83, *JIAEA*, New Series, vol. 1, 1856.

Braddell, T. 'The Europeans in the Indian Archipelago in the 16th and 17th Centuries', in *JIAEA*, New Series, vol. II, no. 4, 1857.

Braunthal, Julius. *History of the International 1864–1914*, tr. H. Collins, K. Mitchell. Thomas Nelson, London, 1966.

Brooke, James. *Narrative of Events in Borneo and Celebes*, vol. I. John Murray, London, 1848.

Brown, J. Macmillan. *The Dutch East Indies.* Kegan Paul, Trench, Trubner, London, 1914.

Boxer, C. R. *The Portuguese Seaborne Empire.* Hutchison, London, 1969.

Burger, H. D. *De Ontsluiting van Java's Binnenland voor het Wereldverkeer.* Veeman en Zonen, Wageningen, 1939.

Cabaton, A. *Java, Sumatra, and the Other Islands of the Dutch East Indies*, tr. B. Mall. Fischer Unwin, London, 1911.

Caddy, Florence. *To Siam and Malaya.* Hurst and Blackett, London, 1889.

Cameron, John. *Our Tropical Possessions in Malayan India.* Smith, Elder, London, 1865.

Campbell, D. M. *Java: Past and Present*, vols. 1, 2. Heinemann, London, 1915.

Careri, G. F. G. *A Voyage to the Philippines.* Filipiniana Book Guild, Manila, 1963.

Careri, G. F. G. *A Voyage Round the World.* (Tr. and publisher unknown.)

Carletti, Francesco. *My Voyage around the World,* tr. H. Weinstock. Pantheon Books, New York, 1964. (A 16th century account of a Florentine merchant who visited the East Indies.)

Caute, David. *Essential Writings of Karl Marx.* MacGibbon and Kee, London, 1967.

Chernyak, Y. *Advocates of Colonialism,* tr. T. Kapustin. Progress Publishers, Moscow, 1968.

Chirino, Pedro. *The Philippines in 1600,* tr. Ramon Echevarria. Historical Conservation Society XV, Manila, 1969.

Chong-Yah, Lim. *Economic Development of Modern Malaya.* Oxford University Press, Kuala Lumpur, 1967.

Christlieb, Theodore. *The Indo-British Opium Trade and the Effect,* tr. David B. Croom. James Nisbet, London, 1881.

Clifford, Hugh. 'A New Collection of Malay Proverb', in *JSBRAS,* no. 24, 1891.

Clifford, Hugh. *In Court and Kampong.* The Richards Press, London, 1927.

Clifford, Hugh. *Studies in Brown Humanity.* Grant Richards. London, 1898.

Clifford, Hugh. 'Rival Systems and the Malayan Peoples', in *North American Review,* vol. 177, 1903.

Clifford, Hugh. *Heroes in Exile.* John Murray, London, 1928.

Colenbrander, H. T., Stokvis, J. E. (eds.), *Leven en Arbeid van Mr. C. Th. van Deventer,* vol. 2. Van Kampen, Amsterdam, 1916.

Cool, W. *With the Dutch in the East.* Java Head Bookshop, London. 1934.

Coope, A. E. *The Voyage of Abdullah.* Malaya Publishing House, Singapore, 1949.

Costa, H. de la. *The Jesuits in the Philippines 1581–1768.* Harvard University Press, Cambridge, Massachusetts, 1961.

Connolly, W. E. *Political Science and Ideology.* Atherton Press, New York. 1967.

Constantino, Renato. *Dissent and Counter-Consciousness.* Malaya Books. Quezon City, 1970.

Craig, Austin; Benitez, Conrado. *Philippine Progress Prior to 1898.* Philippine Education, Manila, 1916.

Crawfurd, J. *History of the Indian Archipelago,* vols. 1, 2. Archibald Constable, Edinburgh, 1820.

Crawfurd, John. *Journal of an Embassy from the Governor General of India to the Courts of Siam and Cochin China exhibiting a view of the Actual State of those Kingdoms.* Henry Colburn, London 1828.

Dampier, William. *Voyages and Discoveries.* Argonaut Press. London, 1931.

Dannenfelt, Karl H. (ed.), *The Renaissance.* Heath, Boston, 1959.

Davidson, J. F. *Trade and Travel in the Far East.* Madden and Malcolm. London, 1846.

Day, Clive. *The Dutch in Java.* Oxford University Press, Kuala Lumpur, 1966.

d'Encasse, H. C.: Schram, S. R. (eds.), *Marxism and Asia.* Allen Lane/The Penguin Press, London, 1969.

Deutscher, Isaac. (ed.), *The Age of Permanent Revolution: A Trotsky Anthology.* Dell, New York, 1964.

Deventer, M. L. van. *Geschiedenis der Nederlanders op Java,* vols. 1, 2. Tjeenk Willink, Haarlem, 1886, 1887.

Deventer, M. L. van (ed.), *Het Nederlandsch Gezag over Java en Onderhoorigheden sedert 1811,* vol. 1. Martinus Nijhoff, 's-Gravenhage, 1891.

Dharmapala, Anagarika. *Return to Righteousness,* ed. Ananda Guruge. Ministry of Education and Cultural Affairs, Ceylon, 1965.

Doornik, J. E. *Vrijmoedige Gedachten over Neerlands Indië en over de Regering van den Gouverneur-Generaal van der Capellen.* Sulpke, Amsterdam, 1826.

Doren, Charles Van. *The Idea of Progress.* Praeger, New York, 1967.

Drewes, G. W. J. 'De Biografie van een Minangkabause Peperhandelaar in de Lampongs', in *VKITLV*, vol. 36. Martinus Nijhoff, 's-Gravenhage, 1961. (Text in Dutch and Malay.)

Earl, G. W. 'Steam Routes through the Indian Archipelago', in *JIAEA*, vol. V, pp. 441–450, 1851.

Earl, G. Windsor. 'Handbook for the Colonists in Tropical Australia', in *JIAEA*, New Series, vol. IV, 1863.

Easton, L. D.; Guddat, K. H. (eds. trs.), *Writings of the Young Marx on Philosophy and Sociology.* Double Day, New York, 1967.

Eaton, B. J. 'Agriculture', in R. O. Windstedt, (ed.). *Malaya.* Constable, London, 1923.

Eredia, E. G. de. 'Description of Malacca and Meridonial India and Cathay', tr. J. V. Mills, in *JMBRAS*, vol. VIII, part 1, April, 1930.

Evans, H. *Men in the Tropics.* William Hodge, London, 1949.

Fanfani, Amintore. *Catholicism, Protestantism and Capitalism.* Sheed and Ward, London, 1938.

Fanon, Frantz. *Studies in Dying Colonialism,* tr. H. Chevalier. Monthly Review Press, New York, 1959.

Fanon, Frantz. *Toward the African Revolution,* tr. H. Chevalier. Monthly Review Press, New York, 1967.

Fanon, Frantz. *Black Skin White Masks,* tr. C. L. Markmann. MacGibbon and Kee, London, 1968.

Fanon, Frantz. *The Wretched of the Earth,* tr. C. Farrington. MacGibbon and Kee, London, 1965.

Filet, P. W. *De Verhouding der Vorsten op Java tot de Nederlandscht Indische Regeering.* Martinus Nijhoff, 's-Gravenhage, 1895.

Final Report of the Rice Committee. Federation of Malaya, Government Press, Kuala Lumpur, 1956.

Fores-Ganzon, Gudalupe. *La Solidaridad,* vol. 1, 1889. Tr. into English with Spanish text. University of the Philippine Press, Quezon City, 1967.

Foster, William (ed.). *The Voyage of Sir Henry Middleton to the Moluccas 1604–1606.* Hakluyt Society, 2nd. Series, LXXXVIII, London. 1943.

Fryke, C.; Schweitzer, C. *Voyages to the East Indies.* Cassel, London, 1929.

Furnivall, J. S. *Netherlands India.* Cambridge University Press, London, 1939.

Furnivall, J. S. *Colonial Policy and Practice.* Cambridge University Press, London, 1948.

Galaisiere, G. J. H. J. B. Le Gentil de la. *A Voyage to the Indian Seas.* Filipiniana Book Guild, Manila, 1963.

Gatmaitan, M. S. *Marcelo H. del Pilar.* Munoz Press, Quezon City, 1965.

Geuns, M. van. *De Opiumcultuur in Nederlandsch-Indie, eene Nieuwe Bron van Inkomsten.* J. H. de Bussy, Amsterdam, 1903.

Goens, Rijckloff van. 'Reijsbeschrijving van den Weg uijt Samarangh nae de Konincklijke Hoofdplaets Mataram'. *BTLVNI*, vol. 4, pp. 307–350, 1856.

Goens, Ryckloff V. van. 'Corte Beschrijvinge van 't Eijland Java's, in *BTLVNI*, vol. 4, 1856.

Gonggrijp, G. *Schets eener Economische Geschiedenis van Nederlandsch-Indie.* Bohn, Haarlem,1928.

Gonggrijp, G. L. *Brieven van Opheffer.* Leiter-Nypels. Maastricht, 1944.

Gonggrijp, G. 'Value Curves and the Lowest Level of the Indies Economy', in *Indonesian Economics.* Van Hoeve, the Hague, 1961.

Gorer, Geoffrey. *Bali and Angkor.* Michael Joseph, London, 1936.

Graaf, H. J. de. 'De Regering van Sunan Mangku-Rat I Tegal-Wangi, Vorst van Mataram', in *VITLV*, 2 vols. 33, 39, Martinus Nijhoff, 's-Gravenhage, 1961, 1962.

Graaf. H. J. de. 'De Regering van Sultan Agung, Vorst van Mataram', in *VKITLV*, XXXIII, Martinus Nijhoff, 's-Gravenhage, 1958.

Gras, N. S. B. 'Capitalism—Concepts and History', in F. C. Lane, J. C. Riemersma, (eds.), *Enterprise and Secular Change*. Richard D. Irwin, Illinois, 1953.

Groeneveldt, W. P. *Notes on the Malay Archipelago and Malacca compiled from Chinese Sources*. W. Bruining, Batavia, 1876.

Guerreiro, J. J. de Vellez. 'A Portuguese Account of Johore', tr. T. D. Hughes, in *JMBRAS*, vol. XIII, part 2, October, 1935.

Gullick, J. M. *A History of Selangor*. Eastern University Press, Singapore, 1960.

Gullick, J. M. *The Story of Early Kuala Lumpur*. Donald Moore, Singapore, 1956.

Haan, de. *Oud Batavia*. A. G. Nix, Bandoeng, 1935.

Haan, F. de. *Priangan*, vols. 1–4. Bataviasch Genootschap van Kunsten en Wetenschappen, Batavia, 1910–1912.

Hamilton, Alexander. *A New Account of the East Indies*, 2 vols. Argonaut Press, London, 1930.

Handbook of British Malaya 1930. Malayan Information Agency, London, (undated).

Handbook of the Netherlands East-Indies 1930. Department of Agriculture, Industry and Commerce, Buitenzorg, Java, 1930.

Hasegawa, Nyozekan. *The Japanese Character*, tr. John Bester. Kodansha International, Tokyo, 1965.

Herrera, Fray Diego de. 'Memoranda', in *The Colonization and Conquest of the Philippines by Spain*. Filipiniana Book Guild, Manila, 1965. (Compiled by Editorial Board.)

Herskovits, M. J. *Cultural Anthropology*. A. A. Knopf, New York, 1955.

Herzen, Alexander. *Selected Philosophical Works*, tr. L. Navrozov. Foreign Languages Publishing House, Moscow, 1956.

Hill, A. H. 'The Hikayat Abdullah', in *JMBRAS*, vol. XXVIII, part 3, June, 1955.

Hobson, J. S. *Imperialism*. Allen and Unwin, London, 1938.

Hoetink, H. '"Colonial Psychology" and Race', in *JEH*, vol. XXI, no. 4, 1961.

Hooker, M. B. (ed.). *Readings in Malay Adat Laws*. Singapore University Press, Singapore, 1970.

Horowitz, I. L. *Philosophy, Science and the Sociology of Knowledge*. C. C. Thomas, Illinois, 1961.

Hourani, George F. *Arab Seafaring in the Indian Ocean in Ancient and Early Medieval Times*. Khayats, Beirut, 1963.

Huan, Ma. *Ying-Yai Sheng-Lan* (The Overall Survey of the Ocean's Shores), tr. Feng Cheng-Chun, ed. J. V. G. Mills. Cambridge University Press, London, 1970.

Humphreys, J. L. 'A Collection of Malay Proverbs', in *JSBRAS*, no. 67, 1914.

Husain, Zakir. *Capitalism*. Asia Publishing House, London, 1967.

Iongh, D. de. *Het Krijgswezen onder de Oostindische Compagnie*. Stockum en Zoon, 's-Gravenhage, 1950.

Ireland, Alleyne. *The Far Eastern Tropics*. Archibald Constable, London, 1905.

Jackson, R. N. *Immigrant Labour and the Development of Malaya*. Government Printing Press, Federation of Malaya, 1961.

Jagor, Feodor. 'Travels in the Philippines', in Austin Craig, (ed.), *The Former Philippines thru Foreign Eyes*. Philippine Education, Manila, 1916.

Jansen, M. H. 'Gedachten over den Handel van den Indischen Archipel voor de komst de Europeanen', in *TNI*, vol. 2, pt. 1, 1849.

Johnson, Harry M. 'Ideology', in David L. Sills, (ed.), *International Encyclopaedia of the Social Sciences*, vol. VII, Macmillan, Free Press, U.S.A., 1968.

Jonge, J. K. J. de. *De Opkomst van het Nederlandsch Gezag over Java*, vols. 2–13. Martinus Nijhoff, 's-Gravenhage, 1864–1888.

Kato, Masuo. *The Lost War*. Alfred A. Knopf, New York, 1946.

Kawasaki, Ichiro. *Japan Unmasked*. Charles E. Tuttle, Tokyo, 1970.

Keddie, N. R. *An Islamic Response to Imperialism*. (Political and Religious Writings of Sayyid Jamaluddin al-Afghani.) University of California Press, Berkeley and Los Angeles, 1968.

Kennedy, Raymond. *The Ageless Indies*, John Day, New York, 1942.

Keppel, H. *A Visit to the Indian Archipelago*, vols. 1, 2. Bentley, London, 1853.

Khaldun, Abdul Rahman Ibn. *The Muqaddimah*, tr. ed. F. Rosenthal. 2 vols. Routledge and Kegan Paul, London, 1958.

Kidd, Benjamin. *The Control of the Tropics*. Macmillan, New York, 1898.

Kiernan, V. C. *The Lords of Human Kind*. Weidenfeld and Nicolson, London, 1969.

Kluckhohn, C. 'The Study of Culture', in D. Lerner, H. D. Lasswell, (eds.), *The Policy Sciences*, Stanford University Press, California, 1951.

Kohl, J. F. Halkema. 'Colonial Nationalism', in *Indonesië*, vol. VII, no. 1, 1953–1954.

Kolakowski, Leszek. *Marxism and Beyond*, tr. J. Z. Peel. Pall Mall Press, London, 1969.

Kolff, G. H. van der. 'European Influence on Native Agriculture', in B. Schrieke, (ed.), *The Effect of Western Influence on Native Civilizations in the Malay Archipelago*. Kolff, Batavia, 1929.

Kyi, U Khin Maung. 'Western Enterprise and Economic Development in Burma', in *Journal of the Burma Research Society*, LIII, no. 1, June, 1970.

La Motte, Ellen N. *The Opium Monopoly*. Macmillan, New York, 1920.

La Motte, Ellen N. *The Ethics of Opium*. Century, New York, 1924.

Lenin, V. I. *Imperialism, the Highest Stage of Capitalism*. Foreign Languages Publishing House, Moscow (undated). Eleventh impression.

Leur, J. C. van. *Indonesian Trade and Society*. W. van Hoeve, the Hague, 1955.

Lichtheim, G. *Imperialism*. Allen Lane Penguin Press, London, 1971.

Lichtheim, G. *The Concept of Ideology and Other Essays*. Random House, New York, 1967.

Linton, Ralph, (ed.). *The Science of Man in the World Crisis*. Colombia University Press, New York, 1950.

Little, R. 'On the Habitual Use of Opium in Singapore', pp. 1–79, in *JIAEA*, vol. II, 1848.

Lodewycksz, Willem. 'D'Eerste Boeck', in G. P. Rouffaer, J. W. Ijzerman, (eds.), *De Eerste Schipvaart der Nederlanders naar Oost-Indie onder Cornelis de Houtman 1595–1597*, vol. 1. Martinus Nijhoff, 's-Gravenhage, 1915.

Logan, J. R. 'Memoirs of Malays', (Che Solliman's Narration), in *JIAEA*, vol. II, no. VI, June, 1848.

Logan, J. R. 'The Present Condition of the Indian Archipelago', in *JIAEA*, vol. 1, pp. 1–21, 1847.

Low, J. 'Notes on the Progress of the Nutmeg Cultivation and Trade from the Early Part of the 17th Century up to the Present', in *JIAEA*, vol. V, pp. 470–487, 1851.

Lüthy, Herbert. 'Colonization and the Making of Mankind', in *JEH*, vol. XXI, no. 4, 1961.

Luzzatto, G. *An Economic History of Italy from the Fall of the Roman Empire to the Beginning of the 16th Century*, tr. P. Jones. Routledge-Kegan Paul, London, 1961.

Mabini, Apolinario. *The Philippine Revolution*, tr. L. M. Guerrero. National Historical Commission, Manila, 1969.

MacMicking, Robert. *Recollections of Manila and the Philippines.* Filipiniana Book Guild. Manila, 1957.

Madariaga. Salvador de. *Englishmen, Frenchmen, Spaniards.* Oxford University Press. London, 1949.

Majul, Cesar A. 'Social Background of Revolution', in *Asian Studies*, vol. IX, no. 1, April, 1971. (Manila.)

Majul, Cesar A. 'A Critique of Rizal's Concept of a Filipino Nation', in Leopoldo Y. Yabes, (ed.), *Jose Rizal on His Centenary.* University of the Philippines, Quezon City. 1963.

Malaysian Digest, vol. 1, no. 2, July 14, 1969. Federal Department of Information, Kuala Lumpur.

Malcolm, George A. *First Malayan Republic.* Christopher, Boston, 1951.

Mannheim. Karl. *Ideology and Utopia.* Routledge-Kegan Paul, London, 1948.

Mannoni, O. *Prospero and Caliban,* tr. P. Powesland. Methuen. London, 1956.

Manrique, Sebastian. 'The Travels of Fray Sebastian Manrique', in the same volume, G. F. G. Careri. *A Voyage to the Philippines.* Filipiniana Book Guild. Manila, 1963.

Maquet, J. J. *The Sociology of Knowledge.* Beacon Press, Boston, 1951.

Markham, C. R. (ed.). *The Voyages of Sir James Lancaster to the East Indies.* Hakluyt Society, London, 1877.

Marsden, W. *The History of Sumatra.* Oxford University Press. London, 1966.

Marx, Karl: Engels, Friedrich. *The Holy Family,* tr. R. Dixon. Foreign Languages Publishing House, Moscow. 1956.

Marx, Karl: Engels, Frederick. *The German Ideology.* Part One, ed. C. J. Arther. Lawrence and Wishart, London, 1970.

Marx, Karl and Engels, Friedrich. *The German Ideology,* ed. R. Pascal. Lawrence and Wishart. London, 1938.

Marx, Karl: Engels, Frederick. *On Colonialism.* Progress Publishers, Moscow, 1968.

Marx, Karl: Engels, Frederick. *Selected Correspondence.* Foreign Languages Publishing House, Moscow. (undated).

Marx, Karl: Engels, Frederick. *On Religion.* Progress Publishers, Moscow, 1966.

Marx, Karl: Engels, Frederick. *The Russian Menace to Europe.* Ed. and selected by P. W. Blackstock, B. F. Hoselitz. Free Press, Glencoe. Illinois, 1952. The title was chosen by the editors.

Marx, Karl and Engels. Frederick. *The German Ideology,* ed. S. Ryazanskaya. Progress Publishers. Moscow, 1964.

Masselman, George. *The Cradle of Colonialism.* Yale University Press, New Haven, 1963.

Masselman. George. 'Dutch Colonial Policy in the 17th Century', in *JEH*, vol. XXI, no. 4, 1961.

Mas. Sinibaldo de. *Report on the Conditions of the Philippines in 1842.* III. Tr. C. Botor, ed. J. Palazon. Historical Conservation Society. Manila, 1963.

Mas. Sinibaldo de. 'The Character of Friars', in E. H. Blair, J. A. Robertson, *The Philippine Islands 1493–1898,* vol. XXVIII. Cleveland, Ohio, 1903–1909.

Maunier, Rene. *The Sociology of Colonies,* ed. tr. E. O. Lorimer. Routledge and Kegan Paul, London, 1949 (vols. 1, 2).

Maxwell, W. E. 'Malay Proverbs', in *JSBRAS*, no. 1, 2, 1878; no. 3, 1879; no. 11, 1883.

McNair, F. *Perak and the Malays.* Tinsley Brothers, London. 1878.

Mead, Margaret. 'National Character', in A. L. Kroeber (ed.), *Anthropology Today.* University of Chicago Press, Chicago, 1953.

Mead, Margaret. 'The Study of National Character', in D. Lerner, H. D. Lasswell, (eds.), *The Policy Sciences*. Stanford University Press, California, University Press, California, 1951.

Meijer, R. P. *Max Havelar, 1860–1960*. University of Melbourne, Melbourne, 1960.

Meilink-Roelofsz, M. A. P. *Asian Trade and European Influence in the Indonesian Archipelago between 1500 and about 1630*. Martinus Nijhoff, the Hague, 1962.

Mendenhall, T. C., Henning, B. D., Foord, A. S. (eds.), *The Quest For a Principle of Authority in Europe: 1715 to the Present*. Henry Holt, New York, 1948. Ch. X, 'Imperialism'.

Merton, Robert K. *Social Theory and Social Structure*. Free Press, New York, 1969.

Metzger, Walter P. 'Generalization about National Character: An Analytical Essay', in Louis Gottschalk. (ed.), *Generalization in the Writing of History*. University of Chicago Press, Chicago, London, 1966.

Middel, R. Brons. *Kesah Pelajaran Abdoellah bin Abdelkadir Moensji dari Singapoera sampai ka Negeri Kalantan*. Brill Leiden, 1893.

Mohamad, Mahathir bin. *The Malay Dilemma*. Asia Pacific Press, Singapore, 1970.

Moon, P. T. *Imperialism and World Politics*. Macmillan, New York, 1937.

Moreland, W. H. (ed.), *Peter Floris, His Voyage to the East Indies in the Globe (1611–1615)*. Hakluyt Society, London, 1934.

Morga, Antonio de. 'History of the Philippine Islands', Vol. I, tr. ed. E. H. Blair, J. A. Robertson, *The Philippine Islands 1493–1898*. Vol. I. Cleveland, Ohio, 1907.

Morga, Antonio de. *Historical Events of the Philippine Islands*. Ed. Jose Rizal, tr. E. Alzona. Jose Rizal National Centennial Commission, Manila, 1962.

Morga, Antonio de. *Sucesos de las Islas Filipinas*, tr. J. S. Cummins. Cambridge University Press, London, 1971. (Hakluyt Society Series II vol. 140.)

Muller, Hendrik P. N. 'The Malay Peninsula in the Past', tr. P. C. H. van Papendrecht. *JSBRAS*, no. 67, Dec. 1914.

Multatuli (Douwes Dekker). *Over Vrije Arbeid in Nederlandsch Indie*. (Date and publisher unknown.)

Multatuli (Douwes Dekker). *Nog-eens Vrije-Arbeid*. Cohen, Amsterdam, 1914.

Muntinghe. H. W. 'Rapport van H. W. Muntinghe, van 28 Julie. 1813', in *TNI*, vol. 2, Zaltbommel, 1864.

Muntinghe. H. W. 'Het stelsel van Regelmatige Belasting vergelijken met dat van Gedwongen Arbeid en Leverantien', in *TNI*, vol. 13, pt. 1, 1851.

Nadel, G. H., Curtis, P. (ed.). *Imperialism and Colonialism*. Macmillan, New York, 1964.

Narkswasdi, Udhis., Selvadurai, S. *Economic Survey of Padi Production in West Malaysia, Report no. 2*, Collective Padi Cultivation in Bachang, Malacca. Ministry of Agriculture and Co-operatives, Kuala Lumpur, 1967.

Narkswasdi, Udhis., Selvadurai, S. *Economic Survey of Padi Production in West Malaysia, Report no. 1*, Selangor. Ministry of Agriculture and Co-operatives, Kuala Lumpur, 1967.

Narkswasdi, Udhis., Selvadurai, S. *Economic Survey of Padi Production in West Malaysia, Report no. 3*, Malacca. Ministry of Agriculture and Co-operatives, Kuala Lumpur, 1967.

Netscher, E. *De Nederlanders in Djohor en Siak*. Bruijniug en Wijt, Batavia, 1870.

Newbold, T. J. *Political and Statistical Account of the British Settlements in the Straits of Malacca*, vols. 1, 2. John Murray, London, 1839.

Norris, Sir William. 'Malay Amok referred to Mahommedanism', in *JIAEA*, vol. III, 1849.

Parry, J. H. *Europe and a Wider World 1415–1715.* Hutchinson's University Library, London, 1949.

Patani, Haji Wan Mohammed. *Semangat Penghidupan.* Majlis Ugama Islam dan Istiadat Melayu, Kelantan, Kota Bahru, 1922. (Malay in Arabic Script.)

Perron-de Roos, E. du. 'Correspondentie van Dirk van Hogendorp met Zijn Broeder Gijsbert Karel', in *BTLVNI,* vol. 102, 1943.

Phelan, J. L. 'Free versus Compulsory Labour: Mexico and the Philippines, 1540–1648', in *Comparative Studies in Society and History,* vol. 1, pp. 189–201, 1958–1959.

Phelan, John L. *The Hispanization of the Philippines.* University of Wisconsin Press, Madison, 1959.

Pierson, N. G. *Koloniale Politiek.* P. N. van Kampen en Zoon, Amsterdam, 1877.

Pilar, Marcelo H. del. *Monastic Supremacy in the Philippines,* tr. E. Alzona. Philippine Historical Association, Manila, 1958.

Pires, Tom. *The Suma Oriental of Tom Pires,* tr., ed., Armando Cortesao. Hakluyt Society, vol. 2, 2nd Series, no. 90, London, 1944.

Plamenatz, J. *Ideology.* Pall Mall, London, 1970.

Plekhanov, G. V. *Fundamental Problems of Marxism.* Lawrence and Wishart, London, 1969.

Plekhanov, G. V. *Art and Social Life,* ed. A. Rothstein. Lawrence and Wishart, London, 1953.

Ponder, H. W. *Javanese Panorama.* Seeley, Service, London. (Printed in 1942.)

Price, A. Grenfell. *The Western Invasions of the Pacific and Its Continents.* Oxford University Press, London, 1950.

Proceedings and Reports of the Commission appointed to inquire into certain matters affecting the good Government of the State of Selangor in relation to the alleged misuse and abuse of toddy in the coast districts of Selangor. Federated Malay States Government Press, Kuala Lumpur, 1917.

Proceedings of the Committee appointed by His Excellency the Governor and High Commissioner to enquire into Matters relating to the Use of Opium in British Malaya. Government Printing Office, Singapore, 1924.

Puthucheary, J. J. *Ownership and Control in the Malayan Economy.* Eastern University Press, Singapore, 1960.

Raffles, T. S. *Memoir,* vols. 1, 2. Ed. Sophia Raffles. James Duncan, London, 1835.

Raffles, T. S. *The History of Java,* 2 vols. Oxford University Press, London, 1965.

Reed, Anthony. *The Contest for North Sumatra.* Oxford University/University of Malaya Press, Kuala Lumpur, 1969.

Rengers, D. W. van Weldern. *The Failure of a Liberal Colonial Policy.* Martinus Nijhoff, the Hague, 1947.

Report of the Rice Cultivation Committee. Vol. 1. Federated Malay States Government Press, Kuala Lumpur, 1931.

Resink, G. J. *Indonesia's History between the Myths.* W. van Hoeve, the Hague, 1968.

Rizal, Jose. 'The Indolence of the Filipinos', in E. Alzona, (tr. and ed.), *Selected Essays and Letters of Jose Rizal.* Rangel and Sons, Manila, 1964.

Roff, W. R. *The Origins of Malay Nationalism.* University of Malaya Press/Yale University Press, Kuala Lumpur/New Haven, 1967.

Rose, J. Holland. *Man and the Sea.* Heffer and Sons, Cambridge, England, 1935.

Rowntree, Joshua. *The Imperial Drug Trade.* Methuen, London, 1906.

Roy, James A. Le. *Philippine Life in Town and Country.* Filipiniana Book Guild, Manila, 1968. *The Philippines Circa 1900.* XIII.

Rutter, Owen. *Triumphant Pilgrimage,* Harrap, London, 1937.

Rutter, Owen. *British North Borneo.* Constable, London, 1922.

Sande, Francisco de. 'Relation of the Filipinos Islands', in *The Colonization and the Conquest of the Philippines by Spain*. Filipiniana Book Guild, VIII, Manila, 1965. (By editorial board.)

Sastri, V. S. Srinivasi. *Report on the Condition of Indian Labour in Malaya*. Government of India Press, New Delhi, 1937.

Schmalhausen, H. E. B. *Over Java en de Javanen*. Van Kampen, Amsterdam, 1909.

Schrieke, B. (ed.). *The Effect of Western Influence on Native Civilizations in the Malay Archipelago*. Kolff, Batavia, 1929.

Schrieke, B. 'Javanen als Zee-en Handelsvolk', in *TITLV*, vol. LVIII, 1919.

Schrieke, B. *Indonesian Sociological Studies*. Part One. W. van Hoeve, the Hague, 1955.

Schrieke, B. *Indonesian Sociological Studies*. Part Two. W. van Hoeve, the Hague, 1957.

Schumpeter, Joseph. *Imperialism*, tr. H. Norden. Meridian Books, New York, 1958.

Scrivenor, J. B. 'Mining', in R. O. Windstedt, (ed.), *Malaya*. Constable, London, 1923.

Sée, Henri. *Modern Capitalism*, tr. H. B. Vanderblue. Noel Douglas, London, 1928.

Selvadurai, S., Arope, Ani bin., Mohammad, Nik Hassani bin. *Socio-Economic Study of Padi Farms in the Kemubu Area of Kelantan 1968*. Ministry of Agriculture and Co-operatives, Kuala Lumpur, 1969.

Senate Document, no. 265, 59th Congress, 1st Session, *Use of Opium and Traffic Therein*. Government Printing Office, Washington, 1906.

Simmons, J. T., Whayne, T. F., Anderson, G. W., Horacle, H. M. *Global Epidemiology*, vol. 1. Heinemann, London, 1944.

Snyder, Louis L. (ed.). *The Imperialism Reader*. D. van Nostrand, New York, 1962.

Sombart, Werner. *The Quintessence of Capitalism*, tr. M. Epstein. Howard Fertig, New York, 1967.

Stapel, F. W. *Cornelis Janszoon Speelman*. M. Nijhoff, 's-Gravenhage, 1936.

Stapel, F. W. *Corpus Diplomaticum Neerlando-Indicum*. Vol. 6. Martinus Nijhoff, 's-Gravenhage, 1955.

Stavorinus, J. S. *Voyages to the East-Indies*. Vols. 1–3. Tr. S. H. Wilcocke, Robinson, Pater-Noster-Row, London, 1798.

Stibbe, D. G. (ed.). *Encyclopedia van Nederlandsch-Indie*. Art. 'Slavernij', vol. 3. Martinus Nijhoff, E. J. Brill, the Hague, Leiden, 1919.

Stibbe, D. G. (ed.). *Neerlands Indie*. Elsevier, Amsterdam, 1929.

Stockdale, J. J. *Sketches, Civil and Military, of the Island of Java*, London, 1811. (No publishing firm.)

Stoney, B. O. 'The Malays of British Malaya', in Arnold Wright, (ed.), *Twentieth Century Impressions of British Malaya*. Lloyd's Greater Britain Publishing Company, London, 1908.

Straits Settlements Annual Report for the Year 1887. Government Printing Office, Singapore, 1888.

Strausz-Hupé, R., Hazard, H. W. (eds.). *The Idea of Colonialism*. Atlantic Books, London, 1958.

Sultzberger, H. H. *All about Opium*. London, 1884. (No publisher mentioned.)

Swettenham, F. A. *The Real Malay*. John Lane, London, New York, 1907.

Swettenham, F. A. *Malay Sketches*. John Lane, London, New York, 1913.

Swettenham, F. A. *British Malaya*. Allen and Unwin, London, 1955.

Swettenham, F. A. *Stories and Sketches by Sir Frank Swettenham*. Selected by W. R. Roff. Oxford University Press, Kuala Lumpur, 1967.

Sydney, R. J. H. *Malay Land*. Cecil Palmer, London, 1926.

Sze, S. A. *Geneva Opium Conferences*. John Hopkins Press, Baltimore, 1926.

Takizawa, Matsuyo. *The Penetration of Money Economy in Japan*. AMS Press, New York, 1927.

Thomson, J. *The Straits of Malacca, Indo-China and China.* Low, Marston and Searle, London, 1875.

Thomson, J. T. *Sequel to Some Glimpses of Life in the Far East.* Richardson, London, 1865.

Thomson, J. T. *Some Glimpses into Life in the Far East.* Richardson, London, 1865.

Tiele, P. A. 'De Europeers in den Maleischen Archipel', in *BTLVNI*, vols. 25, 1877: 27, 1879; 28, 1880; 29, 1881; 30, 1882; 32, 1884: 35, 1886; 36. 1887.

Tiele. P. A., Heeres, J. E. *Bouwstoffen voor de Geschiedenis der Nederlanders in den Indischen Archipel.* Vols. 1–3. Martinus Nijhoff, 's-Gravenhage, 1890–1895.

Tilman, R. O. (ed.). *Man, State and Society in Contemporary Southeast Asia.* Praeger, New York, 1969.

Tinling, J. F. B. *The Poppy-Plague and England's Crime.* Elliot Stock, London, 1876.

Torchiana, H. A. van Coenen. *Tropical Holland.* University of Chicago Press, Chicago, 1921.

Turner, F. S. *British Opium Policy and Its Result to India and China.* Low, Marston, Searle, Rivington, London, 1876.

Vaizey, J. *Revolutions of Our Time: Capitalism.* Weidenfeld and Nicolson, London, 1971.

Valentijn, F. 'Description of Malacca'. tr. D. F. A. Hervey, in *JSBRAS*, no. 18, June, 1884.

Vandenbosch, A. *The Dutch East Indies.* Erdmans, Grand Rapids, Michigan, 1933.

Vaughan, 'Notes on the Malays of Pinang and Province Wellesley', in *JIAEA*, New Series, vol. II, no. 2, 1857.

Vetch, R. H. *Life of the Hon. Lieut.-General Sir Andrew Clarke.* John Murray, London, 1905.

Veth, P. J. *Java,* vols. I, II. Bohn, Haarlem, 1896, 1898.

Vlieland, C. A. *A Report of the 1931 Census and on Certain Problems of Vital Statistics.* Malayan Information Agency, London, 1932.

Waal, E. de. *Nederlandsch Indie in de Staten-Generaal sedert de Grondwet van 1814.* Vols. 1–3. Nijhoff, 's-Gravenhage, 1860–1861.

Wallbank, T. W., Taylor, A. M. *Civilization.* Vol. 2. Scott, Foresman, U.S.A., 1961. (Fourth edition.)

Wanford-Lock, C. G. *Mining in Malaya for Gold and Tin.* Crowther and Goodman, London, 1907.

Warta Malaysia. Ministry of Information and Broadcasting, Kuala Lumpur:
        vol. 4, no. 1, January 5, 1968
        vol. 4, no. 11, March 14, 1968
        vol. 4, no. 14, April 4, 1968
        vol. 4, no. 17, April 25, 1968
        vol. 4, no. 33, August 15, 1968
        vol. 4, no. 37, September 12, 1968
        vol. 4, no. 43, October 24, 1968
        vol. 4, no. 52, December 27, 1968
        vol. 5, no. 17, April 24, 1969.

Watson, M. *The Prevention of Malaria in the Federated Malay States.* John Murray, London, 1921.

Weber, Max. *Economy and Society.* Ed. G. Roth, G. Roth, C. Wittich. 3 vols. Bedminster Press, New York, 1968.

Weber, Max. *The Protestant Ethic and the Spirit of Capitalism,* tr. Talcott Parsons. Charles Scribner, New York, 1958.

Wertheim, F. W. *East West Parallels.* Quadrangle Books, Chicago, 1965.

Wertheim, W. F. *Indonesian Society in Transition.* W. van Hoeve, the Hague, 1969.

Westerhout, J. B. 'Notes on Malacca', in *JIAEA,* vol. II, no. III, March, 1848.

Wheeler, L. R. *The Modern Malay*. Allen and Unwin, London, 1928.

White, Lynn. *Medieval Technology and Social Change*. Oxford University Press, London, 1958.

Willoughby, W. W. *Opium as an International Problem*. John Hopkins Press, Baltimore, 1925.

Wilson, C. *Annual Report of the Labour Department, Malaya, for the Year 1938*. Federated Malay States Government Press, Kuala Lumpur, 1939.

Wilson, C. *Annual Report of the Labour Department, Malaya, for the Year 1937*. Federated Malay States Government Press, Kuala Lumpur, 1938.

Windstedt, R. O. *The Malays: A Cultural History*. Routledge and Kegan Paul, London, 1956.

Windstedt, R. O. *Malaya and Its History*. Hutchinson University Library, London, 1956.

Windstedt, R. O. 'A History of Classical Malay Literature'. Monograph on Malay subjects no. 5. *JMBRAS*, vol. XXXI, part 3, 1958.

Windstedt, R. O. (ed.), *Malaya*. Constable, London, 1923.

Windstedt, R. O., Jong, P. E. de Josselin de. 'A Digest of the Customary Law of Sungai Ujong', in *JMBRAS*, vol. XXVII, part 3, July. 1954.

Windstedt, R. O. *Malay Proverbs*. John Murray, London, 1950.

Winks, Robin W. (ed.). *The Age of Imperialism*. Prentice-Hall Englewood Cliffs, New Jersey, 1969.

Winslow, E. M. *The Pattern of Imperialism*. Columbia University Press, New York, 1948.

Woodruff, W. *Impact of Western Man*. Macmillan, New York, 1966.

Wright, A., Reid. T. H. *The Malay Peninsula*. Fisher Unwin, London, 1912.

Wright, H. M. (ed.). *The 'New Imperialism'*. Heath, Boston, 1961.

Wright, H. R. C. 'Muntinghe's Advice to Raffles on the Land Question in Java', in *BTLVNI*, vol. 108, 1952.

Wright, H. R. C. *East-Indian Economic Problems of the Age of Cornwallis and Raffles*. Luzac, London, 1961.

Zaide, G. F. *Jose Rizal*. Villaneuva Book Store. Manila, 1961.

Zuniga, Jaoquin Martinez de. *An Historical View of the Philippine Islands*, tr. J. Maver. Filipiniana Book Guild, Manila, 1966.

Abbreviations

ADRSS:	*Annual Departmental Report of the Straits Settlements.*
BTLVNI:	*Bijdragen tot de Taal-, Land- en Volkenkunde van Nederlandsch-Indie.*
JEH:	*The Journal Of Economic History.*
JIAEA:	*Journal of the Indian Archipelago and Eastern Asia.*
JMBRAS:	*Journal of the Malayan Branch Royal Asiatic Society.*
JSBRAS:	*Journal of the Straits Branch Royal Asiatic Society.*
SSAR:	*Straits Settlement Annual Report.*
TITLV:	*Tijdschrift voor Indische Taal-, Land-, en Volkenkunde.*
TNI:	*Tijdschrift voor Nederlandsch-Indie.*
VKITLV:	*Verhandelingen van het Koninklijk Instituut voor Taal-, Land-, en Volkenkunde.*

Index